Seabee 71
in Chu Lai

The Face of Vietnam, 1967. I photographed this 93-year-old Vietnamese gentleman in the summer of 1967 in the village of An Tan, just outside the military wire of our compound. He has seen his country torn apart by political strife and the war machines of invading armies his whole life. Indochina has never known the peace of other nations, only the struggle of combating outsiders attempting to conquer this rich, productive farmland at the edges of the South China Sea. Yet, these Vietnamese persist—they're here, with their families, their farms, their hamlets. The people and the land are one. Invaders come and go. Time is slow in this country, patience is a way of life. Soon, this invader (us), with their machines of war will also leave. Soon, the Vietnamese will rest from the terror of war that has gripped their villages for hundreds of years.

(I wrote the caption to this photograph and it appeared on the front page the July 20, 1967, edition of The Transit. *Seems prophetic today. While the present Communist government curtails the freedoms we fought for, there is now peace and prosperity in this tropical land and it has been this way since the U.S. military left in 1975.)*

Seabee 71 in Chu Lai

Memoir of a Navy Journalist with a Mobile Construction Battalion, 1967

DAVID H. LYMAN

McFarland & Company, Inc., Publishers
Jefferson, North Carolina

All photographs and drawings by the author.

LIBRARY OF CONGRESS CATALOGUING-IN-PUBLICATION DATA

Library of Congress Cataloging-in-Publication Data
Names: Lyman, David H., 1939– author.
Title: Seabee 71 in Chu Lai : memoir of a Navy journalist with a Mobile Construction Battalion, 1967 / David H. Lyman.
Other titles: Memoir of a Navy journalist with a Mobile Construction Battalion, 1967
Description: Jefferson, North Carolina : McFarland & Company, Inc., Publishers, 2019 | Includes index.
Identifiers: LCCN 2019040785 | ISBN 9781476678443 (paperback) ∞ | ISBN 9781476636887 (ebook)
Subjects: LCSH: Lyman, David H., 1939– | United States. Naval Mobile Construction Battalion 71—History. | Vietnam War, 1961–1975—Personal narratives, American. | Vietnam War, 1961–1975—Journalism, Military. | Vietnam War, 1961–1975—Regimental histories—United States. | United States. Navy. Seabees—Biography. | Photojournalists—Vietnam—Biography. | Chu Lai (Vietnam)—History, Military—20th century.
Classification: LCC VA66.C62 71st .L96 2019 | DDC 959.704/34 [B]—dc23
LC record available at https://lccn.loc.gov/2019040785

BRITISH LIBRARY CATALOGUING DATA ARE AVAILABLE

ISBN (print) 978-1-4766-7844-3
ISBN (ebook) 978-1-4766-3688-7

© 2019 David H. Lyman. All rights reserved

No part of this book may be reproduced or transmitted in any form or by any means, electronic or mechanical, including photocopying or recording, or by any information storage and retrieval system, without permission in writing from the publisher.

Front cover: High atop Signal Hill, above the village of Nouc Mon, 12 clicks south of Chi Lai, MCB-71 Seabees from Charley Company prepare the foundation for an Army 60-foot observation tower. The concrete for the foundation, even the tower itself, would be flown in by giant helicopters (photograph by the author). *Back cover:* Journalist (JO3) David H. Lyman, 1967, with a new 35mm Nikon F, a Nikkormat SLR and a Nikonos underwater camera, at work in Chu Lai, Vietnam (author's collection)

Printed in the United States of America

McFarland & Company, Inc., Publishers
Box 611, Jefferson, North Carolina 28640
www.mcfarlandpub.com

Acknowledgments

While most memoirs are the work of a single author, this author has had the help of a dozen Seabees and friends who have willingly provided input, advice, corrections and additions of their own. To them, I am indebted, and express my sincere thanks.

The first person to read what I was writing was a fellow writer/editor, Bonnie Durrance. Bonnie and I have been friends for more than 40 years. She offered to read what I was writing and to provide feedback. I'd send her the draft of a chapter, she'd read it and mark it up with notes: "this is marvelous," or "get rid of this," or "boy, does this need work." Bonnie provided direction to the storytelling. She kept me honest and on track. I, like all writers, often get lost in the process, stumbling around, lost, in the forest.

The bulk of the stories in this book are as I recall them and from referencing what I wrote at the time in *The Transit*, the battalion's monthly newspaper I edited. The names of the Seabees mentioned in these stories are real people, as are the events. I began by dictating the printed stories into my iMac, which typed them as I read. That part was easy. Then came the rewriting, as I struggled to include reflections of my personal involvement.

Once Bonnie and I could see the shape of the book, I sent it off to an editor at my eventual publisher. The editor responded, saying the publisher would be interested ... if the book was more about Vietnam and less about my career in the seagoing Navy. Back to the drawing board.

After a few months reworking the structure, adding more content, I shipped off a draft to a few of my fellow Seabees, asking for their input. I wrote to *Seabee Magazine*, asking if they had someone there who might read and comment on the military jargon. The editor sent me to Terry Lukanic, who had written two books on the Seabees in Vietnam. Terry volunteered to read and correct my draft. He's been a great help, as was Seabee Builder Barry Putt from Seventy-One's Delta Company, who also read the manuscript and provided corrections and comments.

Gerald (Pete) Peterson, BU2, the clerk for Charlie Company, wrote back sharing a few stories, as did Bob Timerson, EA3, from Seventy-One's Engineering Department. Dennis Smith, HM, a corpsman in Seventy-One's medical unit, provided information on the medical terminology and identified faces in my photographs. My former assistant, John Cliett, JO3, and Tom Widmark, EO3, with whom I shared the darkroom, responded with a few of their recollections. John Allworthy, EO2, clerk from Alpha Company, and Lt. Jim Dougherty, the S-2 Intelligence Officer, have also been helpful.

Jerry Montecupo, BU2, and John Allworthy, EO2, the clerk from Alpha Company, have been organizing the battalion's alumni gatherings over the years and have managed to assemble a roster of former Seventy-Oners, with addresses and emails. I used their roster to track down 'Bees that I knew. The first one I called was Dick Stapleman, EO3, who plays a large role in this book as he was a buddy throughout my time with the 'Bees. Dick knew how to get hold of Tuffy Lake and gave me his phone number. I called and Tuffy and I have shared rather lengthy phone conversations resulting in more stories and details to fill in the gaps.

To the Seabees of MCB-71, if you recognize someone in a photograph, or some statement that needs correcting, or expansion, I'd deeply appreciate hearing from you. You can e-mail me at DHLyman@mac.com. If there is a second edition, I will make updates as needed, as well acknowledge same on the website www.Seabee71.com.

My editors at McFarland, David Alff and Dylan Lightfoot, could not have been more helpful. David provided feedback and direction on structuring the book; Dylan Lightfoot straightened out my prose and alerted me to details that might have otherwise lead readers to confusion. Profound thanks to McFarland for bringing my memoir to life.

Table of Contents

Acknowledgments v
Glossary ix
Preface 1

1. All This to Avoid the Draft? 5
2. Off to Sea, with a Camera 10
3. I'm Going to Be a Seabee 18
4. Training for Combat Duty 30
5. Waiting to Deploy 40
6. Hello, Vietnam! 48
7. Life in This 'Bee Hive 62
8. The Battalion 77
9. The 'Bees Get to Work 92
10. Close Calls Come in Many Sizes 133
11. Outside the Wire 147
12. The Vietnamese People 159
13. Civic Action Program 168
14. Putting the Pieces Together 177
15. The End Is in Sight 195
16. The Last Month in 'Nam 206

Appendices: The End Is Never Really the End 213
   The Faces of Vietnam's Future 213
   What Happened to MCB-71? 214
   Lessons Learned 214
   Our Commanding Officers 215
   What Are the "Boys" Doing Now? 217
   The One Who Didn't Return 220
   The History of NMCB-71's Pacific Deployment
      in World War II 220
Index 227

The difficult we do right away. The impossible may take a bit longer.
—Seabee attitude to assigned tasks

Glossary

Following are definitions for Navy terms, slang and abbreviations you may find in this book.

AFR—Armed Forces Radio
ARVN—The Army of the Republic of Vietnam
AWOL—Absent Without Leave
BU—Builder
BUPERS—Bureau of Naval Personnel
CA—Construction Apprentice
CDR—Commander, officers rank third up the chain
CE—Construction Electrician's Mate
CEC—Construction Mechanic
CO—Commanding Office
CPO—Chief Petty Officer, E-7, E-8 and E-9
DMZ—Demilitarized Zone, between South and North Vietnam
DPPO—Direct Procurement Petty Officer. These were experienced construction workers inducted into the Seabees with a petty officer rate and pay grade
E-1 to E-3—Unrated enlisted men. Seaman Recruit (E-1), Seaman Apprentice (E-2), Seaman (E-3)
E-4 to E-6—Enlisted pay grades, Third to First Grade Petty Officers
EA—Engineer Assistant
EO—Equipment Operator
EOD—Explosive Ordnance Disposal
FTN—Forget the Navy (or perhaps something more expressive)
Gunny—Marine Gunnery Sergeant
HN—Hospital-man (Corpsman)
I CORPS—Often pronounced "Eye Corps," the northernmost military section of South Vietnam
IPOs—"Instant Petty Officer." Slang for construction pros who went through four weeks of military schooling to become petty officers. The official designation was Direct Procurement Petty Officers

JO—Journalist Petty Officer, now obsolete, replaced by Mass Media Specialist (MC)
LCDR—Lieutenant Commander
LCU—Landing Craft, Utility
LST—Landing Ship, Tank, larger than an LCU
LT—Lieutenant
LTJG—Lieutenant Junior Grade
MAA—Master-at-Arms
MACV—Military Assistance Command, Vietnam
MAG—Marine Air Group
'Nam—Vietnam
NMCB—Naval Mobile Construction Battalion
NSA—Naval Air Station
OCS—Officer Candidate School
OIC—Officer in Charge
P&E—Planning and Estimating
PAVN—the People's Army of Vietnam, aka the Việt Minh. The U.S. used the abbreviation NVA for the North Vietnamese Army
POD—Plan of the Day
ROK—Republic of Korea
RVA—Republic of Vietnam Army
RVN—Republic of (South) Vietnam
S&S—*Stars and Stripes* military newspaper
SATS—Short Airfield Tactical Support
Skipper—the Commanding Officer
SOP—Standard Operating Procedure
TAD—Temporary Additional Duty
UCT—Underwater Construction Team
UNREP—Underway Replenishment
USMC—United States Marine Corps
VC—Viet Cong, Communist insurgents from South Vietnam
XO—Executive Officer, second in command
YN—Yeoman

Preface

The license plate on my 2005 Tahoe has a Vietnam Veteran insignia. It draws little attention, but when it does, it's usually from a fellow Vietnam vet. For example:

"Where and when?" asks Steve Beverage, a neighbor farmer down the road, I've known Steve for years, but never knew he was a Vietnam veteran, nor he me—until I drove into his farm stand for tomatoes and corn and he spotted my license plate.

"Chu Lai, 1967," I reply. "Navy journalist, JO3, assigned to a Seabee outfit. We built bases for the Marines, Army, and the ROK [Republic of Korea] Marines. You?" I ask.

"I was in-country from October '68 to '69," he tells me. "Six months in Vung Tau, then another six months in Fire Base Camron, up on the Cambodian border."

"What were you doing there?"

"I was with the 136 Assault Helicopter Company, assigned to the First Cavalry. I flew Hueys, or Slicks, for six months, then gunships for the last eight months," he replies.

It always starts out this way, and is occasionally followed by a swapping of recollections: the heat, the food, the fellowship, the boredom followed by narrow escapes, and the VC and the VA. Sometimes that is the end of the conversation. One or both of us not wanting to talk about it.

"I wouldn't want anyone to go through that experience," the former gunship driver adds. "But I am glad I did it. I have it behind me."

I agree with him. The Vietnam War was a terrible time for us young kids, and for the nation as a whole. Despite how bad the war was for the U.S. and for the Vietnamese, for me it was a "rite of passage." As a budding journalist, I was curious. I wanted to experience what a war was like. I wanted to photograph and write about a war, to hear the guns and smell the cordite.

I'd been born at the beginning of World War II and remember both VE and VJ days. My brothers and I played war in the woods behind our lakeside lodge while the Korean War played out in black and white on television. We religiously watched the documentary series *Victory at Sea* on television every Sunday. I read Leon Uris's *Battle Cry,* and Richard Tregaskis' *Guadalcanal Diary* while in college. As a young man, I wanted to know more about myself. Did I have the courage to face capture, or even death? Could I actually kill another human being? This was my chance to find out.

I joined the Naval Reserves in 1963, primarily to avoid the draft and stay out of a foxhole in Vietnam. With my background and education in journalism, I wound up a JO3, Journalist Third Class. In 1966 I was commandeered off a Navy ship because a newly forming Seabee outfit, Mobile Construction Battalion 71, needed a journalist. I was not a real Seabee, I was a "fleet-bee," one of the office guys from the fleet. It was my job to publicize the outfit's accomplishments—to write stories and press releases and to photograph, edit and lay out a monthly newspaper, *The Transit*. These were mailed to the folks at home and to other military units to brag about what our boys were doing. Truly, I was more PR hack than journalist.

A Seabee outfit is a Naval Mobile Construction Battalion—similar to a MASH outfit in the Korean War (as seen in the movie and television show). With 800 officers and men, we could "bug out" and set up camp in some remote location to build what the Marines, the Army, the Air Force needed to fight a war.

Since World War II, the Seabees have not only had to build things while a war was raging around them, they also often had to defend themselves and what they had built. Therefore, to become Seabees, recruits—who are primarily carpenters, plumbers, truck drivers, electricians and heavy equipment operators—must go through combat training with the Marines. All of us fleet-bees went through that same training, and in the spring of 1967, off we went to build a war in Vietnam.

I had one of the best jobs in the outfit. I got to visit construction projects up and down I Corps area, from Da Nang to Quang Ngai. I followed my guys from project to project, making notes, taking photographs, conducting interviews. We built roads and bridges, runways, barracks, mess halls, officer and enlisted men's clubs, hospitals—entire camps (or cantonments) for the men who were actually doing the fighting.

I got shot at, almost blown up by a road mine, and spent many a night hunkered down in the mortar pit next to my office as rockets and mortars rained down on the Marine airstrip next door. I joined convoys through territory controlled by the VC, and spent time in hamlets and fishing villages photographing the Vietnamese people. I walked through the streets of Da Nang talking to myself about what a fool I was for being there, alone in a war zone and feeling acutely the danger I was in.

Each month I edited and laid out pages of *The Transit*. What I wrote had to be approved by the officers, then I'd fly up to Tokyo to spend a few days at the *Stars and Stripes* printing plant to typeset and print the newspaper. While there, I got to explore Japan and its culture and I came to know a few Japanese people.

As I flew and drove around Vietnam visiting the projects and getting to see what my outfit was building, I saw firsthand the massive power of the U.S. military. We were building entire cities—huge airport complexes, harbor facilities, road systems—all to win a war against an enemy that had no air force, no navy, no helicopter gunships, no jeeps or tanks. This was an enemy that carried its war on its back through the jungles and mountain passes, wearing sandals they made from the treads of old truck tires—what were called Ho Chi Minh sandals. On my last trip to Tokyo, I flew on a C-141 KIA (killed in action) flight. More than 100 dead servicemen were with me, their remains resting in shiny aluminum coffins. It was only then I realized the war we were building in Vietnam was so deadly. More than 11,000 American Marines, Army soldiers and airmen died in action in 1967, the year I was in Vietnam.

A few months ago, I figured it was time I wrote a memoir of my experience. Besides, my two teenage kids kept asking about what I'd done in that war. More than 50 years have passed, an entire lifetime, but memories remain; and I had help. I'd brought back thousands of negatives of pictures I'd shot in Vietnam. I had pages of notes and copies of *The Transit*, the newspaper I wrote and edited. This material has followed me as I've moved over the years. Recently, looking through those contact sheets, a photograph would jog a memory and scenes, conversations and entire stories would flood in. And so, I began to write.

Sources and Research

As I struggled with the idea of writing a book, a memoir, I realized there was a lot about the war—and the Vietnamese people—that I did not know. A friend suggested I watch the PBS series *Vietnam* by Ken Burns and Kim Novak. I was reluctant, but found it on Netflix, and watched the episode that covered 1967. I realized then just how much I didn't know, so I proceeded to watch the entire series.

Next, to write a memoir, I thought perhaps I should read a few. I found plenty of memoirs on the Vietnam experience on the Internet, written by former Marines and Army grunts. McFarland, the publisher of this book, has more than a hundred on their website. There are even more on Amazon. I bought and read a few. I could only find three that had anything to do with the Seabees.

Asphalt and Blood is a novel by Warren Bell, a former Seabee officer stationed near Hue during Tet in 1968. It's well written and self-published, and tells the story, based on true events, of a fictional Navy civil engineer, LCDR Kevin Corcoran. This Seabee officer is the Operations boss for an MCB building roads in and around the city of Hue, near the DMZ. There's a romance with a Vietnamese woman, and dark intrigue as the Tet Offensive is launched by the VC and the North Vietnamese Army. Bell's story is full of details about the Seabees, construction, the city of Hue itself and the politics. Good read.

Shovels and C-Rations is a small self-published memoir by Charles Thompson, a BU2, stationed below Monkey Mountain in Da Nang in 1968–69. You'll find it on Amazon.

In 2008, Terry Lukanic, a former Engineer's Aide Second Class with MCB-74, began assembling a history of what the 20-plus Seabee units did while on deployment in Vietnam. His compilation covers the years between 1967 and 69. The content is based on official battalion completion reports on file with the Navy, along with newspapers like *The Transit* and *Stars and Stripes*. It's available online as a PDF. (The URL is in the Appendix.)

My Story

While more than 20 Seabee battalions served in Vietnam between 1965 and 1970, with more than 26,000 men involved, my story is about only one of those battalions, Naval Mobile Construction Battalion Seventy-One (NMCB-71). It is told from my perspective as the unit's journalist. Remember, this is a memoir, not an "official" history of the Seabees or of my outfit. Others in my outfit will remember events differently and will have their own stories to tell. A few of my fellow Seabees have helped by reading chapters, making corrections, adding comments and sharing their memories. You'll find them listed in the Acknowledgments.

The stories in this memoir should give the reader a good idea of what it was like to experience a tour of duty in Vietnam as a Seabee, the work we did, and the life we led on a military base in Vietnam.

You'll notice some of my photographs, especially those of the Vietnamese people, are square. These I made with a medium-format camera, a Bronica I bought on one of my trips to Japan. The negative is 6 × 6 cm and provides greater detail than the 35mm format I made with my Nikon cameras, which I also bought in Tokyo. The film was Kodak Tri-X.

Chapter 1

All This to Avoid the Draft?

What the Hell Am I Doing Here?

WHUMP! WHUMP! Two explosions invade my dreams. By the time the third *whump* hits, I realize I'm not dreaming—this is real. It's another VC rocket attack on the Marine runway, just over the berm. I kick off the sheet, swing my legs off the cot and fumble around in the pitch-black to find my boots while the siren wails are followed by: "Now hear this, now hear this. Incoming! Incoming! All personnel take cover." More thuds. By now, I'm fully awake.

I slam on my helmet, slip my flak jacket over my left shoulder, throw my ammo belt with its .45 pistol, holster and extra ammo clips over my right shoulder and grab my rifle. I stumble outside the hooch and down the three steps to the sand wearing nothing but my skivvies. It's 3 a.m. on a hot night in Vietnam.

Four strides and I'm at the mortar pit beside my office hut. I slide down the sloped bank of sandbags into the soft sand at the bottom. I lay my rifle aside, strap the ammo belt and holster around my waist, slip my right arm into the flak jacket and close it. I adjust my helmet and fasten the chin strap while sitting on my heels, my butt against one of the sandbags at the bottom of the pit. Two of the HMs (Hospital Corpsmen) on all-night sickbay duty, slide in beside me. No one appears concerned that we are all sitting there in our underwear.

Illumination flares float down on parachutes out over the perimeter a mile or so away. The boom of our Army's 105mm artillery batteries now mixes with the boom of incoming rockets. The U.S. Army guys go to work lobbing shells into the mountains from whence came the rockets. The three of us sit in the bottom of the pit, talking. The flares finally peter out. It becomes quiet. The "All clear!" comes, and we climb out of the pit and plod back into our hooches. But who can sleep with all that adrenaline flowing? I lay on the cot I'd built in my office and think back: How in the hell did I ever wind up here, in Vietnam?

Is This the Summer of 1967?

I'm 27. I should be doing something else with my life at this age. Instead, I'm a petty officer, a Navy Journalist Petty Officer (JO3), assigned to MCB-71 (Mobile Construction Battalion 71). I and 799 other American Navy guys are living in a camp in Chu Lai on the edge of a beach on the South China Sea. The war in Vietnam has been heating up since the early '60s, and we're here to help build what will become another mammoth military complex. There will be more than 60,000 men and a few women nurses stationed here by the time we leave in six months. And we are only one of a dozen Seabee battalions in 'Nam building roads, airfields, barracks, mess halls, warehouses and landing ramps. The Americans have arrived in this small tropical country to show these skinny Vietnamese how wars are fought—and won. It's simple. Just pour in a lot money and young men.

I'm the unit's PR hack. I write stories and make photographs of the Seabees and the projects they are building. Each month I get to fly up to Tokyo to put together our monthly newspaper to show the folks at home and anyone who's interested, what we've been building.

But I'm getting ahead of myself.

How did I arrive here in Vietnam in the first place? Fate or dumb luck?

Essentially, I am here because I wanted to avoid the draft. I joined the Naval Reserves so I wouldn't have to come here, yet here I am. The draft has been around since 1940—men are conscripted for service in the military; many, many young men were needed to fight World War II. The draft was still around, and much dreaded.

Four years before this, in the spring of 1963, I'd dropped out of my last year of journalism school at Boston University. This meant I was eligible for the draft. If you were in college, had a family, had flat feet, suffered from asthma, were too short or had bone spurs, you got a deferment. I had none of these things. I was now a prime candidate for being a "grunt" in the Army. The trouble was, you didn't know where you stood. The local draft board met monthly to draw names and send out letters. If you got a letter, it was off to the induction center, into the Army and a foxhole in Vietnam, a small country in Southeast Asia that we never heard of in geography class in high school. I was not totally conversant on what was going in Vietnam—no one was at that time. We just knew there was something going on in what used to be called French Indochina.

With the draft hanging over my 22-year-old head, I couldn't get a real job or make a career decision. I had to do something about the cursed draft. I was treading water, living in Boston, working as a freelance photographer, producing weekly radio shows on WBCN and WCRB, and working in television as the floor producer and Ring Master on the Bozo kid's show. Evenings, I ran the Unicorn Coffee House, a folk music club on Boylston Street.

That April, a letter arrived from my dad: "A friend in my men's club is on the Draft Board. He told me your number will be coming up next month. Thought you should know. What are you planning to do, if anything? I'd hate to see you shipped off to Vietnam in the Army. Dad."

That next morning, before heading off to the TV station to don my Ring Master outfit and wrangle 50 kids into the "peanut gallery," I walked along Boston's Atlantic Avenue. The street was lined with recruiting offices: Army, Coast Guard, Air Force, Marines, National Guard. I stopped in each, read the literature, talked to the uniformed recruiter about their "deal" and left. I was searching for an alternative to a foxhole and was saving the best for last.

I'd grown up on boats. I was a sailor. I had a copy of the Navy's *Blue Jacket Manual* when I was 15. I was a devoted fan of the TV series *Victory at Sea*. If I was going to join any military service it would be the Navy. So off I went to see what the Navy had to offer.

As I walked to the Navy Recruiting Office in Fargo Building over by the docks, I had time to ponder this decision about volunteering versus taking my chances with the draft. Most guys of draft age just played roulette and waited to get drafted, hoping, I gather, to be passed over. "Well, what can I do?" I'd hear guys my age complaining. "What options are there? Run off to Canada? Sweden? Claim I'm a conscientious objector? Tell them I'm crazy and just want to kill, kill, kill Gooks?"

I have always been befuddled by these guys who let themselves get drafted. What were they thinking, or were they not thinking? You do have some control of your life. It comes through the choices you make, chances you take. You can let others control your fate, or you can stop pissing and moaning about it, and take action, do something. As I walked to the Fargo Building, I was doing just that. I was taking charge of my future. I knew by the end of that day, I would have made a choice, done something to stay out of that foxhole, out of Vietnam.

I arrived at the Fargo Building and found the recruiter's office. I walked in and had a chat with a chief boatswain's mate about my predicament. "You can enlist in the Naval Reserves," he began. "That means one weekend a month, two weeks a year, for three years. After you've worked your way up in rate, you go active duty for just two years." That sounded better than any of the other services. With a few years of reserve duty, I might just complete my degree and apply for Officer Candidate School. I signed up and took the oath that morning.

"I may be getting my draft letter any day now," I added.

"Do not open it. Bring it here to me. I'll deal with your draft board. You are in the Navy now, son." Yes, I realized as I walked through Boston, back to my apartment, I'm now in the Naval Reserve, for the next five years.

When I got back to my apartment at 6 Joy Street on Beacon Hill, my draft notice was waiting. I did not open it, as instructed, and brought it over to the chief the next morning.

So began my five-year career in the Navy, and the beginning of the rest of my life, although I didn't realize it at the time.

The Entire Nation Is Up in Arms!

I had managed, just barely, to dodge the draft by enlisting in the Naval Reserve. Now, what could I do? I had a few years of monthly weekends and two weeks of active training each summer. My civilian career was stymied until I fulfilled my obligation to the Navy. But I was not the only one whose life was screwed up over this "thing in Southeast Asia." The entire nation was in turmoil, and it was getting worse by the month.

Civil Rights issues had been simmering in Boston, and many other cities, since the '50s. In the spring of 1963, the governor of Alabama, George Wallace, declared, "Segregation now, segregation tomorrow, segregation forever." He then attempted to bar Blacks from entering "his" university. In September, Martin Luther King delivered his famous "I Have a Dream" speech to hundreds of thousands on the Washington Mall. Protesters were marching, filling the cities' streets. Riots were breaking out and cities were set ablaze. America was at war with itself.

To all of this I was only slightly aware. That spring, I'd quit my job as Ring Master on the Bozo television show, gave up my role as Curt Goudy's booth producer on the Red Sox's telecasts, turned my radio show over to Robert J. Lurtsema, and moved to Martha's Vineyard Island. With the backing of some friends, I turned a former supermarket into a coffee house—long before there was a Starbucks. The Moon Cusser Coffee

House did sell coffee, along with other beverages and desserts, but it was the folk music that packed the place night after night, all summer long. This was where James Taylor first appeared on stage (at the age of 15) and where Carly Simon and her sister, Lucy, sang "Wynken, Blynken and Nod" on Sunday evenings. Ian and Sylvia, the Country Gentlemen, Jean Redpath, Tom Rush, Ramblin' Jack Elliot, Bud and Travis, Jeff Muldour, Bonnie Dobson, even the Clancy Brothers—they were all there that summer.

Back on the mainland, things were coming apart over Civil Rights. And President Kennedy had his hands full over that small Southeast Asian country, Vietnam.

The Communists from North Vietnam, backed by the Communists in China and Russia, were backing a band of South Vietnam insurgents, the Viet Cong, who were attempting to overthrow the capitalist, free-market government of South Vietnam, whose president, Ngo Dinh Diem, was a Catholic, and corrupt. The majority of the Vietnamese people were Buddhist. Diem was faced with two crises: his own civil rights war with the Buddhists, some of whom were setting themselves afire on the streets of Hue and Saigon, and the Communist Viet Cong.

In May 1961, President Kennedy had sent in helicopters and 400 U.S. Green Beret military "advisors" to "advise" President Diem on how to handle the communist insurgency. President Diem and his younger brother, General Ngo Dinh Nhu, weren't listening to the advisors. In October, Kennedy sent a fellow Boston blue blood, Henry Cabot Lodge, to South Vietnam as ambassador. Diem didn't listen to him either. Early that November, the RVN generals, with the blessing of the ambassador and the U.S. advisors, staged a coup d'état and both brothers were assassinated. (RVN, the Republic of Vietnam, is the common acronym for South Vietnam.) The RVN generals took over the government but over the next two years they were too busy fighting each other for power and control to listen to the Americans.

By the fall of 1963, there were more than 16,000 American Marine and Army "advisors" in Vietnam, supposedly to help the South Vietnam Army (ARVN) with strategy and training. That September (1963), President Kennedy was interviewed by Walter Cronkite for CBS News: "The Americans can help the South Vietnamese government with advisors and materiel," said Kennedy, "but it is their war, not ours."

Meanwhile, back in the Vineyard, I closed up the Moon Cusser after a wildly successful summer and returned to Boston. With a new financial backer and a great idea, I was off on another entrepreneurial adventure. I was going to open a new, larger folk music club on Commonwealth Avenue in Boston's Back Bay. Since protests, marches and rebellion were all the rage, I would call the new club Shay's Rebellion, after a 1786 uprising in western Massachusetts.

All that fall I was drawing up plans, going through the licensing and permitting process, dealing with the Boston City Licensing Board, police, fire marshal, building and code inspectors. I paid little attention to what was happening in Vietnam. Then came the news.

November 22, 1963. Do You Remember Where You Were?

On November 22, Allan (my roommate and high school buddy) and I had just pulled up in front of the Boston Licensing Department. We had a hearing on my license application for Shay's Rebellion. We were about to get out of the car when WBZ radio broke in with a news flash: "The President has been shot." For an hour, Allan and I sat in the car and listened to the event unfold in Dallas. Allan, a news cameraman with WBZ-TV, said, "I think I'd better get over to the station." Our hearing was postponed. Everyone in Boston walked around in a daze.

In quick order, Vice President Lyndon Johnson was sworn in as president, and then the war in Vietnam began to really heat up. More and more American servicemen were sent in—and to do more than "advise." They were engaging the Viet Cong and getting killed.

Shay's Rebellion was never built. My license application kept getting stalled. I later learned why—I was just too naive to realize people were holding out for a bribe. I went back to radio, freelance photography and skiing while attending monthly weekends with the Naval Reserve.

"Dancing in the Street," a Motown single, reached number 2 on Billboard's Top 100 in the summer of 1964. You could sing that innocent-enough dance tune as you walked down the street. It was written by Marvin Gaye, William "Mickey" Stevenson and Ivy Jo Hunter, and performed by Martha Ray and the Vandellas. A "feel-good" song, it was meant to bring everyone together on the street to dance. It quickly became the Civil Rights anthem for social change. Instead of taking to the streets to dance, though, people were taking to the streets in Boston, and in dozens of other cities, to protest, first over Civil Rights, then over the war in Southeast Asia.

In the early spring of 1964 I was off for two weeks of boot camp at the Great Lakes Training Center north of Chicago. My first ride in a commercial jet airline. It was May and I was dressed in my white uniform, black kerchief tied with a square knot around my neck, black shoes shined and that little white sailor's hat perched on the top of my head. I was traveling under military orders, so the uniform was required. At O'Hare airport I and dozens of other U.S. Navy Reservists were herded onto a bus by nasty petty officers—the process of dehumanizing had begun.

I'd read Leon Uris's book *Battle Cry*, about life as a Marine in World War II, so had an idea, rather a dread, of what was coming. First, the barber. My thin, Nordic blond hair was buzzed off my head in less than a minute. No trim around the ears, no cologne, no polite, "How do you like it?" I and the rest of the busload of reservists were now true Navy recruits, no crew cut, no neat trim, just bald.

After two weeks, I returned to Boston and civilian life—my fine blond hair was gone and it never really came back. Now what? I began working at Magnum Film Productions as a photographer and film cameraman. Allan and I shared a one-room apartment on Beacon Street.

That summer, President Johnson signed the Civil Rights Act of 1964, but the protests and marches not only continued—if anything, they intensified—with the increased resistance to the growing war in Vietnam.

Still in limbo, in Boston, I had no idea what was next.

Chapter 2

Off to Sea, with a Camera

In June 1965, with protests filling the streets of Boston, I and 160 other Naval reservists were off on a two-week Reserve Training cruise. We were crammed into a destroyer, the USS *Compton* (DD 705), as it put out to sea. We joined another destroyer from Newport to conduct joint naval maneuvers. We fired off our three-inch guns, came alongside a fleet oiler to transfer fuel, movies and a doctor, then spent a night in Portland, Maine.

By this time, I'd been in the reserves for two years and had advanced to Seaman

The USS *Compton*, DD 705, was a World War II destroyer stationed in Boston as a training platform for Naval Reservists.

Apprentice, E-2. Since I could type, I was assigned to the Ship's Office, under Yeoman First Class Curtis Johnson. While in Portland, I snapped a photo of Johnson fishing off the side of the ship in the harbor. I figured if I gave him a print he might lighten up on me.

The two destroyers cruised north, through the straights of Canso, into the Gulf of St. Lawrence and down the river to Quebec City, where we spent a few days.

A retired Navy Reserve officer and reporter from the *Boston Globe*, Steven Young, was on board to do a story on the cruise. Since I was seen around the ship photographing the crew and the action, he asked if he could see my contact sheets when we got back to Boston. I was honored to be asked. After I processed the film and made contact sheets in the darkroom at Magnum Productions, the reporter came by to see what I had. I showed him my contact sheets and a few of my favorite prints, including the one I'd made of Yeoman Johnson fishing.

"This is Johnson," he exclaimed.

"Yes, Curtis Johnson, the yeoman."

"No, it is President Johnson!"

"Ah ... now that you mention it, he does look a little like the president."

"Can I have this print?" he asked. "I think I know where I might get it published."

"Sure. Let me stamp the back with my copyright."

"I'll share 50/50 with you if it is published," the reporter said. "That okay with you?"

"Sure," I said.

The Photograph That Changed My Life

A month later, the July 9 edition of *Life* magazine carried a full-page photograph of Curtis Johnson on its "Miscellaneous" back page. I was thrilled, of course, except my name wasn't attached. The caption that accompanied my photograph was titled "Fishing in Troubled Waters." The editor's caption alluded to the fact that our president, Johnson, was mired down with a war in Vietnam, problems with Congress and Civil Rights. So, he had taken a rod and reel and "gone fishing." As the Commander in Chief, he could go fishing on any ship he wished, and the caption said this ship happened to be the U.S. *Compton*.... Oops, they got the wrong Johnson. This was Curtis Johnson, Yeoman First Class, USN. No relation.

The reporter and I split the $600

The last page in *Life* magazine's July 9, 1965, issue featured a full-page photo of my portrait of Yeoman Chris Johnson, misidentifying him as President Johnson.

fee from *Life*. A week later, I sold the same photograph to a German magazine for another $300, which I kept.

A few weeks later, the August 22 edition of the *Boston Globe Sunday Magazine* carried a two-page story of our summer cruise, written by Stephen B. Young, the reporter. The article included seven of my photographs. Not bad, I thought. Maybe I could become a journalist in this man's Navy.

The war in Vietnam was beginning to make an impression on me now. In the same edition of *Life* in which my photograph appeared, the editors listed the problems our president was facing:

The City of Saigon was under attack almost daily from infiltrators.

Constant airstrikes on Hanoi seemed to be making little progress in bringing North Vietnam to the peace table.

The government in Saigon was carrying out public executions, had instilled a curfew, and had silenced the press.

By this time, the U.S. had 21,000 troops into South Vietnam. Another 80,000 would likely be there by the end of the year. Other articles in that same magazine carried stories and pictures of dead Vietnamese and Americans, mentioning the possibility of nuclear annihilation.

Chu Lai

A few weeks later, *Life* magazine carried the story of a major operation in Chu Lai, Vietnam, with pictures by combat photographer Tim Page. It was a place I'd never heard of, but within a year I'd come to know this beach on the South China Sea intimately. In May 1965, the Marines and Seabee Battalion Ten came ashore on this deserted beach 60 miles south of Da Nang. In short order, the Seabees built an entire Marine air base just behind the beach. MCB-Ten built barracks, hangers, offices and laid down an 8,000-foot expeditionary airfield for the Marine A4A jet fighters. To protect the new airbase, Operation Starlite, the first major American ground battle of the Vietnam War, was launched in August. The 12-day battle, involving 5,500 Marines, was an attempt to eradicate the Viet Cong stronghold in Van Tuong peninsula in Quang Ngai Province, 12 miles south of the new base in Chu Lai. The operation killed nearly 700 Viet Cong soldiers, while U.S. losses included 45 Marines dead and more than 200 wounded.

Within a year, I would be getting ready to land on that same beach on the South China Sea—Chu Lai, Vietnam.

Advancement

When I received my orders for "active duty" in 1965, it was already late November. By now, I was a Seaman (E-3), one step away from becoming a petty officer. My orders sent me to the transit barracks in Newport, Rhode Island, then off to serve on the USS *Lake Champlain* (CV-39), a Navy antisubmarine carrier. She was berthed at Quonset Point Naval Air Station, across Narragansett Bay from Newport.

2. Off to Sea, with a Camera

My mother breathed a sigh of relief when I told her I was not going to the war in Vietnam.

Aboard the *Lake Champlain*, this "college kid" was assigned to the E&T (Education and Training) Office as a clerk. I could type. I'll say one thing for the Navy, they have a great training program.

The Navy is a technically sophisticated branch of the service, with ships, submarines, planes and weapons systems that need highly trained personnel. To train these technicians, the Navy has schools for every possible trade, along with manuals, workbooks, and an advancement protocol.

You can go to school to become a radio operator, electrician, builder, carpenter, crane operator, bulldozer driver. There are schools for signalmen, coxswain, engine men, weapons systems technicians, electronic technicians, even journalists. Fort Slocum, on Long Island, was the joint services Defense Information School, where newspaper, radio and television reporters and photojournalists were schooled. I would have loved to have spent 12 weeks there, but since I was a reservist with only two years of required active duty, the Navy wasn't about to spend time and money training me only to get a year of service out of me. If you were regular Navy, with three years of service, schools were open to you.

But there was another path the Navy offered for advancement. I could order up a training manual, study on my own, then take a test. If I passed, had the required time in my current rate, and a positive evaluation in my service record, and they had an open billet, I could get advanced to Petty Officer Third Class Journalist. I ordered the Photographer's Mate and the Navy Journalist's workbooks. The Photographer's Mate workbook was mostly about aerial imaging. The Journalism rate was a practical approach to storytelling, and besides, that was what I'd been studying in college. The Navy's approach was less academic than college, with more emphasis on doing, rather than studying. While reading over the Journalist's workbook, I realized I already knew most of what was required.

A few months after I came aboard this floating airport, the ship was ordered to Philadelphia Naval Depot to be decommissioned. Well, that was quick.

I was the last serviceman to leave the ship and found myself reassigned to the USS *Caloosahatchee* (AO-98)—a seagoing gas station. Before departing Philly, I took the Navy test for Journalist, and waited to see if I passed.

The *Caloosahatchee*, a floating 7/11, was based in Newport to refuel carriers and destroyers underway at sea. During these UNREP (UNderway REPlenishment) exercises, we transferred JP-5 fuel for the planes and bunker fuel to drive the ships, as well as food, ordnance, personnel, even movies for the crew, all the while steaming along at 12 knots, the carrier on one side, a destroyer on the other side, hoses carried across the gap between the ships, suspended by cables.

By now, I didn't really mind being in the service. I'd made the transition from civilian to sailor, and all that entails. I was in the "Service." We didn't call it the military. Service was something you did for your country. Like paying taxes.

I've always looked at taxes as the price you pay for being a U.S. citizen. Taxes pay for the roads, airports, harbors, the military, courts, the FBI, NASA, NOAA, the NEA, the NHA and CDC and all the other trappings the government provides. It's the dues you pay to belong. The "service"—in this case, the military—was just another way of paying back. Some people hate paying taxes, or any form of service, and do everything

The USS *Caloosahatchee* steams into a fresh gale. I shot this from the deck of the USS *Champlain* during an UNREP. I made a print, submitted it up the chain of command, and it wound up, framed, on the bulkhead of the skipper's office aboard the USS *Caloosahatchee*. It was there when I arrived for duty.

they can to get out of their obligation. Ironically, it's usually the wealthy, those who derive the most benefit from the system, that refuse to help pay for it.

"Lyman!" The XO shouted to me from the bridge deck. It was July and I was scurrying around on the main deck with my camera photographing the men. "Get up here."

"Yes, sir!" I shouted back, and took the stairs two at a time to the bridge.

"Here. Congratulations, you passed your Journalist test." He handed me a slip of yellow paper from the teletype machine. "We have no billet aboard this ship for a Journalist, so you'll not be spending too much more time aboard with us." I didn't know if he was as pleased as I was, or not. Now all I had to do was wait until some ship or outfit needed a journalist and I would be reassigned.

Later that summer things did change. The *Caloosahatchee* went into dry dock in East Boston for an overhaul before heading to the Mediterranean for a two-year tour. I was not going, and while I was disappointed not to get to see some of the ports in the

Med, I was glad to be getting off that ship. But, if I was not going with the *Caloosahatchee*, what other ship would need me, a soon-to-be Navy Journalist? So, I waited.

I'm Going to Vietnam!

10/08/1966

AUTHORIZATION IN RATE. ADVANCE TO JO3 AS OF THIS DATE.
TRANSFER TO MCB-71, DAVISVILLE, RI NO LATER THAN 15/08/1966 PENDING SEA DUTY

EPDOLANT

It was mid–August, 1966. I'd just returned to the *Caloosahatchee* late on Sunday night from a weekend pass. Pinned to my bunk was a sheet of teletype paper. I ripped off the note and translated the Navy-speak into English. My advancement to an E-4, Journalist Third Class Petty Officer (JO3), had come through. I was being assigned to MCB-71, Davisville, Rhode Island, for SEA duty. MCB, I knew, stood for Mobile Construction Battalion—the Seabees. SEA duty meant … South East Asia. This outfit was heading to Vietnam! EPDOLANT means Enlisted Personnel Distribution Office Atlantic Fleet.

"Whoopee!" I shouted, awakening half the men in the berthing quarters. "I am heading to Vietnam!" Me, a photographer, a journalist. I could not have been happier. My shipmates thought I was nuts.

It took only a few days to finish up my duties on the *Caloosahatchee*. I sewed the JO3 patch on the left sleeve of my various uniforms, stripped off the *Caloosahatchee* patch on the right shoulder, packed up my sea bag and with a smile, saluted the officer of the deck and the ensign, climbed down to the dock yard and walked to my car in the parking lot. I was on my way to a war.

I had a few days of leave before reporting to Davisville, so I drove home to the hunting and fishing lodge my father had built beside a lake.

I parked my car at the top of the hill, ran down the path to the lodge, shouting hello to all, and shedding my dress whites as I went. I slipped on a bathing suit, ran down the steps from the porch to the dock and plunged into the lake. Floating in the clear, cool water, looking up at the blue sky and white clouds, I was no longer in the Navy. I was home, safe and loved. I dove down to the bottom of the lake and swam among the boulders I've known for so long, all thoughts of the *Caloosahatchee*, boot camp, the Navy, wiped away.

At dinner on the porch that evening, Mom asked, "Where is your next assignment? Another ship?" I'd been dreading this question. I knew she would not take the news well.

"I've been advanced to a Journalist Third Class. I've been assigned to a Seabee outfit in Davisville, Rhode Island. I report on Monday."

"What's a Seabee outfit?" asked my younger brother Lee.

"A Mobile Construction Battalion. We build stuff for the Marines and the Navy," I said.

"So you'll be in Rhode Island?" my Mom said, with a tone of relief.

"Yes, for a little while. We have about six months of training, then the unit will be going to Vietnam." There, I'd said it. Silence followed. The war was on television, with film footage of combat, fire fights, helicopters landing to drop off men, or, a "dust-off," helicopter lifting wounded from an LZ. Everyone knew what the war in Vietnam was like.

"You told us you were going to stay away from the war, here on the East Coast." Her voice now carried a mother's concern for her firstborn.

"This is a construction outfit, Mom," I said, in a confident voice. "We'll be on a base far from the front." My youngest brother, Carl, sat silent. He was quietly crying. He was convinced his big brother was going to war and would get killed.

"Look," I tried to explain to my family, "this is not actual combat duty. I'm the PR guy for the battalion. I'll be safe inside the perimeter. The Marines, the Army … they do the fighting."

"But will you be near the war?" my next brother asked. "You could be killed."

"Yes, my outfit will be near the war," I said. "We'll hear it. But this is no more dangerous than climbing mountains, or some of the crazy things we've done as kids. This is my chance to photograph and write about something really important. Yes, it's risky, but so are many things." Was I attempting to convince them, or myself? What did I really have to worry about?

I was going off to a war, to see what it was like. As long as I had to serve my country in the military, this would be more exciting than living on a ship at sea, with nothing to look at but the horizon.

Dad finally spoke. "Do you believe in this war? Do you know why we are fighting a war there? It's an awfully small country to be fighting over." Dad had been too young for World War I and too old for World War II, but his first son, my half-brother Buzz, had been a belly gunner on a B-24 over Germany in that war. I knew Dad had worried a great deal about Buzz in those days. Even I worried, though I was only four years old in 1944.

"We are fighting to stop Communism," I replied. I'd heard politicians use this expression to explain the reason for this war. "We are defending the South Vietnamese from the North Vietnamese Communists who want to take over."

The reason the U.S. was in a war in South Vietnam was beyond me. Like many kids my age, I was not overly political. I really hadn't given the war much thought, but I did want to see what it was like. I was envisioning a black-and-white war, like the one I'd seen on television, like the series *Victory at Sea*, or the war films of the '50s. That was the war I thought I was headed for.

Besides, I'd been playing war with my brothers and neighbors up in the woods behind our lake lodge for years when we were pre-teens. It was fun. No one got killed, and we all came home for dinner.

Yes, I knew there was a risk, but I've always been drawn to physical adventures—climbing mountains, skiing, sailing, SCUBA diving, driving too fast. This, I thought, was just another way to see what the world was like, what I was made of.

The Games Boys Play

Are all us guys risk seekers? Is that why we are over here? Daring some VC sniper to try and waste us? To see how much fear we can absorb without going bonkers?

Scaring ourselves and each other was a game we played all through high school and college. We'd drive down a country road on a starry night, with the car's headlights off, steering by the night sky we could see between the trees on either side of the road. It scared the bejesus out of the girls. All the better, as they'd grab you and hold on tight.

We'd see the glow of an oncoming car long before we'd see their lights, then turn our headlights back on.

My friend Allan, one of my brothers and I had climbed to the top of Mount Washington one winter, with crampons and ice axes, all three of us roped together. It took eight hours to reach the weather station at the top. The meteorologists there allowed us in to come in, get warm, have a cup of tea, then said we'd have to leave in order to get back down. It was dark by the time we reached the tree line and after 9 p.m. when we finally got back to the car. I had to walk down stairs backward for a week, my upper leg muscles hurt so much.

We almost "bought the farm" one winter when the three of us climbed Mount Madison. We started too late, ran into a blizzard after dark, and got lost above the tree line. Then Allan got a cramp and one of us had to carry him, while the other carried the packs. We eventually found the hut at the top by sending one of us out, tied to a rope, to sweep the black, barren mountaintop until the rope got caught on a cairn—a pile of rocks indicating the trail. Then there was the summer we worked on perfecting an IED to celebrate the 4th of July. We set it afloat in the middle of the lake, on a square of plywood lashed to an inner tune. The raft was piled high with magnesium shavings. Around 9 that evening the time-delayed fuse (a cigarette) set off the device with one hell of a *BANG*, setting the magnesium ablaze that then shot straight up into the night sky, raining down as a shower of sparks for five minutes. We could have killed ourselves a dozen times with the crazy stunts, adventures and mischief we got ourselves into. Skiing down unmarked trails, hanging off cliffs without protection. I'll not even mention the girls, and the businesses we started, which mostly failed or were abandoned—all just to find out what we could and probably should not be doing. We were just curious teens.

So, now I was heading off to Vietnam, the greatest risk game there is—a war. But I was not going to be in it, I was going to be behind it, one of the support guys, in the "rear echelon" that included many more men than would be out there doing the fighting.

What did I have to worry about?

Chapter 3

I'm Going to Be a Seabee

It was Monday morning, August 18, 1966, when I drove up to the front gate of the Seabee base in Davisville, Rhode Island. I showed my ID card and orders to the Marine guard, who waved me through, pointing to the base HQ. I parked my Campbell's-tomato-soup-orange VW in the visitor's lot, and with orders in hand walked into the first-floor offices. I was in my dress blues, a third-class petty officer now, a new JO3 rating patch on my left shoulder.

I was processed in, told where the barracks and the mess hall were, and where to check in with my outfit—a single-story office building lost amid all the other wooden buildings. Davisville is a sprawling military base, contiguous with Quonset Point, the naval air station, where the USS *Lake Champlain* had been berthed. I was in familiar territory.

I found the barracks, was shown to a bunk with its attendant locker where I dropped my sea bag and was given a mess hall chit, then I was aimed in the direction of Building A2. With orders still in hand, I walked across the grounds to A2 where MCB-71 was housed. This turned out to be the Regimental HQ. The yeoman at reception pointed to a desk in back, among rows of desks in a large room.

"That's your outfit over there," he said. I walked over, stood at attention and handed over my orders to a First Class Petty Officer, an EO1, an Equipment Operator. He was dressed in work blues. He looked up as I announced myself: "Third Class Journalist David Lyman reporting for duty as ordered." The petty officer was a non-commissioned officer, so there was no need to addresses him with a formal "sir." The older man looked over my orders, sat back and eyed me.

"Well, welcome. I suppose. Right now MCB-71 is just you and me, son. We are it. The entire battalion. The last person I need right now is a journalist. I need a yeoman, a personnel man, someone who can type and process in the men arriving for this new battalion. Can you type?" he asked.

"Yes," I said. "I worked in the Personnel Office on the USS *Lake Champlain* for a few months. I can handle the processing in."

"Good. That's your desk over there. We have 700 men and a bunch of officers to check in over the next two months, or so I'm told. Your job is to process the paperwork, get them assigned to the barracks and training schools."

"Is there an officer on board?" I asked.

"No. I'm it."

"I'll need a typewriter, filing cabinets, supplies, copy machine."

"Fill out a chit and I'll sign it. Until an officer arrives," he said, "I guess I'm in charge here."

Davisville, the Naval Seabee base in Rhode Island, had a scattering of single-story, wooden buildings left over from World War II, with a few parade grounds and rows of two-story brick barracks. You would think, with all the construction experience the Seabees have, that the base would be, well, nicer. Quonset Point, next door, was in far better shape. I got to know these buildings as I went in search of office supplies. There's a large mess hall, Regiment HQ, the BOQ (Bachelor Officers Quarters), a movie theater, and a snack bar selling beer and soft drinks—we called it the "geedunk." It's a Navy thing. Three Seabee battalions called Davisville home. The Navy had two other Seabee bases, one in Gulfport, Mississippi, and a third in Port Hueneme, California.

The next day, I was busy setting up an impromptu personnel office. I found an empty filing cabinet in the back room and moved it into my space at a desk across from the First Class. I asked around and found an Olivetti typewriter. I found the Mimeograph and Ditto machines, arcane duplicating technology dating back to the days of Edison. I "procured" file folders, stationery, and service jackets to hold the men's records. The next day men began arriving. I was ready. Thankfully they came in ones and twos and not all at once.

By the end of August, I had an assistant, Seaman Ron Reedy, a hefty Brooklyn Irishman who helped with the checking in process. He was good at it.

"Here. Fill this in," Reedy instructed, "and this and this, sign here and there, no, not there, here." There were forms on which to list next of kin, page twos, chow passes and liberty cards, forms for the BOQ and COMRATS, forms for schools, forms for berthing and forms for breathing.

"Oh, yes. Now that you're here," Reedy added, "welcome aboard the US Naval Mobile Construction Battalion 71. And, yes ... we'll all be going to Vietnam in the spring."

By early September, the men were arriving by tens and twenties, every day. They came from Port Hueneme, the DPPO school over at Quonset Point, and Naval reserve units in Brooklyn. They came from destroyers, aircraft carriers, and fleet oilers. They came from the "Ice" (the U.S. Antarctic Research Base). They came from OCS and the CDC school, some came from Vietnam. They were fleet sailors, Seabees, old salts and young boots just out of recruit training. The bulk of the men had been working in the construction trades just a few weeks earlier but were now in the Navy through the DPPO (Direct Procurement Petty Officers) program. Those of us from the fleet called these new petty officers IPOs, Instant Petty Officers. They included carpenters, electricians, plumbers, steel workers, heavy equipment operators, mechanics, well drillers, and explosives technicians who had just completed four weeks of Naval Petty Officer training. Five weeks before, they had been on high-paying civilian construction projects, but now they were Seabees, if in name only—later they would have the opportunity to prove what it was to be a real Seabee.

"Pete" Peterson, a BU2 from North Dakota, arrived in late August. There were only about 70 men in the whole battalion then. When it was discovered that Pete (his real first name is Gerald) could type, Chief Otterson grabbed him as Charlie Company's clerk. When a new steel worker or builder checked in, I'd send them over to Pete, who assigned the builders to the first or second platoon, and the steelworkers to the third platoon. Charlie Company had three squads per platoon, with 13 men in each squad. By mid-September Charlie Company had 120 men.

Pete already had a two-year degree in industrial drafting when he joined the regular Navy in January 1966. So the Navy sent him off for 12 weeks of Builders "A" School to learn how to build stuff the Navy Way. But he seldom got to build anything, as he was stuck in an office, except when he got to join a convoy security team or join a team of builders for a day or two.

Pete was a busy man over in Charlie Company by the time Ensign T.W. Bones arrived to be the company's Officer in Charge (OIC). Seabee builders were arriving by the twos and fives, daily. Pete was busy assigning them to training sessions on base and keeping track of where each man was. He lost one guy and mistakenly reported him AWOL. Pete later remembered he'd sent the guy off to leadership school in Newport the previous week.

After officially becoming part of this still unofficial naval unit (the battalion was not yet commissioned), the Seabees and Fleet-bees were interviewed, classified, assigned to companies, given barracks assignments and added to various lists. There were lists for schools, for duty sections, watch schedules and lists for military training at Sun Valley—the nearby combat training facility. Reedy and I were busy 'Bees.

By the first of September, there were 300 men on board and a handful of officers. Yeoman Reedy and I were replaced when two real Personnel men arrived to take over. Reedy was assigned as the yeoman/clerk for the unit's chaplain, LT Dennis. I went off on to my next job, editor of the POD.

The Seabees—We Can Do!

In those first few days of processing-in the men, there was little else to do. I first got bored, then became curious about what these Seabees were really all about. I'd heard that

A company of Seventy-One Seabees march off to chow between rows of Davisville barracks, October 1966.

Seventy-One was to be one of the battalions to be "re-commissioned" and that the original Seventy-One had served in the Pacific in World War II.

What better way to satisfy my curiosity than to write about it? But you can't write about something you don't know anything about (not that I haven't tried). So I had to go out and do some research.

I asked around the regiment and found there was an old Seventy-One veteran living in the area who'd served in the Pacific during World War II. He had a copy of the unit's cruise book and loaned it to me. As I read through it, I realized that you can't wage a war without there being engineers and construction workers to build things and to fix things that have been blown up. The journalist who put the book together was a good writer and he told the story of the original Seventy-One's two years of action in the Pacific. It was compelling reading. From this book, I wrote up a brief history of MCB-71 and included it in the check-in packet for the men arriving—to help the men understand the heritage they were joining. (See the Appendix for an excerpt of that history, with a link to a PDF of the cruise book.)

A Brief History of the Seabees

A Seabee outfit, or Naval Mobile Construction Battalion, is sort like a MASH (Mobile Army Surgical Hospital) unit, as seen in the popular movie and TV series. It is a self-contained unit of around 800 men and officers with its own cooks, office personnel, chaplain, engineers, architects, construction workers, doctors, and a monthly newspaper. As a mobile unit, we can "bug out" at any time, move halfway around the world, set up camp, and build anything the military wants—an entire Naval base if necessary, although that might require two battalions.

The Seabees were formed in 1942, and if you have ever watched John Wayne in the 1944 movie *The Fighting Seabees*, you'll see Hollywood's dramatized version of the Seabee history. It's a period propaganda movie, but it does hold a germ of truth. As World War II got underway, the military needed roads, runways, barracks, mess halls, hospitals, even basketball courts. The Marines needed landing and port facilities to offload supplies, equipment and more men. The civilian contractors and the men doing the building were ill equipped and not trained to defend themselves when their project came under attack, so the Seabees were formed as a military construction arm of the Navy. The Marines and the Army have similar engineering units, but the Seabees were the outfits to call.

While the majority of the Seabee units were building facilities on islands in the Pacific, Seabees were among the first to go ashore on the beaches of Normandy on the night of June 6, 1944. They came ashore under cover of darkness to blow up the steel and concrete barriers the Germans had built in the water and on the beaches to forestall amphibious landings. During the landings, 10,000 Seabees installed pontoon causeways over which tanks, trucks, jeeps and materiel flowed shore.

The name "Seabees," and the bumblebee that represents them, was originated by Frank Iafrate, a civilian draftsmen and cartoonist working at Quonset Point Naval Air Station in Rhode Island in the early '40s. Mr. Iafrate was asked to sketch a Walt Disney–type character for a new construction unit. He first thought of a beaver but realized beavers run at the first sign of trouble. The bee was perfect; it could sting. The bee cartoon was approved by the Navy, and Sea and Bee, standing for Construction Battalion (CB) was incorporated with the new insignia. Mr. Iafrate himself later enlisted in the Navy as a Seabee.

The Seabees in Vietnam

The Vietnamese had been at war with one enemy or another for more than 2,000 years—the Chinese, Mongolians, French, Japanese and each other, South versus North. As early as the mid–1950s, U.S. Navy Seabees were assigned to help move a million North Vietnamese, mostly Catholics, down to South Vietnam, in what was called the "Passage to Freedom." In 1956, a team of Seabee Engineers was assigned to survey the roads from South to North. They traveled by jeep, on foot, and by pack mule over rough terrain for months. What they found was devastation. World War II bombing raids, and sabotage from the Viet Minh and a more recent guerrilla group, the Viet Cong, had destroyed bridges and blown up large sections of road.

In 1963, a secret Navy Seabee team arrived in Vietnam to work with U.S. Army Special Forces, the CIA and the South Vietnamese military to begin constructing camps, runways, roads, port facilities, landing ramps for LSDs, and helicopter pads to combat a growing invasion from the North. In 1965, MCB-Ten came ashore with the Marines, landing on the beach of Chu Lai, to establish what would become a military city of over 60,000 men.

As the conflict between North and South heated up, more military infrastructure was needed: runways, landing strips, more base camps, roads and barracks, hospitals. Old World War II MCB units were being re-commissioned and put into action. By 1967, the year we arrived in 'Nam, there were 20,000 Seabees in-country. By the time we left in the fall of '67, there were 21 Seabee battalions building military facilities all up and down Vietnam.

But before we were to arrive, there was a lot this new battalion needed to learn, so off we went to train.

Life in the Seabees

By October, I was beginning to feel more like a Seabee. I was required to dress like one. "Clothes makes the man," they say. Never thought much about that until I'd been in the Navy for a few months, when I noticed I was beginning to feel more like a sailor. Perhaps the uniform does have something to do with it. I was proud of my shiny shoes, the perfect square knot in my black rayon kerchief, the fit of my bell-bottom trousers. We sailors from the fleet had five uniforms: dress blues, work blues, dress whites, work whites, and dungarees—all needing attention, cleaning, ironing, folding and stowing. I was just getting used to shipboard uniforms when the Navy ups and gives me another uniform, my drab green Seabee uniform. Let me tell you about these duds.

The U.S. Marines get hand-me-downs from the Army and Navy, the Seabees get hand-me-down from the Marines. The Army and Marines get M16 rifles in Vietnam, we get an M14, rifles that go back to the Korean conflict. The Army and Marines get jungle fatigues and jungle boots; we get heavy-duty green fatigues left over from a Korean winter campaign. Our lace-up black leather boots sweat all day.

3. I'm Going to Be a Seabee

We "fleet rates" had to replace our work blues and whites, depending on the season, with these Marine hand-me-down green duds. They were uncomfortable, needed a gallon of spray starch and a hot iron to get them past inspection. Even our skivvies (underwear) were green.

The dress code involved "blousing" the pant legs of our fatigues over the boot tops. This meant wrapping a screen door spring around the top of each boot, hooking the ends together, and tucking your trouser leg under the spring—to keep out the snakes and jiggers, or so they told us.

The cap we wore was of little use, but like our white sailor caps, each man shaped his to suit. During maneuvers, or outside the perimeter in Vietnam, we were required to wear a steel helmet with its removable inner liner and camouflage fabric outer cover. You could heat up a can of C-rations in your helmet, use it to shave in, piss in, or drink beer from. I painted "PRESS" on both sides of my fabric cover, hoping the enemy would see I was a non-combatant, and not shoot me.

Dress blues (right) were replaced by hand-me-down green duds from the Marines (left).

Everyone had to wear a flak jacket when outside the "wire," the perimeter, in Vietnam. These brick-lined vests weighed 22 pounds and were supposed to protect your torso from grenade and mortar fragments. They did not hang low enough to protect the privates.

To show what rate or rank we were, we wore a metal chevron pin on our shirt lapels and cap. Our Navy belt buckles, even our lapel insignias, had to be blackened so as to not shine or draw attention, in case the VC were watching. Over our right breast pocket was our last name, embroidered, and over the left was embroidered "US Navy."

Officers were not to be saluted in the combat zone, so as to not draw attention to a superior officer—prime targets for snipers. We were getting ready to deploy and live in Vietnam.

The Unit's Structure

Like Most Seabee outfits, Seventy-One had five companies: Alpha, Bravo, Charlie, Delta and H, or Headquarters.

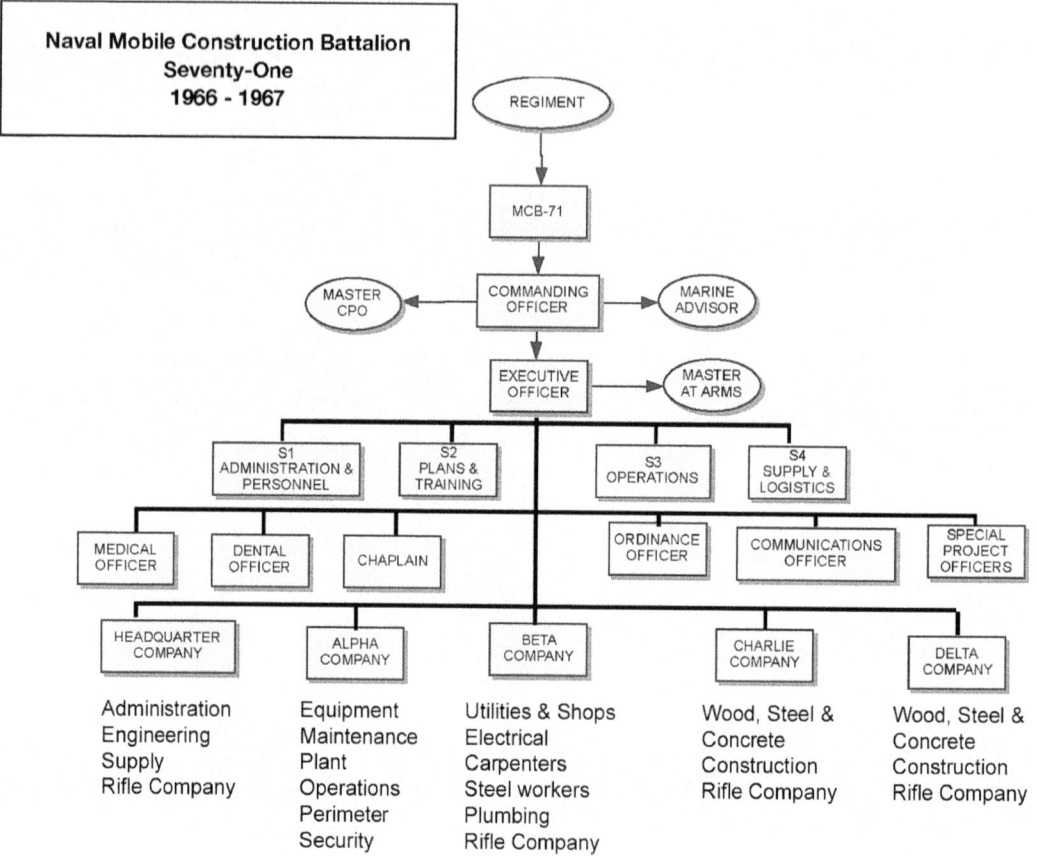

Organization of a typical Seabee battalion.

Alpha, our largest company, included dozer, scraper and grader operators, truck drivers, mechanics, rock drillers, quarrymen, asphalt and cement plant operators and road builders. Alpha Company also provided our base security once in-country, with the guys standing four-hour watches at machine gun positions around our perimeter.

Bravo, Charlie and Delta companies were made up of builders, utility men, steel workers, and other construction rates. These guys built *vertical* projects out of concrete, wood and steel. They would be cutting up 2 by 4s, nailing up plywood, erecting steel buildings and installing metal roofs; they'd be rigging com wire, putting in electrical systems and lighting, fixing air conditioners and the generating and refrigeration plants.

Most of the men, around 80 percent, in A, B, C and D companies were DPPOs, Direct Procurement Petty Officers. I'll tell you about these chaps in a minute.

Hotel Company, aka Headquarters, aka HQ, would be full of men who had come from the fleet, from the regular going-to-sea Navy. They included yeoman, personnel men, postal clerks, bursars, barbers, storekeepers, cooks, corpsmen, even a journalist. Some of these fleet rates had no idea what MCB meant on their orders. Could it have been Nuclear Missile Command Boat or Naval Mine Control Boat? They found out the minute they stepped off the bus in front of the Seabee sign at Davisville.

There were three distinct groups of personnel in our Seabee outfit: The officers, about 20-plus of them. They included ensigns who had just finished OCS or an ROC program, and were as green as the rest of us. The older officers who ran things included Lieutenants Junior Grade (LTJG), Lieutenants (LT), Lieutenant Commanders (LCDR) and two Commanders (CDR), the CO and XO.

Chiefs—older enlisted men who had been in the Navy for ages—there were about ten of them. They ran the companies and teams in the field. Then there were the rest of us enlisted guys (E-2 and E-3), from non-rated to Third, Second and First Class Petty Officers, (E-4, E-5 and E-6).

We also had a Marine "Gunny," a Marine Gunnery Sergeant, whose job it was to oversee our combat readiness, the unit's weapons, security bunkers, convoys and the military side of our unit. Not only do the Seabees build things in a combat war zone, they are also training to defend themselves and what they build.

Instant Petty Officers (IPOs)

I was about to turn 27 that fall (1966), right after Thanksgiving, old for an enlisted man, but not in this outfit. Most of the Seabee petty officers were in their 20s, even 30s. A few of the chiefs were in their 50s—some had served in World War II. These "gray beards" had a great deal more savvy than most of the officers.

The DPPOs (Direct Procurement Petty Offices) were E-4, E-5 or E-6; enlisted men who had years of civilian construction experience before they joined the Navy. These construction pros were recruited for their experience and entered the Navy's DPPO program, to wind up as petty officers, depending on experience in their trade. We called them IPOs, Instant Petty Officers, because their training in the military's way of doing things was only a four-week boot camp.

As the IPOs arrived and checked in, they were teamed up with others of their rate, assigned to a company; the company clerks assigned each to a platoon, then a squad. Each platoon was under the command of a Chief or a regular Seabee First Class, who had made the Navy a career.

I got to watch the men in their squads and platoons go through a bonding process, which included team exercises, and a great deal of unofficial "one-ups-men-ship" in the barracks and at the bars. I noticed most of the guys were gregarious. They felt comfortable as part of a team. I didn't. I never joined a team in high school or college. I was always the manager or scorekeeper. I was never one of the actors in a school play, always the stage manager. Being a photographer and a writer fits my personality. They are solitary professions. I am comfortable being alone, always have been, even growing up in a family of four boys. So being crammed in with 800 other guys in our unit, or on shipboard, took a bit of getting used to.

My Buddies

Two months after arriving at Davisville I could call myself a Seabee. I had made only a few friends, but then that's all you really need anyway. My buddies included Jim Reedy, the now chaplain's yeoman; Wally Skop, a YN3 from Kingston, New York, a real cut-up; and Dick Stapleman, an equipment operator from Idaho. Dick was the commanding officer's driver, responsible for the CO's car. After dropping the CO at the officers' quarters in the evening, he'd swing by the barracks and pick up the rest of us for a ride to the bar. There were others—Hanratty who worked in Admin; Wagnor, an engineering assistant; Widmark, who worked in the darkroom with Knupp, the photographer's mate (who I didn't get along with). The officers were another group entirely. Above us in the chain of command, they had been made "officers and gentlemen" by an act of Congress, while we were merely the proletariat.

Four of us developed code names: Raunchy Reedy, Scuzzy Skop, Slimy Lyman, but Stapleman was just Stapleman. We four remained buddies all the way through training, deployment and our return to Davisville. But the week after I was released from active duty and moved to a ski town in Vermont, I hardly heard anything from the team again—until now.

My half-brother, Buzz, who was a gunner on a B-24 in World War II, mentioned the same thing. After his war, no one wanted to be reminded.

The Plan of the Day

That first week in September, only two weeks after landing in this Seabee outfit, the Executive Officer (XO) checked in. As I was processing him in, he asked, "Who here can type? I want to get out a POD, every day." This was not the first time someone has asked me if I could type. First time I heard it, I was a brand-new E-1, a seaman recruit on the first day of our "indoctrination" into the Navy.

A second-class boatswain's mate stuck his head into the classroom where 30 of us brand new E-1 Seaman Recruits were learning how to address officers, salute properly and fold our uniforms. "Anyone here able to type?" I looked around. No hands. Sheepishly I raised my hand.

"You can type?"

"Yes."

"You're the college kid? Right? Get down to the XO's office. They need a Yeoman. They can't use you, get your butt back here. Understand?"

"Yes, sir!" Off I went on a slightly different track from the rest of the recruits. "College kid"—that nickname followed me for the rest of my Navy career. With my black-rimmed, "Clark Kent" glasses, my thin frame and blond hair, I looked more intellectual than I was—a college dropout. But I knew how to type. I'd perfected my hunt-and-peck technique as a billing clerk working part-time at U.S. Rubber Company in Chicopee Falls (Massachusetts) while in engineer college. Typing was required when I got to journalism school at Boston University. Even though I never did learn to touch type (I still have to look at the keys), I can type 40 words a minute, with moderate typos. That one skill not only helped me in the Navy, it laid the groundwork for the career I'd choose to do for the rest of my life—write.

This time, the question was coming from the XO, Commander George Brown, a Naval Civil Engineer. He was a soft-spoken officer whose orders sounded more like suggestions than commands. He also looked more like a banker than a blood and guts officer of a military battalion. "Yes, sir. I can type," I replied. "I'm the unit's journalist, sir."

"As soon as we get a personnel man in here, I'd like you to get out the POD," CDR Brown said. The XO (Executive Officer) is second in command and the officer who actually runs the battalion.

The Plan of the Day (POD) is like the unit's daily newspaper. It's a printed schedule of what's supposed to happen the next day. "I can't run this battalion without a POD," he said, smiling.

By the end of September, there were enough officers and men on board so we moved to our own building. When a real personnel rate arrived to take over the processing in, I moved into a small office just down the hall from the CO and XO to better assume my new "official" role as editor of the POD.

Since I was the second person to join this new Seabee battalion, I knew everyone, knew the base, knew how to get things done, knew where to find stuff. I was Radar O'Riley, the admin corporal in M*A*S*H, the one who knew what was going to happen before it happened.

In my new role as POD editor, I spent my mornings gathering details. I made the rounds of each company office, checking in with the company clerk about their plans for the next day. Afternoons, I checked in with the XO to find out what he wanted in the POD for the following day.

A lot of the POD was standard stuff, the day and date, the major officers, who was to be the OOD, the OPS officer, and Master at Arms. Then came the schedule for that day, beginning with reveille, breakfast, officers' call, muster by company, inspection and instructions, then the work that was to be done that day.

There were schools for the tradesmen, work details for the recruits, projects to undertake by platoons and squads. Then lunch. All by the clock. After lunch, more assignments, projects, instructions—all this to keep the outfit informed and running on time.

After I'd gathered the details from each company, I'd type up a rough draft for the XO to review and edit. He's pass my draft by the CO, and they'd both make changes and additions. I'd then type up a smooth "master," the XO would review and sign it, then hand it back to me, and I went to press. Getting the daily POD printed was also my job. Thankfully I'd learned the process on one of my last ships.

Office Technology

"If we need a few copies," instructed the yeoman first class in the personnel office on the carrier, "you use carbon paper. Good for three or four copies." He was overweight, and by the stripes on the forearm of his jersey he'd been in the service for most of his life—one stripe for every four-year hitch. He also had a permanent crook in the forefinger of his right hand, where a coffee mug resided. These E-6 lifers do very little actual work, mostly they yell at the E-3s and E-4s who do the work, but they do know what's to be done.

"If an officer needs more copies, you have two options," the yeoman instructed. "Ditto or Mimeo." He showed me two machines on a table in the corner, each the size of a large bread box. "You know how to use those?" he asked.

"Yes," I said, "I used them in the office at the tire plant where I worked when I was in college."

"We'll soon find out how much the college kid knows," he said. "The CO needs this set of instructions typed out and he needs 50 copies. You can handle that?"

"I can try," I said.

The Ditto machine, or "spirit duplicator," is a simple machine, but it has its limits. To duplicate reports, orders, instructions, you type the text onto a top sheet of paper to which a blue carbon sheet is attached. As you type the letters, the blue carbon is transferred to the back of the top sheet. This sheet, or stencil, is fixed to a drum on the Ditto machine. As you crank the handle, sheets of plain paper are fed under a roller where they are dampened with alcohol. The damp sheet is then passed under the drum where the stencil transfers some of the blue carbon from the top sheet. These stencils were good for about 20 copies before the carbon was used up.

The next option for generating multiple copies is the Mimeo, or mimeograph machine, a technology going back to Edison in 1888. This machine was in general use in schools, churches and offices around the world for more than half a century, until the current generation of "copy machines" arrived.

This process also involved typing, or drawing, on a special stencil. As you type, the letters form small perforations in the top sheet. This stencil is placed on a drum, which contains a gooey black ink. As the drum rotates, clean sheets of paper are pressed between the inked stencil and the bottom drum. Ink is squeezed through the tiny holes in the stencil onto the fresh paper. This process could generate hundreds of copies before the stencil wore out.

Fixing a typo, and I created many, was not easy, but it could be done with the bottle and small brush of "Wite-Out."

"This man's war is all about technology," added the yeoman. "Got to know how things work. You got to know how to dismantle and clean your weapon, fight a fire on a ship, read a radar screen. Back here in the office it's the same thing. It's about machines. If we didn't have these machines, you'd be using a quill pen and ink, and the grunts out on the line would be killing each other with bows and arrows, but then I guess those are a rudimentary form of technology as well."

The kids today have no idea how difficult it was to do things back then, especially in the tropics, with no air conditioning and a war going on all around you.

My father taught me how to use tools: saws, chisels, draw shaves, a hammer, planes, a level and plumb bob to build boats; photography meant I needed to learn chemistry, optics, the mechanics of the shutter and the iris. Some of these ancient tools and technology I still use, but much of the technology has changed, and drastically. Those who come lately to the creative process know little or nothing about the technology that came before. Construction, photography, printing, radio and television, all of these technologies have experienced major transitions, and while I and my fellow journalists embrace the new, we also have a fond affection for technology on which we cut our teeth.

At the bottom of each day's POD was space for "Announcements." This was where I got to be creative and exercise my journalistic training and sense of humor. I started including interesting events on the base, movies at the theater, a report on evening touch football games between the officers and enlisted men. I had to use nicknames for the officers, and disguise the actual events. There was gossip making the rounds, humorous screw-ups within the battalion, news about who was doing extra duty over the weekend.

One week in November, the skipper was called to Regimental HQ and questioned about the un-military nature of his unit's POD. "All I can say," said my skipper, in his (and my) defense, "is that our POD is read by everyone in the outfit, and by most of the men in other units as well."

The March to Town

During one of our POD meetings, the skipper and XO were discussing what could be done to bring the entire battalion together for an exercise to build esprit de corps. As the public relations guy, I suggested a march into Providence, a distance of 17 miles, to raise awareness for UNICEF. It would get us great press.

"That's a bit too long," said the XO.

"How about a march to Warwick? That's only seven miles."

"That's better."

"I'll alert the media," I offered, "tell them this Seabee outfit is marching for UNICEF. We can carry a large sign. Make people along the way aware of what we were marching for." The Skipper and XO went for it. I had the carpenters make two large signs and our sign painter did the lettering.

The entire battalion, all 800 men and officers, turned out in full combat gear, rifles, packs, helmets and boots. They formed up, and with the skipper and XO leading, off they went, out of the base, up U.S. Highway One, heading north toward Warwick.

Of course, *I* wasn't going to do any marching; after all, this was my idea. I commandeered a jeep and with my buddy Stapleman driving, we shadowed the march so I could photograph the column of men on their way into Warwick. My photographs appeared in the Providence newspapers the next day, and we got a mention and a photograph on television. The men were none too happy with me and my idea of a seven-mile march in full combat gear, on a warm October day, but the XO and CO were pleased with the press coverage and a "well done" from Regimental Command.

That fall was a study in confusion, but by October 4, we were an official military unit. There was a formal commissioning ceremony, with marching, speeches by admirals, the CO, the XO and a blessing by the chaplain.

A second class yeoman arrived in the battalion, and I was relieved of my POD editorship and relegated to one of the smaller offices in the rear of the building. Then off I went for two weeks of basic combat training.

Chapter 4

Training for Combat Duty

Welcome to Mudville

"Ready on the left. Ready on the right. All ready on the firing line. You may commence firing when your target faces you."

The drill instructor's harsh command was followed by pure silence. Then all hell broke loose as twenty M14 rifles opened up with a fusillade of 7.62mm slugs hurtling to their targets. The firing continued for a full minute, filling the air with a deafening din. It was a cold November morning and we were in Sun Valley—not the posh ski resort in Idaho, but a scruffy, good-for-nothing, gravel pit in Rhode Island, ten miles from our warm barracks back at the base. This combat training facility was run by a team of hard-nosed Marine sergeants. They were nastier than the biting wind that was sweeping in off Narragansett Bay, a wind filled with the sound of small arms fire, the sound of war.

A platoon of cold and shivering Seabees were lying on frozen ground squinting down the barrels of their M14s, getting used to the sights on the barrel, the trigger pull, the kick, and the noise. This was just one of hundreds of exercises we went through in preparation for our combat duty in Vietnam—a place as unlike this freezing grey New England landscape as one could imagine.

As the units' journalist, historian and scribe, I had to complete this training with the rest of the men in Hotel Company—but I got to carry along my camera. This two-week training was an introduction to the weapons of war. We learned how to heave a M61 grenade—and duck. We fired our rifles, the .45-caliber service pistol, grenade launchers. We learned to watch out for the back blast from a 3.5 anti-tank rocket launcher (bazooka). This firing exercise was the last day of week one. Earlier that week had found us in classrooms back at the base, listening to and watching a Marine sergeant show us how to dismantle, clean and reassemble our own M14s and the M60 machine gun—until we could do it blindfolded. There were classes in combat formations, hand-to-hand combat, map reading, camouflage, silent hand commands, and we heard lots of war stories by the sergeants who had recently returned from Vietnam.

Week Two—the real test was about to begin. Our warm classrooms, barracks and beers at the base geedunk every night was to end. We boarded the grey buses Monday morning at 4:30 a.m. on a cold November day. The steel barrel of my M14 was too cold to touch, and I was too cold to talk. We were all just too cold. I stomped around in my service boots, trying to keep warm, as did the 20 other men waiting with me.

It was a 20-minute ride to Sun Valley, our new home. We piled out of the buses, formed up into ranks, a familiar routine now. Morning was still night when the Marine

4. Training for Combat Duty

instructor led us to a line of six Quonset huts, each big enough for a squad. They were cold, more like iceboxes than barracks. A small oil-burning heater stood in the middle of the hut. With luck, it might give off some heat. There were rows of cots arranged along the walls, and a footlocker for each—this was home?

I was told to find a rack, a dusty mattress on a wire frame, and to inspect my second-hand "782" gear. This was a conglomeration of mud-covered equipment: a web belt, canteen, ammo pouch, a salty combat helmet, well-worn poncho and a knapsack. My squad and I didn't have time to dwell on the sorry state of our combat equipment, as the instructor entered with orders for setting up our lodgings and posting today's routine. A routine that looked as if it would take three days to complete. By the end of that first day, we felt as if it had.

We learned that you can see a cigarette lit at 400 yards, hear a bolt go home in a rifle at 300 yards, hear whispers at 200 yards. We watched flares of every description light up the night—old friends once we were in Vietnam. My platoon and I sat through classes in night sounds, patrol movements, first aid, and battle dressings, as we learned to use most of the equipment used by the Marines in combat. There was marching and more marching. Lunch every day was a box of C-rations for each man, followed by marching, classes and more marching. It was to be a full week, but thankfully just one week; the Marines get six weeks of this—ouch!

"You think this is bad," said our drill sergeant, "wait until you get your sorry asses down to Camp Lejeune, where the real guerrilla training begins. You'll all be crying to be back here in comfortable Sun Valley." This was just a "basic" introduction to combat Seabees might need if they were attacked on a building site. After all, "we build, we fight to protect what we build" was the Seabee's motto since World War II.

Dinner at Sun Valley was a team exercise. The sergeant dropped off a case of C-rations in our Quonset hut. The case contains 24 small C-ration boxes, enough food to sustain 24 men for 12 hours. Each individual box contained a few cans—the "main course," which could be a can of succulent pork slices or delicious beans and meatballs, or chicken and noodles or our all-time favorite: lima beans and ham, ugh! There might be a very small can of peaches, or fruit cocktail, a packet of crackers, and a few luxury items: toilet paper, chewing gum, five cigarettes and a packet of coffee mix. We began to look on these luxuries as the highlight of our day. We'd fill a large pot with water, put it on the oil heater in the middle of the room to get hot, then each of us dropped our cans of dinner in the hot water to take the chill off. There would always be a lot of bartering as we swapped dinners or exchanged cigarettes for peaches. We became experts at opening our tin cans with a military P-38, a small and simple can opener that we hung on our dog tag chain. By the end of the week each man was the proud owner of their own P-38—the sign of a trained combat killer.

Tuesday we found ourselves belly down on the frozen ground, rifles cradled in our arms before us, crawling forward on our elbows under live fire and barbed wire. This was the infiltration course. We were harassed all afternoon, sniffing colored smoke grenades and were yelled at. A rope bridge spanned a gully—a foot rope to inch along on, another rope, chest high, to hold on to for balance. One Seabee didn't lean out, but pulled back on the hand rope, sending five of his buddies into the mud 10 feet below, and entangling the others in the two ropes. It took six instructors a half hour to untie the troopers.

Our training went on. We were taught the "high crawl," the "low crawl," how to "hit the deck." We were yelled at, cursed at, sworn at. The frozen ground and the barbed wire pulled and tore our combat duds, scraped the skin off our elbows, the smoke-screen laid down by the instructors burned our eyes, but as each man crossed the log barrier at the end of the course he was pulled to his feet, brushed off and allowed to stand with the rest, yelling encouragement to the man behind, still trapped in the barbed wire maze.

We didn't lose anyone during the four-hour night compass exercise, but it was nip and tuck in the back woods that night. This "Orientation Course" requires your squad to follow a set of instructions, in the dark, from mark to mark, using only a compass. Our instructors assured us that we were so stupid that they were already getting prepared for an overnight search for lost patrols.

Thursday was our BIG day—both platoons marched off into the Rhode Island backwoods, down "The Road to Paris." We were harassed by the aggressors, our Marine instructors. This was the war games part of our training. It was fun, but there was hard frozen ground into which we had to dig foxholes for the night—and it was a cold night to live through. Flares lit the sky, keeping us awake and on watch. There was small arms fire somewhere out there in the darkness. We ate cold C-rations, as lighting a fire would give away our location and draw gunfire. Friday morning, we filled in our foxholes, gathered up our gear and marched back to our Quonset hut. There was a hot meal waiting, a written test to fill out, and an hour to clean quarters before the buses arrived to cart these 30 battle-seasoned, combat-hardened, bragging heroes back to base and a shower.

Crawling in the mud during combat training.

Down and Dirty with the Marines

The training of a fighting man takes a lot of sharp orders, equipment, time, yelling and money—things the Marines have aplenty.

The Seabees are a Navy unit, like the Marines. Most of the building the Seabees do is for the Marines, but in Vietnam, we would be building and repairing things for the

4. Training for Combat Duty

Training on a rope bridge.

U.S. Army, Marines, Air Force, the Korean and Vietnamese Army, and the Vietnamese civilians in the villages near our base.

Since we would be in the combat zone, we might occasionally be called on to defend what we were building, as well as ourselves. So off we went to spend three weeks with the Marines in Camp Lejeune, North Carolina. They knew how to fight.

In January, the entire battalion boarded half a dozen C-130 transport planes and flew to the Marines training facility in North Carolina. We were leaving cold, snow-covered New England, and were looking forward to a balmy time in the South. We didn't get it. We were met with snow, rain, mud, and more cold. In the retelling of our Lejeune story at bars and future cocktail parties, these three weeks would take on glorious and grand proportions. But here is an accurate account of those January days in the southern pines of North Carolina—just for the record.

We landed at Cherry Point, North Carolina—the Marine Air Base near Camp Lejeune. We enlisted men crowded aboard man-hauls, 35-foot tractor trailers with few windows, more like cattle cars, for the hour-long trip, standing up all the way, to our home south of the Mason-Dixon line. We arrived at Stony Bay Camp, a small World War II compound stuck at the extreme southern section of the huge Marine training facility. We were housed in small, white concrete huts, each with its own kerosene heater and racks of musty mattresses on rusty steel cots. The showers and toilets were in separate cement block huts, a short walk away. This was problematic. Making the three-minute dash to the head to pee in the middle of the night, in six inches of snow, meant getting dressed. A few men elected to run the distance in skivvies and barefoot. A few others just snuck around the back of the hut and peed in the bushes. Some were caught and given extra duty.

At Stone Bay Camp we were self-contained, except for the chow hall, and the bar which required a 15-minute hike through the woods to the rifle range complex. We called the path the Burma Road.

The Fleet-bees that had served aboard ships found this a real treat. We were ashore. We could switch into our civilian duds after chow and make our way to the EM club for a pitcher of beer. We'd then stumble back down the Burma Road in the dark. It's a miracle no one was lost.

Our first days of Marine training were wet. We sat on wooden benches in an outdoor classroom, rain dripping from the pines, drizzling off helmets, running down the backs of our necks, rusting the barrels of our M14s. The Marine instructors were a no-nonsense bunch, from the officers all the way down to the Jarheads. They took their mission seriously. We, on the other hand, a hastily thrown together bunch of former construction workers, well ... we were a little less formal. Marines must suffer from bad hearing, for there was a lot of yelling, barking and in-your-face shouting. It was all we could do to keep a straight face.

Marine instructors help a squad of Seabees learn how to operate the M60 machine gun on the firing line in Camp Lejeune.

We learned how to yank the pin on an M26 grenade, throw it and duck. We threw smoke grenades and shot grenades off the end of our M14s. To break up the routine, there were afternoon war games, as our Marine instructors took us into the North Carolina woods for squad maneuvers. We crawled around in the mud, under barbed wire, while live .50-caliber bullets whizzed overhead. Under conditions like these, my cameras stayed dry inside my camera bag. These six days of infantry training wore on as we learned more about freezing in North Carolina than coping with the topical heat we'd encounter once in Vietnam.

Our days were full of this stuff, but in the evenings, after dinner, we climbed into civilian duds and relaxed. By now, MCB-71 had been together for three months, chiefs, officers and enlisted. We were becoming a unit, teams were bonded, friendships were made. There was a movie theater up at the rifle range, along with the EM Club. You had a choice: a movie or beer. You couldn't do both, for the movie got out about the time the bar was required to close. I saw few films, electing to fuel my imagination with a pitcher of beer and a bag of Doritos. The bar ran out of beer most nights following our invasion. The Marine who managed the place said that he'd never sold so much beer.

My regular drinking buddies, Reddy, Skop, Wagnor and Dick Stapleton, and a few of the guys from engineering and the survey department made the hike up the Burma Road nightly, but it was the hike back in the dark that was the challenge.

A couple of guys from A Company got their hands on a few small booby-traps and mined the Burma Road one night. They strung tripwires across the path and waited in the underbrush for the fireworks. A bunch of officers making their way back from the nightly movie tripped the wires and the resulting bangs scared the living daylight out of them. There was a lot of laughing and yelling, as the officers chased the enlisted men through the woods back to camp. Now, I wasn't part of these shenanigans, but being in the general vicinity, I was considered an accomplice by association, and had to stand guard duty a few nights with my buddies.

The rivalry between the officers and "certain" enlisted men didn't end there. Toward the end of our time in Lejeune, a few partying Seabees starting down the Burma Road broke into song as they passed the officers' quarters. About halfway down the trail, a bunch of be-slippered and hatless officers in their underwear caught up with the revelers and collected ID cards. I escaped, as I was a few steps ahead. What do they say about outrunning a hungry bear? You only have to run faster than the guy behind you.

The second week of training saw most of the battalion broken up into small groups for specific training schools. The surveyors, being good with trigonometry and the surveyors' transit, went to mortar school, where they dropped a mortar round right on top of the old dead tree the Marines had been aiming at for years. The Marines would have to find a new target.

The guys from A Company shot a half million dollars' worth of small arms ammunition and rockets. Marine cooks were teaching our cooks how to set up a field kitchen to feed us. Our corpsman underwent advanced training in field medicine, while the ETs and RMs attended Field Communication School. I got to see it all, as I made the rounds with the XO or CO in a jeep photographing what our men were doing.

The training at Camp Lejeune was geared for the not-too-bright teenage boot, fresh out of Parris Island. The Seabees, for the most part older, in their early and mid–20s, were a little more on the ball. So the training went rather fast, at least that's what the Marines told the CO and XO.

I joined a platoon of Seabees for two days of guerrilla warfare training, and not only learned a lot, but it made for a good story. We got a first-hand taste of what it would be like when we got Vietnam. We experienced an ambush, making all the mistakes any green Marine would make. We hid behind the truck.

"Get off and away from the truck," the Marine yelled at us. "Hit back, and hit back hard and fast. Lay down a blanket of protective fire." This sounded dumb to me; the truck was protection. Then, it was explained. "The truck is an easy target for small arms, a grenade or mortar. Get off the trucks and into the bush. Fire back, and fire low. A round going overhead is nowhere as scary or as effective as one hitting the ground in the enemy's face. A ricochet is more apt to take out an enemy than a round overhead." Our Marine instructor had had two hitches in Vietnam, so we listened. "This is a new type of warfare being waged in Vietnam. Get ready."

We invaded a typical Vietnam hamlet, and were introduced to booby-traps, bungee stakes, hidden pits and tunnels.

"Don't pick up a souvenir, it'll be wired to a grenade."

"Don't step on what you can't see."

"Don't trust anyone, even the kids."

"This is not a walk through the park. This is a war zone."

This is what the Marine told us as we crept through the make-believe Vietnamese village. His warnings had a bite. I drank all this in.

In the early '50s, I'd played war with my brothers and neighbors in the woods behind the lake. We'd watched television news and saw what was going on in Korea. The afternoons found us sneaking around in the woods, with our BB guns, hiding behind trees and old stone walls, springing ambushes on each other, setting up trip wires, digging foxholes, throwing live firecrackers.

Our EOD (Explosive Ordnance Disposal) guys got to blow up a lot of stuff, using a variety of compounds. They worked with Composition C, planted road mines and detected mines the Marines had hidden on a road or in a village. We all got to chuck hand grenades and fire standard-issue semi-automatic M14s and the newer M16s. When it was time for us to do the John Wayne Course, we loaded up with live ammunition, and with our rifles on our hips, our left hands on the barrel to keep the rifle from elevating when on automatic, we crept along the trail. Plywood cut-outs representing the enemy popped up from a ditch, or out from behind a tree. We shot at the enemy until a cut-out of the president popped out. You weren't supposed to shoot the president.

One night, toward the end of our training, the entire battalion put on a night fire display for the generals. We shot M60 machine guns, mortars, M14s, M16s, anything. The shower of fire lasted ten minutes and lit up the night. The sound was ear-splitting. I made a series of long exposures, capturing the glow of the tracers as they streaked down range. Tracers ricocheted off borders and tumbled through the air, creating a staccato trace. The time exposure illustrated awesome firepower. Tracers are a burning dab of magnesium at the rear end of every fifth bullet, creating what looks like a glowing fire hose. The person firing the round can see the tracer, but the person standing in the way can't.

The War Games

Operation Moon Pie (the name our operations officer, LCDR Martin, gave to our war game exercise) got underway on the Monday morning of our last week. The battalion unloaded from the man-hauls and began the march down a dirt road into the North Carolina woods to set up base camp. This was an exciting time. Each man had a full clip of M14 blanks in his rifle and watched the woods intently for signs of an ambush, which never came. This was the start of our last week of training with the Marines, a three-day bivouac out in the open. It was great fun, even if there was no beer, only C-rats, and ice-cold water to shave in.

I'd played this war game as a kid. Dad had taught each of us each how to hunt and care for a rifle. He accompanied us into the woods, pointing out tracks, feces deposits

4. Training for Combat Duty

Operation Moon Pie: Pup tents, sleeping bags, C-rats, and the fun of summer camp in the North Carolina woods.

where deer have passed, places where we might wait for the deer or rabbits to pass. He told us stories of hunts he'd been on in Vermont. The stories must have been true, for our lodge and his workshop on the hill behind the lodge contained numerous stuffed animals he'd bagged.

In our pre-teen years, my younger brother Lee and I would go on a hunt after school. We'd flip a coin to see who would be the hunter and who would be the hunted. Either role was challenging and emotionally thrilling. The hunted would take off into the woods, up to the mountain, or along the edge of the lake, the summer cottages now closed for the season. Five minutes later the hunter left to follow, to find and overtake the hunted. There were ambushes to set and avoid, a great game of hide and seek, only this time, we carried our BB guns, and would fire at the aggressor. Usually we were too far away to hit anyone, but just the word "Gotcha!" would end the game and we'd debrief the exercise on our way back to the lodge for dinner. Innocent as it was, it was a good preparation for the war game I now found myself, and my entire battalion, engaged in.

That afternoon, the battalion arrived at what was to be our campsite and we began setting up. I found a spot for my two-man tent and made camp. I dug a drainage trench around my tent, to keep any rain from getting inside and soaking my nice, warm, down-filled sleeping bag. I had an extra pair of dry socks, a fresh tee-shirt and my "douche kit." I was all set.

I pitched in to dig the latrine, a slit trench, what would serve as our public toilet. This was a ditch—a foot wide, two or three feet deep, ten feet long—over which you straddled, your pants and skivvies down around your knees, hoping for the best. Once done, you were required to shovel some of the loose dirt over your deposit.

Alpha Company was charged with perimeter security. Equipment operators set up machine gun bunkers and hunkered down, waiting for the attack they knew was coming.

Revealing yourself over the slit trench was best done at night, for the privacy darkness provided.

Our camp site had the air of a circus setting up. There was a perimeter to establish and machine gun nests to build. The EEGs and the RMs strung communications wire through the trees from the CP (Command Post) to Alpha Company's machine gunners, who were busy digging in and setting up their .60-caliber machines. The rest of us dug foxholes, unloaded trucks and stacked supplies. The cooks set up a field kitchen and began preparing to feed us. We ate C-rats for lunch. There was no shower, and you had to shave holding a mirror in one hand, the razor in the other, your steel helmet full of cold water hanging from its strap on your tent pole.

The first night we stood watch and waited for the enemy to attack. Nothing.

This was how our three days of war games were spent. Our Ops OIC, LCDR Roger Martin, had devised the plan for these field exercises, which involved squads of Seabees leaving camp every morning to perform construction tasks back at the rifle range, then returning in the evening. This simulated more realistically what the teams would be doing in Vietnam.

"This war is a lazy man's job," one Seabee wrote home. "For those not out on construction job, there is little to do in this camp during the day. After breakfast of lukewarm boned turkey, cheese and crackers, we policed the area, then crawled into our tents and napped." During the night, everyone was kept awake, listening and watching for harassment by the aggressors off in the woods. The camp was attacked on a couple of occasions but the CP remained intact. One of the bunkers reported to CP they were under automatic weapons fire and requested permission to return the fire. The neighboring bunker called in reporting that their M60 had a jam and they couldn't stop firing.

So it went. We were camping out, on summer vacation—the only things missing were fishing rods and a stream.

The XO returned to camp one afternoon and was stopped by one of our security patrols on the road. His jeep didn't have the required windshield sticker. He was harassed and searched before someone came out to identify him.

"Well, we were just doing what we were told to do," said one of the Seabee guards. The XO was not laughing.

"Ya, no exceptions, sir. Just follow instructions," said the other Seabee.

The final night of our field exercise we were attacked. The battle went on for over an hour. The attackers, Marines in training, bent on capturing the CP and the officers inside, tried to gain access through the perimeter line. They came close, but Alpha Company's machine guns, firing blanks, stopped them. Flares floated down in the night sky, smoke grenades were thrown, but the breeze blew the smoke away. There was a lot of yelling and guns going off.

"Cease fire! Cease fire! They've withdrawn," came the word from the CP. We had repelled them. This brought a lot of shouting and firing into the air. The casual observer might have mistaken this war game for a Fourth of July celebration.

Next morning, we folded our tents, filled in the fighting holes and slit trenches, packed up the field kitchen, removed the comm wires, dismantled the machine guns, boxed up the remaining ammunition, and loaded our trucks. Before we could leave for a shower, the entire battalion was required to police (pick up) the entire area: "Make it look as if we'd never been here."

That following day, all day, we drilled, we marched, we rehearsed the manual of arms, ironed uniforms, and polished boots for our "Pass and Review" ceremony. This must have been an important occasion, for the reviewing committee included the Camp Lejeune commanding general, Major General J.O. Butler. If you have ever watched the 1940s film *The Fighting Seabees* with John Wayne (some of which was shot on our base in Davisville, Rhode Island, in 1944), you know that we Seabees are not prone to spit and polish, or orderly formation. Most Seabees, except us "fleet-bees," were really civilian construction workers dressed up to look like sailors. But we somehow pulled it off. The battalion marched, paraded, stood at attention, trooped back and forth, dipped flags, and "eyes righted" right along with the best Marine units.

The training had been strenuous and at times exhausting. In the end, all of us were glad for the training, but were also happy that our three weeks among the Marines was over. Our thoughts were on getting back to the afternoon party with free beer. The party lasted well into the night. EO1 Roop took on a challenge and drank his combat helmet full of beer. Seabees do know how to party.

Chapter 5

Waiting to Deploy

Cinderella Liberty

"I'm leaving," Dick said. "I'm getting out of here. I'm going home. I haven't been paid in nearly two months. My wife and kids have run out of money."

"You haven't been paid?" I asked, as if what the Navy was paying us amounted to anything. But Dick had a wife and kids back in Idaho.

"Those f—— guys in Personnel lost my service jacket [personnel file]," he said. "Without it, I can't get paid, my allotment can't be sent to my wife."

"How long has this been going on?" I asked.

"More than a month. I can get my old job and make some real money for a few weeks. More than this outfit is not paying me."

"Now hold on, Dick," I warned. "You can't just leave. You'll be arrested for desertion and thrown in prison."

Lt. Billy Dennis, our chaplain, whose office was directly across the hall from mine, heard my conversation with Dick and came over.

"Sit down, Dick," he said in his kindest voice, as he closed the door.

Dick Stapleton was one of those IPOs, a heavy equipment operator from Idaho, and the captain's driver. He didn't have much to do during the day, only pick up the skipper in the morning and return him to the BOQ in the afternoon, so he hung out in my office. Dick had been driving earthmovers on mining sites before he joined the Seabees. A nice guy with a wife or two back home and a few kids. The reason I say a "wife or two" was that he had married three times—twice to the same woman. Anyway, the personnel office had misplaced his file, and without a file, disbursing (e.g., the paymaster) could not issue Dick his bi-monthly pay. After a few months of no money to send home, Dick was frantic. He took his responsibility to his family seriously, and what he was getting paid in the Seabees was a fraction of what he was making as a civilian equipment operator. With no money coming in, he was in limbo and getting desperate. He was now in my office threatening to go AWOL.

"I hear you," said the chaplain, "and want to help. You have a few options, none of them good. You are not getting paid, and you can't leave, but there is a possible solution. Now, what I'm about to tell you, you did not hear from me." Dick and I sat and listened. Dick held his head in his hands. "It's sort of like a Cinderella Liberty. Put in for a four-day liberty pass—not leave. Pack your sea bag and fly home. Work for a month. We'll call you when they find your file, or when the unit is about to depart, then get back here. But, do not unpack your sea bag, and keep an open return ticket. When you get back here, you'll go before Captain Mast, or be court martialed, but for being AWOL, not for desertion. There'll be no prison time, you may lose a pay grade or have to do time on the honey bucket crew. Keeping your sea bag and airline ticket as proof you planned to return, not desert. Understand?" Dick nodded and thanked the chaplain. I slapped Dick on the back and told him I'd call with any news.

Dick found out he could fly home, standby, if he had $100. Tuffy, one of the guys in Engineering, loaned him $90 and I gave him the other $10. He would need an official-looking military liberty pass to fly standby. Since I knew how to prepare such orders, that was no problem. I typed up a set of orders and Dick fudged the CO's signature. He tore up the fake orders as soon as he was on the plane.

Dick arrived home and immediately went to work driving a loader for the same mining company he'd worked for before, earning four times what the Navy would have paid him, if they'd found his file.

His file did turn up, lost behind a filing cabinet. The chaplain called Dick with the news. Dick took his sea bag down to the local recruiting office and turned himself in. The Navy flew him back to Davisville. Not much happened after that, but in June, while we were in 'Nam, the Navy finally got around to hauling Dick before a court martial. The trouble was, Dick had fallen through the cracks and no one knew how long he'd overstayed his liberty pass. There were no records, so they charged him with a day and a half. They docked him some pay, which he wasn't getting anyway, and reduced his rate. They added 30 more days to his two-year hitch. Dick never did serve time on the honey bucket detail. He was too valuable driving a dozer.

The First Edition of The Transit

The battalion returned to Davisville from North Carolina, our training with the Marines behind us. We were now a fighting Seabee unit. While most of us waited for our departure to Vietnam, our advance party took off in March, to familiarize themselves with our new base in Chu Lai. The rest of us packed up our offices and equipment, completed schools, or went on leave, or mostly just waited—all of February, then March. There was little to do; all the equipment and supplies had been packed and shipped, and all the offices were closed, except for mine.

It was time we told the folks at home what their boys had been up to, and where we were heading. My principal role in the outfit was to edit and publish a monthly newspaper, officially called the unit's "Family-Gram." I had enough stories and photographs of our training, the recommission ceremony and general news to fill a 12-page tabloid newspaper. The CO, XO and the chaplain each wanted to write a column. The back page contained a checklist of what each family and serviceman needed to do before departure. The XO wanted to know how I intended to get this newspaper printed, and how much it would cost.

Creating a newspaper is a complicated project, I told him. It involves typesetting, design and layout, proofing, headlines, photographs and captions. We would need a name and a front-page banner for the publication. Then, when the type is set and the proofs ready, we could get the paper printed at an offset printing plant. I knew the process and how much it would cost. I'd learned how to produce a tabloid newspaper earlier that winter while on Christmas leave skiing at Mount Snow in Vermont. I was working in the resort's PR office in exchange for a lift ticket.

My high school buddy Allan was the staff photographer, and Dick McLernon, the resort's marketing director, gave the two of us the job of producing the first edition of *The Mount Snow Valley News*. McLernon felt the valley community needed a newspaper, and he wanted the ski area's name on it. Allan found a letterpress shop in the Boston area that set type for the college newspapers. Misty Theolopos, the Greek proprietor, had set up Collegiate Press in a small two-story brick building, behind a delicatessen on a nondescript street in Somerville. Misty's shop had three Linotype machines, a Ludlow headliner, a proof press, and counters for laying out the pages for a newspaper. Allan and I knew nothing, so Misty taught us. Everything we did was in hot, molten lead, heavy slugs of lead. We learned how to use a pica rule, spec body text, fit headlines and sub-heads, arrange lead body text in columns, separating the columns by one-point lead strips of lines to lead the reader's eye around the page. There were rules to follow, and rules to bend. We learned about "slug lines," two or three words at the head of a story set in a single chunk of lead.

The Linotype machines were large, ingenious devices the size of refrigerators, with keyboards like a typewriter. The operator would read the editor's text from a sheet of paper, type the letters on the keyboard, triggering a series of matrices, each a separate letter, to come sliding down into a holder. The operator then proofread the line to ensure it was set correctly, then sent the line of matrices over to a channel into which molten lead flowed, creating a two-inch-high slug with the raised letters on top. As the slug was formed, it joined others, inline to a galley tray. As the slugs accumulated, the galley began to look like it might actually say something. Trouble was, you couldn't easily read it—the lines were in mirror form.

This mechanized process dates back more than 100 years. Before then, type was set by hand, each letter placed individually into a galley. This was the way all printed publications were created as far back as Gutenberg. Working with galleys of lead slugs, headlines of lead, one-point lines to separate stories, provided me with an understanding of page layout and design. It forced me into using clean, organized pages of text and images.

Allan and I worked around the clock for two days, moving little bits of lead around on the make-up table. Finally, Misty announced he'd had enough of our fussing about and that our 12 pages looked good enough. We were ready for a final proof. Each page, made up of 50 pounds of lead slugs, was transferred to a small imprint press, black ink was rolled over the surface of the lead type, a clean sheet of proof paper was inserted into the press's roller, and off came a clean copy of each page. What a great feeling it was to see our work. The only thing missing were the photographs. They'd be added later at the printing plant.

When the proofs were dry, we carefully wrapped them up and drove to Lowell Offset Printers, 50 miles away in Lowell, Massachusetts. Here, our pages were photographed on a large "process camera" and turned into negative film. The photographs we wanted inserted into the pages were also re-photographed and turned into screened negatives. The pages and photographs, now negatives, were "stripped" together in large sheets of orange paper, then exposed to a sensitive aluminum plate with a carbon arc. The plates attached to drums on the offset press, the press got up to speed, turning out 10,000 impressions an hour. We only needed 3,000. It was a short run.

Allan and I loaded bundles of *The Mount Snow Valley News* into the company's station wagon and drove back to Vermont, dropping off stacks of the newspaper at bars, restaurants and inns as we drove up through the valley.

We stopped at the last bar for a beer, and as the newspapers were snapped up and read by the skiers, we were rewarded for our efforts by watching the readers pore over our work. That has always been one of the most satisfying parts of this job, watching people read your stuff.

The whole process was hard work, but I loved it. It was gratifying to see the pages come together, like a jigsaw puzzle. At night my dreams were filled with huge letters, lead slugs, entire paragraphs set in molten lead floating around me, chasing me, rolling over me, stamping out words on my bare skin.

The technology of communication has always fascinated me. As I've said, I'd been studying journalism in college before I dropped out. My professors were academics, more interested in studying the process than using any of the technologies to actually create something. I'd already learned how to make photographs, and produce and host radio programs, but this printed communication was new.

While college attempted to teach me the theory of communications, it was here at Misty's letter-press shop that I got my hands dirty, learned typesetting and the mechanics of communication.

The Transit *Comes to Life*

With this basic knowledge of how to get my battalion's newspaper produced. I approached LTJG Smith, OIC of HQ, as well as the CO and XO, and explained what was needed. They authorized the expense, I wrote up my TAD orders, and off I went to Misty's to get the battalion's first newspaper produced.

This took three days.

I designed a logo for the masthead, calling the publication *The Transit*, with a silhouette of a Seabee surveyor and his transit at one side and the battalion's seal on the other side. The name stuck, and is still used today.

Misty helped me design and set type for *The Transit*, which was then printed at Lowell Offset Printing. I piled 3,000 copies, the minimum order, in the back of my VW and drove back to the base. The tabloid was passed out among the men and a bunch of us stuck on mailing labels and *The Transit* was off to relatives, other Seabee units and the military brass.

That done, I put in for three weeks of leave, drove up to Vermont, moved in with Allan and his wife, Sally, and settled into three weeks of civilian life. I worked in the ski resort's PR office in exchange for a ski pass. I wrote news releases, took photographs, skied, partied and produced one more edition of the *Valley News*. While civilian life was preferable to Navy life, I was actually looking forward to spending the next seven months in Vietnam. I was curious to see what all the fuss was about, and I wanted to write about and photograph what I would experience there. I wasn't as scared as I was excited. I knew my unit would be behind a perimeter, and not engaged in actual combat, but I would be doing what I'd wanted to do since I was 12—telling stories and making photographs people would actually see and read.

the TRANSIT

1943 U.S. NAVAL MOBILE CONSTRUCTION BATTALI(

Vol. I No. 1 — (Family Gram)   THE TRANSIT

Seabees Learn

It is said that men fight the hardest when they are defending their own. This is never truer than in the case of the Seabees, Navy constructionmen who have found themselves fighting for their lives on the roads and airstrips they have built around the world. Defensive fighting is a specialty with the 'Bees, they are trained in it, they practice it, and when the time comes, they are ready to use the tactics and fighting skills taught them by their Marine instructors. One Seabee outfit, Mobile Construction Battalion 71 from Davisville, Rhode Island (home of the Atlantic Seabees) has just completed three weeks of defensive training and is now back home.

Training for the Seabees begins with advanced infantry combat. Marine instructors from the First Infantry Training Regiment at Camp LeJeune, North Carolina took MCB 71's Seabees into the cold rainy woods of North Carolina to teach them the techniques of war. The use of their M14 rifle, the rocket launcher (known at the bazooka), grenades, defensive movements and aggressive tactics, how to lay ambushes and fight them off, how to search prisoners and how to creep through the woods at night without a sound. These were the subjects of the Seabee's first week - conventional warfare. Rain and mud, mud and rain. The sandy clay turned into a quagmire as 800 Seabees trudged the foot paths of Camp LeJeune. The climate, much colder than any South Asian country, was nevertheless just as wet as a Vietnam monsoon. The rain poured down- the training went on.

After a 60 hour week of cold wet training the sun came out on the coast of North Carolina to dry out MCB 71's Seabees. the second week of training found many Seabees in special classes: 106 recoilless rifle, the 3.5 rocket launcher, 81mm mortar, Anti-guerrilla warfare and M60 machine gun. One Seabee, Robert T. Lloyd, came within three points of bettering the Marine's M60 machine gun record, the second highest mark shot on the course. On the 81mm mortar course one MCB 71 Sea-
Continued on page four

"Eyes right!" standard-barer for MCB 71's ALPHA Company tips his colors as his company passes the reviewing stand during the Battalion's Pass-in-Review ceremonies at Camp LeJeune, North Carolina.

4 Months Of Training Nears End

Four months of training, special schools' classes, lectures, indoctrination - training, training and still more training. Since commissioning last fall the Battalion has had but one purpose - to prepare itself with an organization, and prepare its men with individual training. The Training Department, under Lieuntenant R. W. Gray and Matser Chief E. F. Otersen, has been at the center of this vast training schedule. It has been their task to assign the Battalion's 800 men to the various schools and classes run by Davisville's Construction Training Unit and Military Training Department.

With over half of the rated men in the Battalion obtained directly from the nation's construction industry this past summer - through the Direct Procurment Petty Officer program - there was no the need for as much basic construction training as with other units. Training took the form of advanced schools for many of the men, with specialized schools in everything from airfield design to building of a railroad.

The equipment operators received driving time on every possible type of heavy hauling equipment, plus rock crushers and even forklifts. Construction mechanics, the nuts and bolts men, learned to fix the simplest part to the largest diesel engins. Our EA'S, Engineering Aids, attended railroad building school, airstrip layout classes and drafting courses. Builders built structures as small as a tool shed and as large as a concrete warehouse. The Utilitymen, Construction Electricians and Steel Workers were briefed on the type of work they could expect to do for the fleet and fleet Marines while serving as a Seabee.

One of the most useful training procedures was the use of "crew training", developed and used on the West Coast, MCB 71 was the first to make use of this principle here at Davisville, Rhode Island. Crews, or teams, are sent out on a training project, much the same as will be done on our future deployment. This use of crew training was even incoporated into
Continued on page six

"Ambush right!" Convoy bailout part of the Anti-guerrilla warfa(rines at Camp LeJeune. (Story a

107 Seabees Re

The Advance Party, compris will be leaving the Davisville ar Battalion's future deployment sit tion that will effect a smooth ta our fellow Seabee unit sometime

The Party will cover five phase each gaged to help our futu work, projects and living cond tions "in-country ". The BEE (Battalion Equipment Evaluatic Program) is a joint inventory all rolling stock of the unit bein relieved. That which will be le behind, parts needed, repair wor to be done and additional equip ment to be ordered are the r(sponsibility of the Advance Party.

A representative from each con pany is included in the Party. The will familarize themselves with th projects of their counterpart Among these projects are airfie maintainance, quary and roc crushing plant operation and c(ment plant improvement.

The first page of the first edition of The Transit, February 1967.

When the three weeks were up, I returned to the base and packed up my office for the flight to 'Nam. But before we left I had to get laid.

Getting Laid

Getting laid in the late sixties was not as easy as it is today. The act itself is pretty much the same, although internet porn may have upped performance expectations a bit. Back in the sixties, sex was still pretty much a taboo subject in polite conversation; well, except for the guys who couldn't stop talking about their latest conquest. Girls were scared stiff of getting pregnant, contracting one of many sexually transmitted diseases, getting dumped by their partner, or gaining a reputation as a slut. Men—boys—they really didn't know what they were doing most of the time, figuring what feels good to them must feel good for her. "T'aint necessarily so," even today.

So, I went at the task of getting laid seriously. After all, I was in Vermont, at a ski resort, among young, single, attractive women who were looking for mates, even if just for the weekend. Trouble is, I had no idea how to go about chatting up a girl. I knew nothing of the complicated art of seduction. My buddy Allan was good at it, but he wasn't about to share his secrets with me. He was now married, with a baby on the way. So I had to make my own way.

I'm often too eager. My emotions trample on my better judgment and I blow a possibility. Or I'm too shy and turn away. Females have always found me "intellectually interesting," and I have a lot of female friends and associates, but few want to get into bed with me. I'm not gay, nor do I lack a sex drive—I'm as horny as the next guy. I'd dated numerous young ladies in high school and college, but the farthest I'd gotten was a handful of bra. I'm just not good at seduction. I don't understand the female psyche. I was raised in a household of men on the edge of a lake, with my three brothers and a woodsman dad. Mom did her best, getting me to attend dancing school at 14 so I could learn how to hold a girl while dancing, but I've never known how to talk to a woman into bed, not back then in the sixties. The few women who have understood me, have been patient, so I've learned a great deal about women since then.

That winter I was bent on getting laid. Lucky for me, I found an attractive and very sexy local girl from Wilmington. She was fun and found me "interesting"—at least that's what she told me. I guess you could say she took pity on me, or felt it her patriotic duty to ensure that I was not to be sent off to war and certain death a virgin.

One night, driving back to the lodge where she was working, we took a detour to a vacant lot to "park." It was snowing and was turning cold. We climbed into the backseat of the company station wagon to snuggle, and began fooling around in earnest. The car began to cool off just as we were getting heated up. Time was of the essence. I had a condom I'd carried with me for years. We all did. Stuffed inside our wallets, its bulge or impression a telltale announcement to everyone that we were "prepared," like any good Boy Scout. Well, by the time I got the ancient device out and opened, it came apart in tatters. So much for preparation and protection. By this time, the car was cold and so were my hands, which didn't help any in the foreplay phase of seduction. She kept complaining and urging me to hurry.

I'll not bore you with the rest of the rather brief encounter, only to say it was a penetrating experience, one that I'd rather not relive.

I was on a plane to Vietnam four days later, the memory of my first sexual experience still fresh in my mind. She and I never wrote each other afterward.

Off We Go to War

We stood in rough formation in front of the barracks, sea bags and personal stuff on the ground next to us. It was April 4, 1967. We were leaving chilly, damp Rhode Island for Vietnam. Piles of dirty snow lined the parking lot, reminding us of what we were leaving. We were heading to the tropics.

My worn-out camera bag hung over my shoulder. It contained my Topcon 35mm SLR camera with a 28mm lens. There was also a normal 50mm lens and a telephoto 200mm in there, each wrapped up in chamois. I had a light meter, and a few rolls of Tri-X film and a small strobe flash. The gear was a few years old, but it was what separated me from the rest of the men in the outfit.

We loaded our gear and ourselves onto a bus, and I found a seat. It was a ten-minute ride to the airfield over at Quonset Point NAS, where we unloaded next to a huge, silver, C-141 transport plane. We marched up the loading ramp, piled our sea bags along the fuselage and were told to find a seat. I was on my way to Vietnam, with 80 other guys from MCB-71.

It took nine of these huge birds the next few days to get the entire battalion to 'Nam. The accommodations on the planes were spare—web seats in rows, two porta-potties

Waiting. Bundled up against a chilly Rhode Island wind, we wait. Within 24 hours, we'll be halfway 'round the world, landing in the 100° heat of Vietnam.

5. Waiting to Deploy

aft, and our gear piled along the side of the plane. There were no windows to look out, no flight attendants, no complimentary beverages, no inflight movies, just a line of water coolers strapped to the bulkhead. The plane's crew handed out wrapped sandwiches. Most of the guys brought magazines and a few had cards—groups of poker players huddled together. I had a book: *Where Eagles Dare,* a World War II suspense novel by Alistair MacLean. It lasted just long enough to get us to Alaska.

The C-141 lifted off and climbed to 36,000 feet, five miles up, heading northwest to Alaska. It was a boring eight-hour flight up to Elmendorf Airbase outside Anchorage. The plane landed, taxied to a military terminal and we were told to get up and march off the plane, only to stand around in the cold air, white-capped mountains in the distance, while the plane refueled. That took an hour. Back aloft, and after another eight-hour flight, we landed at Yokota Air Force Base, 15 miles outside Tokyo, Japan—arriving in the middle of the night. We again stood around outside during refueling, but it was getting warmer. From Japan to our base in Vietnam was a five-hour flight.

Chapter 6

Hello, Vietnam!

The First Taste of Combat

As one of the last planes bringing Seventy-One to Chu Lai approached the runway, the VC began a mortar barrage that hit the south end of the runway. Two of our Seabees who'd arrived earlier, in the advance party, construction workers Anthony Lake and CMA Charlie Lawrence, were there guarding boxes of equipment for MCB-40, awaiting shipment back to the States. Mortar shells burst within 30 yards of the two men, sending shrapnel rocketing off the boxes. The men immediately took cover and got on the radio to report the event to the Command Post. This was their first experience of what life would be like in Vietnam. The two received commendations for their cool, appropriate actions and proper use of radio phraseology, which they had learned from the Marines a few months earlier.

Arriving in Vietnam

It was morning when our C-141 set down on the concrete runway at Chu Lai. It had taken us 26 hours to get here. We'd passed through 12 time zones, gone over the international dateline, and arrived the next day, having traveled 13,000 miles, halfway around the world.

The plane taxied to the terminal, an open-air hanger next to the runway. Each of us shouldered our sea bags and marched down the loading ramp into a blast furnace. The temperature on the runway was well over 100°F. The humidity was 80 percent. The air was heavy and thick with moisture. It was hard to breathe. It was hard even to see. We squinted into a white sky, the sun lost somewhere up there amid a milky haze. The harsh, tropical light was blinding. Not a speck of blue.

We stood in loose formation, waiting, looking around. We'd landed in a huge military complex. The landscape—as flat and sandy as Cape Cod—was not fit for anything but this airstrip. What trees remained were short, scruffy pines. We'd left chilly Rhode Island yesterday, (or was it two days ago?) and today I was sweating—I'd be sweating for next seven months.

We boarded a line of six-bys, dump trucks, for the fifteen-minute ride to our base. The line of trucks snaked along a paved road out of the airfield area, passing planes, rows of helicopters on their pads, munitions bunkers. We passed Quonset huts, small wooden cottages called hooches, with their tin roofs, as well as warehouses, many vehicles, and

6. Hello, Vietnam!

As we stepped off the plane, we were met with a blinding glare of tropical haze. The mountains, lost in the haze, held the VC enemy. The 9th Marine Engineers' camp lay just beyond the base perimeter.

the occasional basketball court. There were 40,000 other military servicemen here; Marine and Army battalions, each in their own camp with rows of barracks, mess halls, warehouses and fenced-in supply depots—all this military infrastructure went by in a blur. It was too much to take in.

As the trucks rose up over a grade, I caught a glimpse of the South China Sea, silver-blue, stretching east in the haze. Below the knoll lay our base, Camp Shields, an orderly village of huts stretched out along the beach, facing northeast. It had been built two years before by MCB-Ten and was named after the first Seabee to be killed in action in Vietnam. Our camp was right where any bunch of GIs would want a camp, on the beach within the sound of the surf washing in from the sea. It was neatly laid out, clusters of huts divided by streets and walkways. The first building to go up? The bar.

My truck pulled to a stop in front of a platoon of Seabees from MCB-40, their sea bags by their sides. These were the guys we were replacing, waiting to depart on the truck and the plane on which we'd just arrived. They were shouting encouragement and warnings to their replacements, what to watch out for.

"You poor bastards! Wait until the in-coming begins to rain down."

"Watch out for the girls in the village. They got the clap."

"This dump is now all yours!"

I was too far gone, having been cramped up and sleepless for 24 hours, to care.

Members of our advance party had arrived a month earlier and were there to show us around. In small groups, we were introduced to the washing-up facilities, a concrete slab with a tin roof and no walls, a long sink down the middle with banks of faucets on

Enlisted men's quarters (hooches) neatly spread out along a sandy beach.

either side. The showers were semi-private booths with a short shower curtain over the entrance. The entire camp had a temporary summer "beach colony" atmosphere, as if a strong wind would wipe out the place. Sand was everywhere, under foot, in the hooches, in your bed.

The urinals were 55-gallon drums with the ends removed, set into the sand, with diesel fuel floating on top of the urine. These provided little privacy, just a plywood barrier on three sides. The toilets were another matter. These were six-hole privies, simply outhouses. Each seat was directly over a 55-gallon drum that had been cut in half and onto which handles had been welded. Each day the honey bucket crew would wrestle the full drums out, dump the contents onto the ground, pour on kerosene and light them up. So much for sanitation.

There was a large mess hall and adjacent galley, an amphitheater with benches facing a stage and screen for the nightly movies and the occasional USO stage show. The camp was laid out in a grid, with streets and walkways leading to clusters of hooches. The chiefs and officers had quarters at opposite ends of the beach, behind the razor wire perimeter. The crew's quarters were crammed into the center of the camp, the admin and medical hooches were located at the south end of the village, near the chapel and parade grounds where we mustered each Sunday.

Those of us who had just arrived were fed and given 24 hours to overcome jet lag. We were exactly on the other side of the world from Davisville—12 hours difference, and a day earlier.

I found my hooch, a plywood hut housing a squad of other guys from Headquarters Company. The first-class yeoman in charge assigned us our spaces. Mine was a semi-private cubicle in the corner by the front door. There was a cot, a tall locker for my gear and rifle and little else. Most men had carved out what privacy they could by re-arranging

6. Hello, Vietnam!

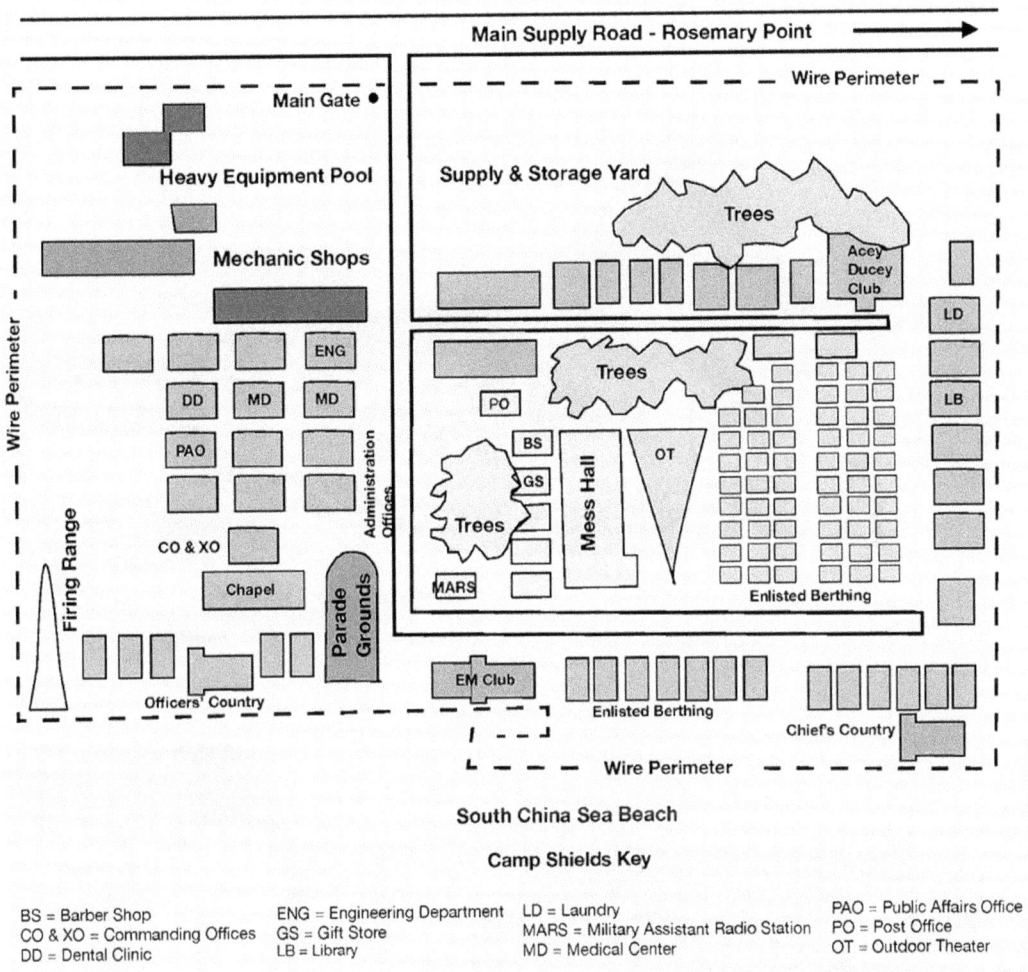

Camp Shields layout.

lockers, hanging curtains or bamboo blinds over the entrance. The lockers separating each cubicle were wallpapered from floor to ceiling with *Playboy* centerfold pinups. There was an aisle down the center of the hooch, from the front to the back door. The bottom half of the walls of each hooch were sheets of plywood, the upper half, screens. Plywood shutters were propped up with a stick to let air through the hooch, and were lowered to keep out the rain when showers swept in off the sea. The roofs were corrugated tin, which just transferred the sun's heat inside during the day, and the sound of clattering of rain at night.

My Public Affairs Office

Rested, I found my office space in one of the "Admin" hooches on the east side of the village. Sick Bay was on one side, a mortar pit on the other side, next to the CO's

Top: My Public Affairs Office hooch, attached to the darkroom, with a handy mortar pit close by. *Bottom:* My messy office. Note the custom-built cot on the right where I slept each night.

quarters. Only half of this single-story cottage was the PAO (Public Affairs Office); the other half was the photographers' air-conditioned darkroom. When I walked up the four steps and opened the door, the space was empty—no desks, no furniture, no shelves, no filing cabinets, no lights. For three days, my two assistants and I scurried around camp getting what we needed. We acquired items from supply or we simply "comshawed" them (a Navy term for acquiring stuff outside of normal channels, such as: on long-term loan, or borrowing without permission), and we got chairs from as-yet unoccupied offices.

The first thing I did was plug in the small Sony radio I'd brought, and searched the band for stations. Got to have tunes while working. The Armed Service Radio came in loud and clear, patched through from their studio in Saigon.

My team and I borrowed plywood and tools from the carpenters and got to work building our own desks, counters and shelving. I built a drafting table on which to lay out the battalion's monthly newspaper. We unpacked our container of equipment shipped over from Davisville and set up shop. We had two Olivetti typewriters, files, darkroom gear and photographic supplies. There were reams of cheap yellow newsprint paper for typing up drafts, boxes of photographic paper, 100 rolls of Tri-X film and archival sleeves for filing my negatives.

This space, open on three sides with screened windows and shutters, and a single door, became home. The partition between us and the darkroom was soon filled with photos and notes on possible stories, a map of the enclave and the surrounding villages. A creative person needs a certain amount of clutter around to feel at home. It was here I wrote articles, drew up what *The Transit* pages might look like and edited my photographs. But since I needed privacy to write, and my assistants were there all day, I wrote mostly at night.

I had two assistants in PAO, John Cliett and Jimmy Jackson, both SNJOs, which meant they were one step away from becoming JO3s. These two did the basic work of a Public Affairs Office, wrote and mailed out releases to hometown newspapers in the States when men re-enlisted, were advanced in grade or won an award. They produced a weekly news bulletin that was "mimeographed" and distributed around the camp. My primary job was to photograph, write, edit and lay out the monthly newspaper.

After a month of mostly interrupted sleep back in the hooch, I'd had it. I couldn't deal with the snoring, the comings and goings all night long, or the first class yeoman who ran the hooch with a loud voice, insisting everyone be up at 5:30 a.m. I also did not like the general lack of privacy, so I packed up and moved to my office. I built a cot by the door and slept there, undisturbed, for the rest of our tour.

Building a War

"Jump in, Lyman," shouted LCDR Roger Martin, the operations officer (S-3). I was standing by the mechanic's shop with my camera bag when the officer pulled up in his jeep. "I'm heading out to make the rounds of the sites. XO says he wants to you to tag along. I have a dozen sites to visit before lunch," he said. "Need to be back for an operations meeting at noon." I climbed in beside the lieutenant, clutching my camera bag in my lap. No seat belts in these open World War II jeeps. Off we went to explore the sprawling military base.

When we arrived on this sandy beach on the South China Sea in April, there was

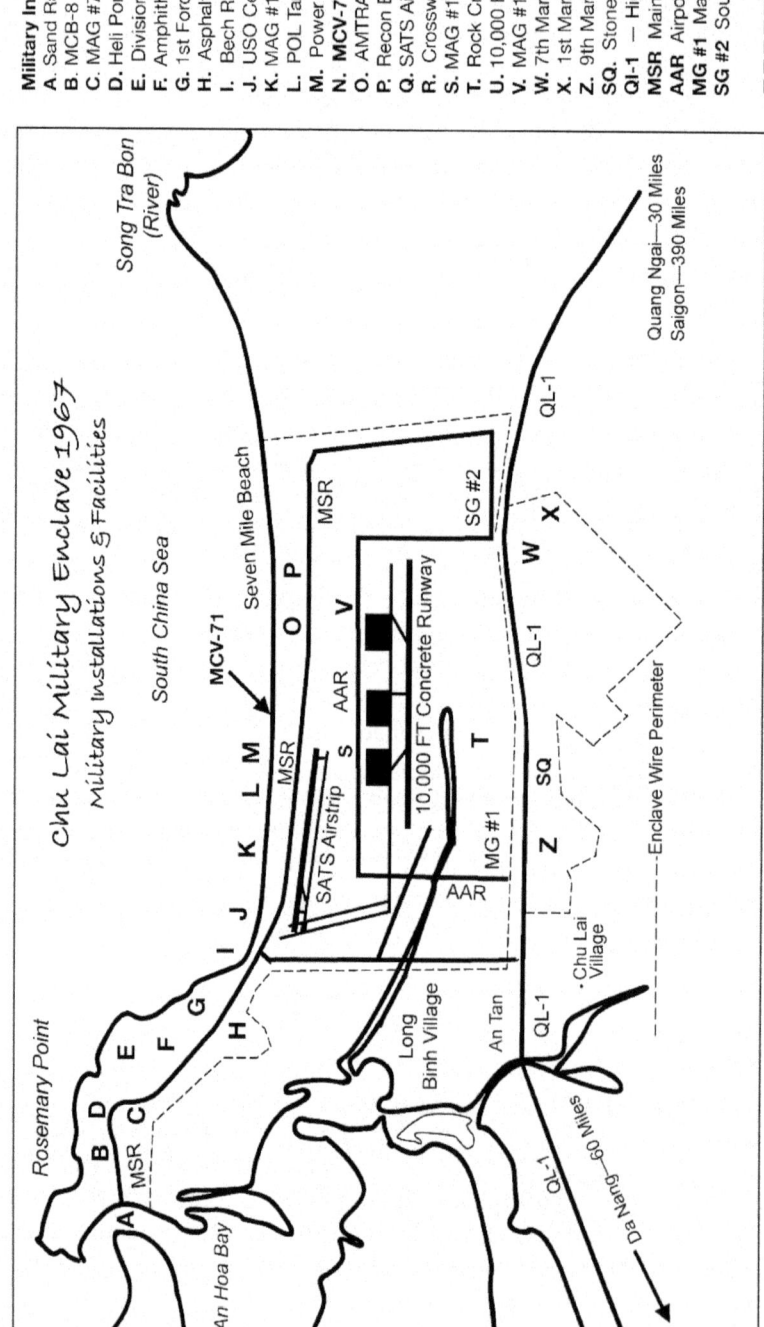

The Chu Lai base.

already a lot going on. The 5th Marine Regiment had moved its headquarters from Da Nang to Chu Lai, with 17,000 men. The Republic of Korea Marine Brigade was here as well. Task Force Oregon included:

- 3rd Brigade, 25th Infantry Division
- 1st Brigade, 101st Airborne Division
- 196th Light Infantry Brigade
- 2nd Squadron, 11th Armored Cavalry

Just as Seventy-One was arriving, the 196th Light Infantry Brigade had pulled into Chu Lai. The task force headquarters was activated on April 12, and by April 17, the 196th had commenced Operation Lawrence, to the west of the air base. By the end of April, the task force had assumed control of the Chu Lai tactical area of operations. There were close to 40,000 men stationed in Chu Lai, in various camps scattered over the 10-square-mile enclave. By mid-summer 1967, there were 60,000 men stationed in Chu Lai. That's more people than live in Portland, Maine, for chrissakes!

We were just one of two Seabee battalions here. That's more than 1,500 construction guys—and still we couldn't build stuff fast enough to keep up with the military surge. We were building a war machine on the sands of Chu Lai on the scale of a major World War II campaign.

LCDR Roger Martin and Seventy-One's advance party had already been here for six weeks, getting the lay of the land, inspecting the equipment and facilities we would inherit from MCB-40 when they turned Camp Shields over to us. The lieutenant knew what was

A squadron of Marine A-4 Skyhawks, parked at MAG 13's (Marine Air Group) SATS airfield. We'd be repairing this jet fighter runway regularly for the next seven months.

going on. I had no idea. I was about to get an education. As we drove north to Rosemary Point, along a two-lane paved road, the lieutenant provided a running commentary.

"There's an ROK [Republic of Korea] Marine brigade moving in and we need to build them a camp," he said. "There's two hospitals on the drawing board," he continued, rattling off more projects. All this I heard, but didn't register. My mind and my eyes were too busy drinking in the sights. The base went on for miles, over sand hills, along the beach, the sparkling sea off to our right. We passed camp after camp. Jet fighters were taking off in a continual stream, helicopter gunships skimmed the treetops overhead. We arrived at the Sand Ramp, a landing and staging area on the beach below Rosemary Point. Landing craft, LSTs and LCUs, were lined up on the beach, their front doors down, forklifts scurrying in and out, off-loading pallets of stuff, stacking them in a receiving area that looked like a small town. It was all too much to take in.

"The Marines have launched Operation Union," the lieutenant added. "It's a search and destroy mission up in the Que Son Valley, someplace between us and Da Nang. It's going on now." I would learn later that the operation didn't go well. More than 100 Marines were killed, but there were some 800 North Vietnamese Army regulars and Viet Cong killed.

"Task Force Oregon," the lieutenant went on, "has one mission: to protect this Marine air base, which provides fighter support for our ground troops on search and destroy missions into the highlands of Eye Corps." It was in these valleys and mountain passes that the North Vietnam Army and VC were building a path, the Ho Chi Minh Trail, to supply their forces in the south, near Saigon.

We drove over to the main concrete runway, on the south side of the base. This is the runway on which we'd landed, and it was used by large cargo C-141 and C-131 planes, and the Phantom bombers which were dropping ordnance on North Vietnam targets.

"By the end of May," the lieutenant said, "there will be so many men stationed here in Chu Lai, I don't know where they're going to house them all. It'll mean four new bases scattered over this 10-square-mile sand pit."

LCDR Martin and I stopped a dozen times to look at possible sites marked on his map. I photographed the topography for later examination, and on we went.

"Some of these building sites will require additional roads," he said, talking to himself as much as to me. "Drainage will be an issue when the monsoons come."

The Skipper Outlines the Work

Early May, a hot Sunday morning. The entire battalion was at muster, standing at parade rest on the concrete basketball court. Inspection of the troops, including the officers, had just ended and our CO, CDR Coughlin, stepped up to give us a pep talk.

"Seventy-One is now fully engaged," he said, in as military a voice as he could muster. "To get the projects Regiment has given us, we will be working alongside MCB-Six." This was the other Seabee battalion a few miles up the beach on Rosemary Point. He continued, outlining the workload ahead. He explained that we would be building roads, hooches, offices, wardrooms, clubs, mess halls and kitchens, medical facilities, a surgical hospital and an evacuation hospital, installing a communications system, drilling for water and installing water supply and sewage disposal systems. Detachments were forming. One was already in Quang Ngai. Another would be leaving that week for projects in Saigon.

While all this new construction was going on, the battalion would be fixing roads, installing culverts to improve drainage and repairing damage to the runways whenever needed. The Marine Air Wing and Air Force needed ordnance bunkers built to store and protect their bombs and other explosives. This would require crushed rock, asphalt for the roads, concrete for foundations. We would be operating a stone quarry, a laterite pit, rock crushing, and asphalt and concrete plants.

Our eyes glazed over. This was all too much to comprehend, standing there sweating. Someone passed out, just crumpled up there on the concrete, either due to dehydration, a hangover, or the sheer demands of this old man's war.

What Lay Ahead for This Seabee Outfit

You can't build without something to build with. So, lumber, materials for Quonset huts and steel Butler buildings, steel matting for the runways, pipe, toilets for the officers,

CDR Coughlin, our CO, addressed the troops on Sunday mornings.

were shipped to Da Nang from the States on freighters, off-loaded, and reloaded on LSTs and LCUs, to make their way south to the Sand Ramp at Chu Lai. LCDR Patterson (S-4) was our Supply OIC. He was in charge of this never-ending stream of materials. Our trucks were making round trips to the amphibious landing area at the Sand Ramp, around the clock, bringing back equipment, supplies, building materials, fuel and food. At the staging area, forklifts moved around pallets of beer, drums of fuel, motor oil, spare parts, entire jet engines, medical supplies, and coffins.

In addition to the two Seabee outfits, the 9th Marine Engineer unit and an Army Engineer unit were here, adding an additional 1,000 construction men. These outfits were building artillery installations, repairing or installing bridges, sweeping the highway for mines and building camps on hilltop forts for the land forces.

A Marine All-Weather Fighter Attack Squadron, VMA AW-533, arrived in May with a flight of A-6A Intruder all-weather attack aircraft, to provide air support for Marines in I Corps, and to deliver ordnance to targets in North Vietnam under all weather conditions. They would need a control tower, refueling and ordnance pads, offices, barracks, briefing rooms, along with water and sewage systems, communications and electricity.

In the months to follow, I would get to see a lot of what the military brass had planned for their war machine. I photographed construction projects, made notes and interviewed builders, chiefs and officers at the worksites for *The Transit*. It took a few weeks of rambling around the Chu Lai Enclave to realize how large this base was. It was larger than Davisville and Quonset Point NAS combined—and we were here to make it even bigger. This enclave was only two years old but was only one of a dozen American bases the Seabees, Marine and Army engineers were building in Vietnam. There were now major bases in Phu Bai, south of the DMZ, in and around Da Nang, in Cam Ranh Bay, Phu Cat, Phan Rang, and the Tan Son Nhut Air Base outside Saigon.

I now had a good picture of what my outfit would be doing, and how we fit into the overall scheme of building a war. For a kid from a small town in New England, it was thrilling to be involved in this massive undertaking. I was getting a chance to witness U.S. military might—the sheer amount of material the U.S. was pouring into the war effort was staggering—all this to wage war on a guerrilla force of small people up in "them there" hills. This is what it must have been like during World War II, when the U.S. military arrived on the beachheads with shiploads of men, weapons, ammunition, equipment, tanks, trucks, jeeps and crates of supplies.

Our Seabees could now get to work, and I could begin writing about what they were building. Over the next six months of watching and experiencing what was going on, I began to realize the old men in Washington were making a huge and needless mistake.

A Little History of Chu Lai

On May 6, 1965, the Marines and the Seabees came ashore on a deserted beach 60 miles south of Da Nang. This sand pile had no name at the time, so General Victor "Brute" Krulak dubbed it Chu Lai. Soon the ARVN's (Army of the Republic of Vietnam) 2nd Division and 3rd Battalion joined the Marines. They came ashore in landing craft, just like Normandy, to secure the area. I don't know from what—there was nothing here when they arrived but sand and a few curious locals, who cheered when they landed. The U.S. military brass had big plans for this deserted strip of sand. Things were getting too busy up in Da Nang, and the brass needed another air strip to provide air cover for the ground troops. This vacant beach area was within easy air strike of the DMZ and cities in North Vietnam. There was a protected cove to the north, to provide a landing and staging area. Highway One ran through the area.

On May 7, 1965, the 3rd U.S. Marine Expeditionary Brigade, composed of the 4th Marine Regiment, 3rd Reconnaissance Battalion, elements of Marine Aircraft Group 12 (MAG-12) and the rest of Seabee battalion MCB-Ten, landed and began building an airfield and base facilities.

The SATS Expeditionary Airfield was ready for its first combat mission in just 25

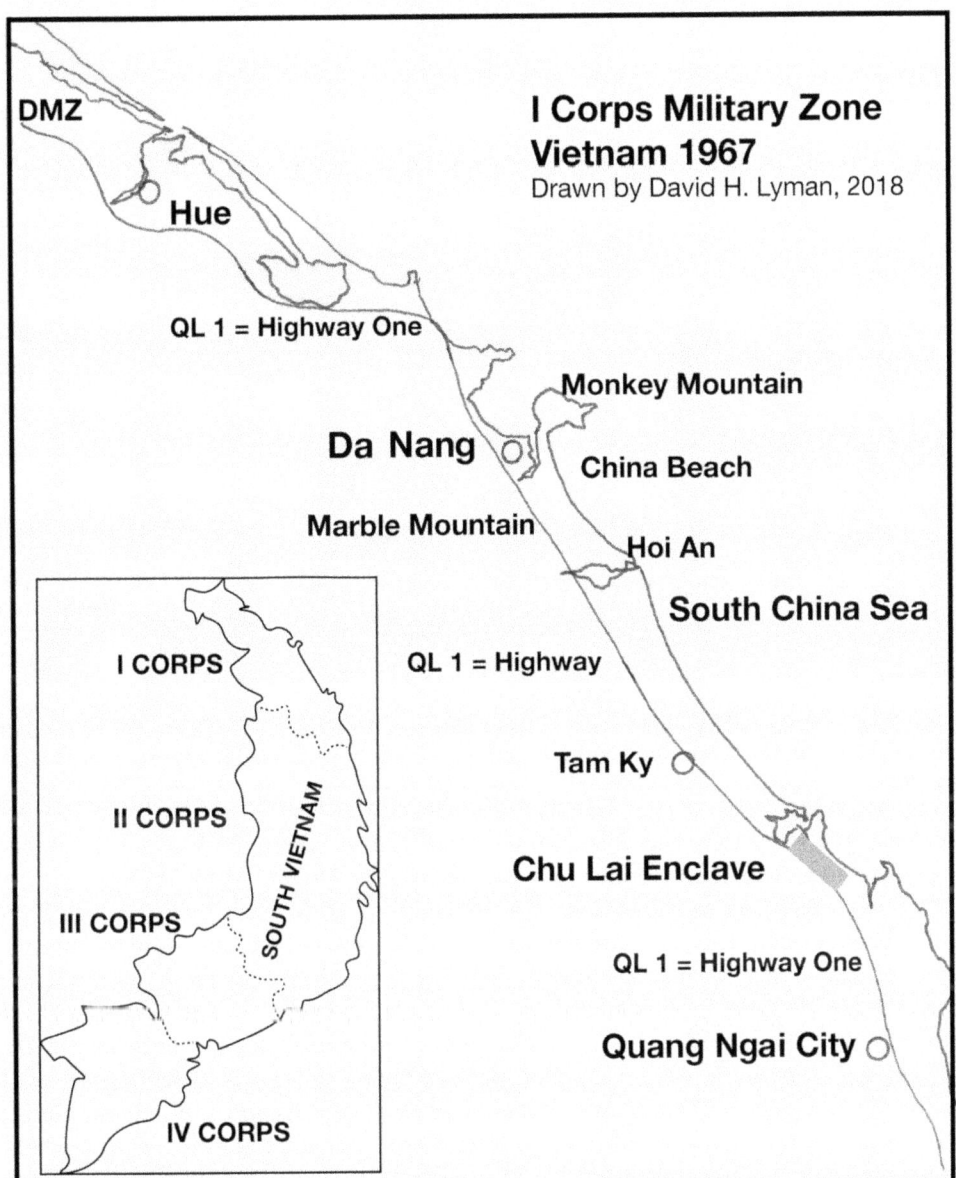

The Chu Lai Enclave was in the northern part of South Vietnam, in the I Corps (Eye Corps) Military Zone.

days. Within a year, this strip of sand had been turned into the Chu Lai Military Enclave. The enclave occupied nearly 15 square miles of sand, between two rivers that flowed down from the mountains to the south and west and into the South China Sea. At the northwest end, where the Trau River emptied into An Hoa Bay and the sea, Rosemary Point, a prominent peninsula, rose out of the sand. From there, the enclave ran along seven miles of curved beach to the Tra Bong River in the southeast. The perimeter then extended south and west, inland for two miles to Highway One and the railroad tracks.

A Marine's A4A Skyhawk from MAG 13 touches down on the all-metal SATS crosswind runway. The machinery in the foreground is the arresting gear equipment used to capture planes landing "hot."

Out past "the wire" were the hills and mountain valleys where the VC and the PANV (People's Army of North Vietnam) were carving out the Ho Chi Minh Trail.

The 9th Engineer Battalion, First Marine Division, arrived in Chu Lai in June 1966, and went about setting up their camp to the south of Highway One, outside of the perimeter wire. This Marine Construction Battalion, like the Seabees, was there to support the First Marine Division combat operation. They built roads and repaired bridges, swept Highway One for mines, erected barracks, operated the cable ferries on nearby rivers, and being outside the Chu Lai perimeter, manned their own security perimeter. (A book on the 9th Engineer Battalion, First Marine Division's deployment to Vietnam, 1966 to 1970, as told by the men and officers who were there, has been published by McFarland, and is available via their website.)

Within a year, the enclave was a major military installation. The Seabees had extended the SATS runway, and added a short crosswind strip, with arresting and catapult gear. The civilian contractors had built a new 10,000-foot concrete runway, with taxiways, parking aprons for fighters and boomers. There was a control tower, along with ordnance bunkers for the bombs. There were camps within the enclave housing brigades of infantry, armored and airborne units, U.S. and ROK Marine battalions, two Marine air wings flying A-4 fighter-bombers, and a Phantom bomber wing. An Army Recon unit was camped right next door to our camp on the beach. On the other side of our camp was a massive fuel tank farm and a large electrical generation plant.

A fuel pipe came ashore from an offshore off-loading platform. This allowed the tankers to off-load JP-5 jet fuel, diesel and gasoline, while remaining out of range of VC rockets. That underwater pipeline leaked, so our UCT (Underwater Construction Team) made more than 80 dives to fix it.

Each of these military units had their own barracks, mess halls, parade grounds, water system, shops, offices and clubs (bars). The Chu Lai Enclave was a regular city and growing.

Chapter 7

Life in This 'Bee Hive

The military, if nothing else, can bring regularity to your life. Reveille was at 5:30 a.m. Breakfast was from 5:30 to 6:30. After breakfast, each company assembled in formation somewhere on the base to be counted—to make sure no one had gone missing during the night. There was a reading of the POD, announcements and team assignments for that day, then it was off to work. Lunch break was midday, 45 minutes, and most of that time was spent standing in the chow line.

We were halfway through the summer, halfway through our seven-month deployment to this tropical paradise. It was hot, very hot. The sea was now too warm to provide any real refreshment. But life went on in this small town on the edge of the South China Sea.

Sunday mornings the bulk of the battalion, 500 men (200-plus Seabees were on detachments somewhere else in Vietnam), assembled for muster, inspection and a pep talk. We stood on the hot concrete basketball court, in the hot sun, sweating in our best uniforms, shaved, with boots shined and weapons cleaned. Inspection was followed by the officers praising us for the effort we showed, upon which followed lectures on safety on the job, safe sex (with whom? we wondered), personal hygiene and the importance of taking our weekly malaria pill. We learned what projects were coming up, which detachments were leaving camp on projects, and more about safety. It was 9 a.m. by the time we were released from muster, when we ambled back to our hooches and get out of uniform. Some headed off to church, others jumped into bathing suits and hit the beach. A few guys climbed into work greens and drove out to the villages on to participate in our Civic Action project, helping put a roof on a local school or church. The bars opened after lunch, and by nightfall, the entire battalion was enjoying a happy, hazy buzz.

The work schedule for a Seabee battalion was so intense, our seven months in Vietnam were credited on our records as a full year's service in the combat zone. Each Seabee battalion served two seven- to eight-month tours, adding up to 14 to 16 months, which was a few months longer in-country than most other military outfits. We also worked a lot harder than non-engineering outfits. We all put in 60-hour weeks of physically demanding labor—that is, all except we desk jockeys.

Day After Day, Week After Week

The daily and weekly grind was mind-numbing, but there was no way we could feel sorry for ourselves—we didn't have time. Being busy, we knew, was a whole lot easier than what the Marine and Army combat units faced; days of waiting and boredom interspersed with intense firefights—bullets, rockets and mortars raining down death.

Pay for an E-5, Second Class Petty Officer, was $315 a month. That included base pay, combat pay, and living outside the States pay. It all added up to $78.75 a week, which came down to $1.31 an hour for a 60-hour work week—and all with no air conditioning! Most of the men in construction would have been making $40 an hour back home driving big machines, pouring cement, welding steel girders together, building skyscrapers … and they wouldn't have anyone shooting at them. I wonder what OSHA would say about the working conditions we faced in Vietnam. Nevertheless, our outfit had very few work-related, loss-time accidents. In fact, we got numerous commendations for our safety record.

Luckily, it was summer and dry—come fall when the monsoon rains arrived, the camp would be wet and soggy. I'm from New England, I know what "mud season" is. I'll swap the mud for this heat any day.

Beach Village on the South China Sea

Camp Shields had everything any New Jersey or Cape Cod beach town had. Our village on the beach had a library, a barbershop, three restaurants, four bars, a general store, three garages, a filling station, a water system, a phone network with operators

A summer rental on the beach at the Jersey Shore? Not likely. It's Charlie Company's line of cottages on the beach, with a view of the South China Sea.

Our sidewalks were made of Marston matting (PSP), used for runways on the coral islands of the Pacific in World War II. The mats, with lots of holes for drainage, were necessary on the soft beach sand of Camp Shields.

(male only), a police force (and even a small security army), a bank, a school, an all-denominational church, a bakery, a post office, a gift shop, a garbage collection service and a sewage system (aka the honey bucket team). We had a complete medical and dental facility, a taxi service of sorts, a travel agency, generator and ice plants, hardware store, supply and lumber yards, even our own oceanside resort. We even had our own weekly bulletins and a monthly newspaper. By mid-summer we had installed a powerful MARS shortwave radio station, connecting our 'Bees with their folks at home (more on this later).

The barbershop, with two chairs and only one barber, was one of the few places in camp with air conditioning. There was only one style of cut—short—but the shop was always full. I figure it was the air conditioning. Next door was a gift shop, run by a local Vietnamese businesswoman and her teenage daughters. They sold Vietnamese-made handicrafts, fabrics and Vietnamese clothing to send home as gifts. You could drop off uniforms for an off-base Vietnamese tailor to make adjustments and sew on new rate insignias. There was a Korean laundry and dry-cleaning service that would pick up and drop off twice a week. To that extent, it was like being at home.

While we did complain, we had it a whole lot better than the grunts in the combat units. We got daily showers, three squares, a bar, and we didn't get shot at—much. The Marines and Army soldiers had to hike into the bush with a 40-pound pack of equipment, carrying food and water for three days, maybe a week. They lived in the bush, no showers, trudging through muddy rice paddies. They slept on the ground, were eaten alive by

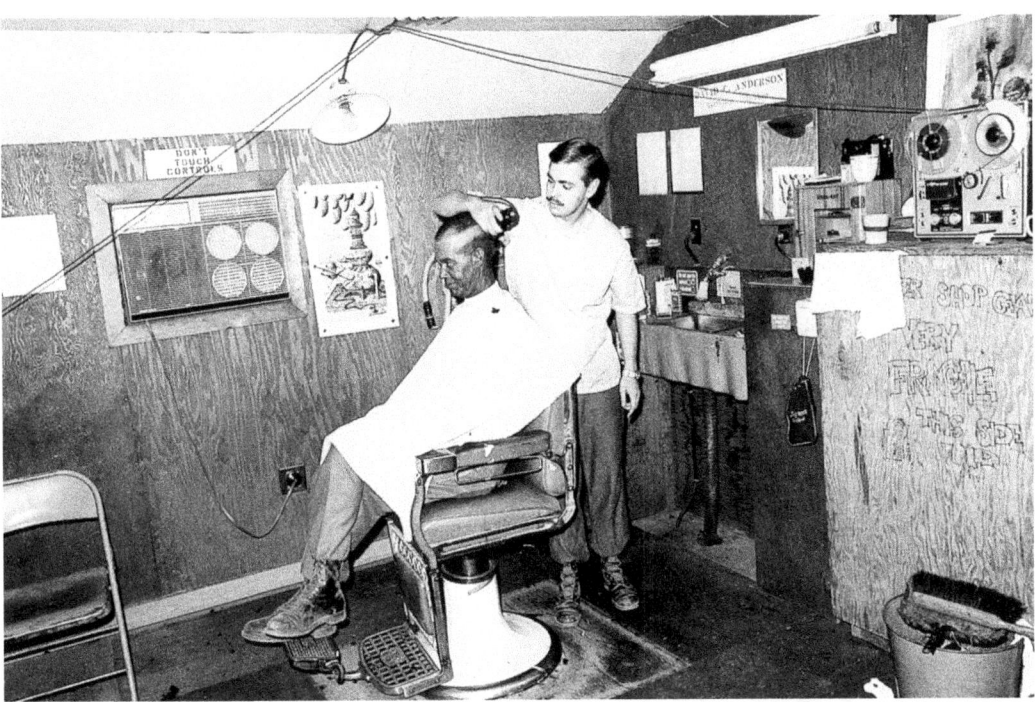

Time for a haircut, a chair is open. David Anderson, SHB 3, buzzes some hair from Chief Carter in the air-conditioned barbershop. There's only one style, and no cologne.

bugs and leeches, dined on C-rations, and drank muddy water that was supposedly "purified" with pills. Oh, and they also got shot at and blown up.

We all shared the heat, the noise, dust, the shits and the petty harassment from those above us, though.

Navy Chow, Navy Grog

Our camp had three restaurants, one for the enlisted men, another for the chief petty officers, and the third for the commissioned officers. I never did get to dine with the officers, where they were served by stewards and didn't need to stand in line like the rest of us.

Each of us had our own personal "mess kit," a six-section steel tray, steel mug and flatware all secured together by a hunk of welding rod and hung on a nail in our office or sleeping quarters. At mealtimes, we would grab our kit and rush to the mess hall, only to stand in line outside. Before entering the mess line, we'd dunk our entire kit into barrels of hot water to sanitize them, then shuffle along in line while the cooks loaded up our trays with standard Navy cuisine. Mashed potatoes, mushy peas and carrots, "horse cock," "shit on a shingle," white bread, pudding for dessert. We sat at long tables, like they do in prison, and shoveled it all down. When the meal was over, we scraped the residue into a garbage pail, rinsed off our kits in another barrel, then washed the kits in a soapy barrel with a long-handled brush, then into another rinse barrel. We did this three times each day.

Chow line in the enlisted men's chow hall.

Drinking ... it's a Navy thing. In the 1800s, sailors on ships of the royal and continental navies got a ration of rum, every day. The rum was mixed with water and lime juice. The cocktail had three purposes.

    1. The booze kept the crew mellow and easier to control.
    2. The lime juice helped prevent scurvy.
    3. Screw-up, talk back, shirk your duty and you were denied your ration. It was carrot and stick.

The Brits kept up the tradition until 1970, the New Zealand Navy until 1990, and the Canadians still continue. The U.S. Navy did away with the tradition before World War II, but that was on shipboard. For units ashore, like the Seabees, the tradition of "hoisting a few" was alive and well. Drinking, being a Navy tradition, was one that we Seabees were more than happy to continue. After all, we were ashore. If we got drunk, we couldn't possibly fall overboard and get ourselves lost at sea. A few of the younger Seabees got their hands on pot, which they purchased from the villagers who worked around the base, but alcohol was the preferred method of unwinding for us older Seabees.

The Social Clubs

There were four clubs, or bars, spread around our base: The Chiefs' Club and the Officers' Club were at opposite ends of the village, along the beach perimeter. The Acey-Ducey Club, for first class and second-class petty officers, was back by the supply yard.

7. Life in This 'Bee Hive

A typical night at the EM Club. Rick Hanratty, DK3, from HQ (left) is tending bar as the enlisted men crowd in to order cans of suds.

The EM Club, for us third class petty officers, E-2 and E-3s, was located by the wire barricade near the beach. MCB-Ten had built this thatched hut on a concrete slab, with palm leaf woven latticework for walls and a thatched roof. The wind blew off the sea through the open, screen-less windows. It opened at 6 p.m. It could have been Club Med, if it weren't for the sounds of war off in the hills.

The club had two rooms, a small one which held the bar and a few tables, and a larger room, with more tables and chairs, card tables and a pool table. The place served cans and bottles of beer from various countries: the customary Stateside brands, plus beers from the Philippines and Mexico, Tiger beer from Singapore and "33" beer from Saigon. There were a few bottles of hard liquor for shots. No mixed cocktails. Getting a buzz on was a nightly occurrence.

I'd saunter in around 8 p.m., lean on the bar while ordering a beer, and survey the crowd to see if there was a table with friends I might join. The discussions around those tables did not involve small arms fire in a rice paddy, "dust-off" extractions and dumb decisions from the officers back at command. These were Seabees, construction professionals. The men talked about beams, siding, roofing options, the lousy mix from the asphalt plant, the condition of our fleet of trucks, road and runway repairs. Oh, they might get around to sexual tales while on R&R and the resulting "medical condition," or what they'd do when they got "out."

My guys were pros and they really liked what they did, for they talked about it incessantly. I guess there was a degree of satisfaction in actually building something—a barracks completed, a road opened, a landing strip fixed and back in operation. It seemed the combat operations outside the perimeter was a thankless affair. The Army and Marine guys had to keep reclaiming the same territory over and over again. It was like bailing out a boat with a sieve.

For me, I was now part of a construction company, building stuff.

The South China Sea

The beach was right *there*. You could hear it. You could smell it. The "Beach for Lunch Bunch" included those of us who wanted to spend a few minutes swimming or floating in the sea. Our base perimeter was completely surrounded by three strands of barbed wire topped with razor wire, with a maze passageway through the fencing to reach the beach. When I could, at noon I'd climb into a bathing suit, wrap a towel around my neck, run to the beach and plunge into the waves. Just a few minutes of being totally immersed in the warm South China Sea was worth the effort. The sea was a meditative place where all the stress of living in a war zone, for a few minutes, was washed away—until mid-summer, when the seawater was too hot to provide much refreshment. On Sunday afternoons, our only time off, the beach was full of men playing ball, swimming, sunning, napping. Some Sundays I went off with our UCT (Underwater Construction Team) to Rosemary Point to SCUBA dive among the coral and the submerged shipwrecks. Twenty feet below the surface, the water was cool. For 20 minutes, I could forget where I was.

From Rosemary Point to the Tra Bong River in the southwest, the Chu Lai beach ran for eight miles. Sunday afternoons found the beach crowded with Seabees.

After dinner, from 5 to 6:30, my routine was to shower, put on civvies and watch a movie in the outdoor theater, or I'd head off to the EM Club for a beer or two, or three.

Sliding into Oblivion

It took an hour or so of drinking before the buzz kicked in. Then it was happy time. Half an hour later I was as lucid as I was going to get. I would feel the Muse approaching. Finishing my fourth beer, I would say good night to my table mates, and make my way back to my office hooch. I would stop for a pee into one of the 55-gallon barrels-in-the-sand that were scattered throughout the camp, climb the steps to my office, unlock the door, enter, reach for the string that hung from the light socket overhead, and turn on the light.

I could sustain this slide into oblivion for another hour, maybe two, before I would fall off the edge. It was during this slide where I was my most creative, teetering on the edge between dreams and reality. Hunter Thompson spent a lot of his time there, invited in through the drugs—the booze no longer strong enough to open the door.

I would sit at my desk, staring at the Olivetti. An idea would materialize out of the fog, or would have followed me from the EM Club. The door would open and in I went. I began to write. I would bang away at the keys for an hour or more, stumbling through the process of capturing a thought, an observation or fragment of a story. I needed to get it on paper before it vanished or I was too far gone to see the keys.

Some of what I wrote, once re-written, might find its way into *The Transit*. Most of what I wrote had nothing to do with the military. I wrote about growing up, jobs I had, girls I dated, hunting in the woods behind the lodge, fishing on the lake as a young boy. I wrote essays, poetry, stream of consciousness. I'd write about the foolish things my brothers and buddies and I did as teens.

I would get an idea for an event in my past, and through writing it out, I would get to relive that time and see if it could tell me anything about who I was then, or who I was now. I was just telling stories, only this time I was the only one listening.

These beer soaked evenings, and in that period between 2 and 4 a.m., when the door might open and dreams come tumbling out, it was all I can do to get a fragment or two down on paper. I'd tried to gain access to these lucid moments during the day, sober, but would rarely break through. Give me a few beers, or a stiff rum, and if I'm lucky I would write something I still liked the next morning.

When my slide would hit bottom, I would be spent, done; the door closed. Even if the dream was still with me, my fingers could no longer hit the proper keys and I knew the session was over. I'd kick off my boots and fall onto the cot in the corner of my office.

The next morning I would be punished with a hangover, but rewarded with something to read. Most of what was left from my night's adventure was crap, unintelligible, incomplete sentences, misspellings, typos, unfinished thoughts that trailed off into nothingness. But if I was lucky, there would be *something* amid all the crap. There might be an idea worth exploring. The novelist John Gardner, in his book *On Becoming a Novelist*, says, "All you have to do to be a writer, is write well enough so that when you read what you wrote, it will bring you back to the 'fictive dream.'" So, I would read over my musings in the morning. There on the page there might be a fragment of an insight, or a sentence or two that makes sense, something to bring me back to that original idea. Those times,

I could use my craft as an editor to shape that raw material into something that was readable, that said something. That's the real work of a writer, rewriting, crafting the idea.

Those mornings, with the aid of two APC tablets, I would be functioning normally by noon. But by 4 in the afternoon, I was again anticipating my return to the EM Club to begin the process again.

I looked at myself occasionally. What did I see? A guy with a drinking problem? Or was it that he had a writing problem?

Or both?

Military General Store

Next to the gift shop was a PX ... a general store of sorts. It sold "luxury" items, like soap, toothpaste, shaving gear, gum, candy bars, batteries and non-alcoholic beverages like Coke. It was here I was introduced to Ting (no, not Tang. Ting), a carbonated grapefruit soda, that I still love to this day. It's hard to get outside of the Caribbean but I hear you can get it on Amazon. The PX was supplied, if you can call it that, by the Army Regional Exchange in Da Nang. They sent down a CONEX container every few weeks full of what they didn't want. Fortunately, by mid-summer an expanded Army PX opened up in Chu Lai that served all the units, but they didn't have the cameras, radios, tape recorders, watches, or the stuff most of us wanted to buy. They even ran out of soap for two weeks.

I found a Nikonos underwater camera up at the PX in Da Nang on one of my trips to the I Corps Press Center. It was the only camera they had at the time, so I bought it. This did come in handy when diving with the UCT boys. When word got around that I flew up to Japan each month to print the newspaper, the boys came by my office to press hundreds of dollars into my hands, with a shopping list for cameras, watches, radios— either to bring back with me or mail to their relatives in the States. I became the unit's black market PX. More on this later.

We got laundry service twice a week, thank God, but the Clayton steam generator used to operate the dryers frequently broke down, meaning we had to hang our wet duds and towels outside in the sun to dry on lines between our hooches.

"Good Morning, Vietnam!"

What a rotten way to start the day.

Each morning, a DJ on Armed Forces Radio (AFR) came on strong with that famous "Goooood Moooorning, Vietnam!" That enthusiastic opening salutation had been coined by Adrian Cronauer, an Air Force DJ at AFR in Saigon. When he toured out in 1966, his replacements just continued on with "Goooood Moooorning, Vietnam!" Cronauer went on to write a book about his radio days in Saigon, which became the basis for the movie *Good Morning, Vietnam*, starring Robin Williams. Those Saigon DJs tried to be positive, inspiring, uplifting. Who were they kidding? They had just reminded all of us where the hell we were, Vietnam!

My small Sony portable radio was tuned to AFR in the office most of the time. This was one of those multi-band radio receivers that could pick up stations all up and down

Vietnam and on the shortwave band further than that, but I couldn't tell from where, 'cause I couldn't understand the language. AFR network was based in Saigon, but there was a repeater transmitter here in Chu Lai, so the propaganda, baseball games and music came in loud and clear.

The news was sanitized, we knew that. The newscaster in Saigon kept telling us we were all doing a fantastic job of beating back the North Vietnamese and bringing freedom to the South Vietnamese. Back home, all was just fine, not to worry. They didn't report on the protests, anti-war marches on college campuses, the flag and draft card burnings. We heard nothing of the taunts and jeering our boys were greeted with when they arrived back home. All we heard was President Johnson telling the American citizens that we were winning this war.

The news from Hanoi Hannah, that female voice from North Vietnam radio, was no better, maybe worse. I could pick up her pleasantly accented voice on the medium band. She provided just as much fake news as we heard on AFR, but from the North Vietnamese perspective. Listening to her, we learned the U.S. was losing the war, the VC were killing our men, blowing up our airfields, attacking our convoys. We should pack our bags and go home. Then she played some marching music, followed by a few country-and-western tunes, and then it was back to more Hanoi Hannah. She tried to mess with our minds. Trying to turn the servicemen against the war, she reminded us our girlfriends were home sleeping with our best friends.

I'd worked in radio before the service, and have always found radio a way to understand the culture I was in. I found what I thought were Vietnamese stations, but since I couldn't understand a word, I never knew for sure. The music, while interesting, sounded like a band of musicians on out-of-tune stringed instruments. The music on AFR was too young for me, mostly rock and roll and lots of country and western. There were a few songs that hit home for all of us. "I've Got to Get Out of This Place" by the Animals was not about Vietnam but it may as well have been. "Chain of Fools" by Aretha Franklin reminded us of the military chain of command we all suffered under. "Leaving on a Jet Plane" by Peter, Paul and Mary was about leaving home for 'Nam. "Green, Green, Grass of Home" by Porter Wagoner reminded us of what was waiting when we got out of "this place," if we ever did. "We Shall Overcome," covered by dozens of performers, maybe even thousands, is about hope, either for the ending of the Civil Rights war at home, or for the ending of this war we were in.

Armed Forces Radio and *Stars and Stripes*, the daily military newspaper, only hinted at what the Marines and Army foot soldiers were up to in the hills and valleys. There was no television on our base, so we never saw what the folks back home were watching. They had a better view of the action than we did. I never saw a Viet Cong, dead or alive, not knowingly. I never saw anyone dead for that matter. We heard a lot of noise, saw flashes of exploding ordnance in the hills, but the war was at arm's length. Some of our detachments scattered around Vietnam saw some action, manned the perimeter and shot back at the VC. I did, only once, but most of us didn't.

What we learned about actual combat we heard from the U.S. and Korean Marines at the clubs we visited up and down the beach. The ROK Marines were a nasty bunch of guys. They hated the VC and had no compunction about slicing off the ear of a dead VC, adding it to a cord attached to their K-bar scabbard—collecting scalps, as it were. I could understand the reason the ROKs did this—it was a notch on their pistol. I found the trophies a bit disrespectful, but then I was not called on to do what these Marines were doing. I gathered some of the U.S. Marines would have liked to collect ears, but it was a court martial offense.

The grunts we met talked about long periods of boredom, waiting for something to happen, orders to come, for the VC to show itself, then there'd be a firefight for a few hours, and the VC would retreat back into the boonies. The Marines would secure a village or hilltop, leave on another mission, and the VC would just creep back in. Some of the men told of dead comrades, fields of dead VC, burned-out villages with dead civilians. As a photographer for my unit, producing a newspaper that would be seen by folks back home, I was told I could not publish pictures of the dead, or of destroyed equipment, or anything the enemy might use against us—or put the military in a bad light. Not that I had the opportunity.

High Stakes Poker

Major pastimes for the men in any war includes playing cards. Illegal poker games took place on our base, and on every base up and down the beach. Some games were just for fun. Others were serious, high-stakes games played with $100 bills. In-country, the government paid us with military scrip, funny money that looked like it came from a Monopoly game. This was the only currency we could use in-country. Outside, the Vietnamese used piasters, a word left over from the French, more funny money. But the high-stakes games were played with U.S. greenbacks. The brass tried everything they could to curtail the illegal gambling. These games, they said, led to fights, men losing their shirts, increased theft of government property, loss of morale.

One ploy the officers tried to de-incentivize these high-stakes games was to tell the post office that greenbacks could not be exchanged for U.S. postal money order. You could buy money orders with scrip, but not with U.S. bills. The officers thought that by stopping the gamblers from sending their winnings home, the games would stop. Right?

Since I was flying to Japan each month, the gamblers would press thousands in greenbacks into my hands with the request to purchase money orders once I was out of Vietnam, and mail their winnings to folks at home. I did this once, but was scared of getting caught so I stopped. It was enough to take a thousand in cash with me each month to Japan to buy cameras, watches and radios, which I either brought back with me, or mailed home to families. Even some of the officers put items on my black market shopping list.

A Letter Home from Vietnam

Many of our guys just never did write home to tell their folks what it was like in Vietnam. So, I wrote a generic "Letter Home" for the second edition of *The Transit*, with photographs, to show the folks what our village by the sea looked like. Here's that text:

Dear Folks…

I realize it's been a long time since I've written, But, with getting settled in here, finding my way around I've been a busy Seabee. I know you all want to know what it's like over here. I'll try to give you an idea.

We stepped off the plane into a damp hot and sticky heat that sucked the breath out of you. After

7. Life in This 'Bee Hive

cold and wintry New England, this was a shock to say the least. Well, the hot weather didn't seem to last long, or I got used to it awful fast, whichever way, it's a lot better now. The dust is bad and it's still as hot, but those things I can live with. The camp is actually like a summer beach resort. Little cottages, with screens, ten of us crammed inside. We have our own cubicles with lockers artfully decorated from ceiling to floor with Playboy centerfold pin-ups. The beach is a stone's throw away. The surf was really heavy when we first got here, but is quieted down a lot since. The swimming is still great, and the water, if you don't mind the little stinging jellyfish, is like the ocean on the Jersey Shore. Although, our work schedule does not leave much time from making like Coney Island. The food is pretty good. Our cooks are something else. The head chef, Oldies, he's called, got himself an award back in D-ville, and he's really turning this Navy chow into something we can eat. No milk to speak of, but there are gallons of "bug-juice" Kool-Aid and iced tea—different colors, but it all tastes the same, like water.

Since we got over here a month ago we've spent two nights in the mortar pits. These are sandbag lined trenches dug into the sand between the hooches (cottages) meant to be bomb shelters. Last Saturday in the middle of the night the VC hit the sand ramp 5 miles up the road with mortars. We're too far inside the Chu Lai enclave to receive any real fire. But, when the sirens blare and the base PA begins shouting "In Coming, In Coming" we all grab our helmets and weapons and dove into the pits. If we did get attacked, all the units, including ours, would go to Condition One: "Everyone man the perimeter." Boy, what a mad scramble that would be. I couldn't find my pants in the darkness, so I grabbed my rifle, ammo belt, helmet and flak jacket and dove into the pit in my skivvies. It didn't bother me, as the rest of the gang was in the same embarrassing situation. Had the VC made it through our lines they would have died of laughter. The only mishap was when one of our chiefs fell into his mortar pit and broke an ankle. The only time there was any real damage to our camps happened when a rocket, meant for the air strip, missed and blew up one of our privies, the 4-holers we call "the head," but that was before we got here. Other than that, it's been pretty quiet around here. At

Marine Gunny SGT Cleylon Camper from Bowmont, Texas, checks out a Seabee's M14, alongside the XO, CDR Brown. SGT Camper replaced Marine Gunny SGT Gene Harrison, who headed back to Davisville to train more Seabees heading to Vietnam.

nights you can hear the Marines, and now the Army, lobbing artillery in the mountains behind the airstrip and occasionally you hear a machine gun popping off on the outer perimeter. There are always a few flares floating down around here turning night into day. There is a war going around here someplace, but so far you can't prove it by me.

When we arrived, they really had us jumping. Three projects for the Army have kept some of us up all night. Seems a little planning would help, but then operational requirements in this war change every day. The only real problem around here is the dust. Yeah, it's everywhere. The boys coming back from a day at the rock crusher, or the quarry are so covered with sweat, dust and salt deposits so bad you can't tell who's who.

Sunday is inspection day. The skipper gives out with the praise and tells how great we're doing, then hands out some awards and looks at our rifles. We've got Marine Gunny Sgt. here—a big honcho in the Marines, who got stuck as the advisor to this Seabee outfit. He goes along with the skipper on inspection, and while he's a real great guy, when it comes to not knowing your rifle's serial number or a speck of dust or sand in the barrel, he sounds like Jack Webb in the *Drill Instructor* movies. He can be a real hard ass.

He's turned a few of the Seabees from Alpha Company into Marines. They sit on the camp's perimeter all night behind a M60 machine gun, keeping the Marines down the beach from sneaking in here to

Left: Caption from *The Transit*: "Judy Larson, an 18-year-old from California, and her USO troop dropped in for a few hours one Sunday in August and won the hearts of the entire 800-man battalion. Judy is a natural singer, great dancer and a real trooper. Her show business father put the troop together and they've been touring Vietnam base camps longer than we've been here. Miniskirts were all the rage that year, and no female performer was allowed on stage without wearing one, not even Martha Raye." *Right*: A Filipino dancer with a USO show entertains the troops.

7. Life in This 'Bee Hive

The villages outside the "wire" were full of kids. Seabees naturally attracted kids, who climbed over the tall Americans, searching for candy hidden in their pockets.

stealing our beer. The VC wouldn't stand a chance of getting past our guys.

Saw my first white girl in 42 days last weekend. The USO brought the "Beauties and the Beasts" to our stage for a show. The group was from New Zealand. Not half bad—not half good either. One of the girls was as fat as Burt the butcher at the Grand Union. The other two were another story. But, it was the kids who really stole the show. Two little Filipino girls, both about 16, and they could dance—put American teenagers to shame.

We have movies most every night, if you like *Batman* and *Gunsmoke*. Once a week we have an hour of infantry training—they show us re-runs of the TV show *Combat*. The bar here is like a typical tropical island hut—without the typical island girls that makes any tropical island typical. The heat here keeps most of us sober, for fear of a hangover the next morning.

They started letting us out of our cages last week. Groups were allowed to go into the local town, An Tan, for a couple of hours. With five bucks of this funny money we call Piaster—I grabbed my rifle and proceeded to win over the local population. It was a disaster. First they don't speak too much English. Second I don't speak Vietnamese at all. But I've never let something like that bother me. With a few expressions I picked up from the Marines, I managed to carry on pretty well with the village's businessman—enough so that I didn't come back empty handed. All you have to know is a few of the basic terms.

"You Number one," means, you're the best.

"You Number 10," means look out, they don't care much for you.

"Never happen," means it's just is not going to happen, simple as that.

"Souvenir me cigarette, chop chop. You number one Seabee, yes?" means give me a cigarette, right now, friend.

There is a wealth of more colorful expressions, but these were picked up from the Marines and they're not fit to print.

The country around here is as flat and sandy as Cape Cod. It's not fit for anything but the air strip we have to keep fixing. But a couple of miles to the south and north the land is a whole lot greener.

The Vietnamese girls were shy, and conservative, but they smiled when they met a Seabee.

Looks like truck farming land in New Jersey, and the people look happier and healthier. There's a range of mountains 10 miles to the west, pretty rugged, especially when you consider the jungles are full of Viet Cong. The girls here are a lot prettier than I thought they'd be. They are all very thin with straight black hair and a rich brown tan. They all wear black slacks and a white shift, that covers them from shoulders to the ankles, and a straw hat.

    Well, it's about time to go. Chow line isn't getting any shorter and I got to take my weekly malaria pills; actually I think it's our weekly dose of Ex-Lax.

    The temperature is supposed to be getting hotter around here, they tell me—up to 130 degrees and that's in the shade. If you can find any shade. R&R is coming up soon. They give us a week to get away and have some fun. I have not decided where to go yet—Bangkok, Hong Kong, Thailand, Tokyo; maybe I'll just sit here on the beach in August.

                                                        Your son.

Chapter 8

The Battalion

Like most Seabee outfits, Seventy-One had five companies: Alpha, Bravo, Charlie, Delta and H, or Headquarters.

Alpha was our largest company, with heavy-equipment operators, truck drivers, mechanics, rock drillers, rock crushers, asphalt and cement plant operators. These guys built *horizontal* projects: roads, landing strips for planes and helicopters, foundations for buildings, culverts and drainage systems; they shaped the amphitheater for Bob Hope.

Alpha and Bravo companies often worked 16-hour days, occasionally throughout the night, repairing the Marine runway that suffered frequent mortar and rocket shelling from the VC in the hills.

Ted Husak and Earl Clark, CMs (Construction Mechanics) from Alpha, use muscle and basic technology to separate a damaged tire from a truck rim. The mechanics in Alpha could rebuild an entire engine, fix a transmission, replace a set of injectors, all to keep the outfit's trucks, dozers, scrapers and other vehicles moving.

Bravo, Charlie and Delta companies were made up of builders, utility men, steel workers, and other construction rates. These guys built *vertical* projects out of concrete, wood and steel. They cut up 2 by 4s, nailed up plywood, installed metal roofs, built furniture and the interiors of officers' clubs. Bravo Company also had a well drilling team, establishing themselves as the most productive crew to spend a deployment in Chu Lai.

In the mornings each company assembled in some sort of formation while the chiefs and officers read off the teams and the day's assignments. Teams of builders headed off to put up buildings, wood or steel; the utility men came along later to erect poles, string wires, install lighting; while metal workers installed corrugated roofs, plumbers installed water and sewage lines. Alpha Company would have already leveled the site, built the access road, dug trenches for the pipes, and poured cement for concrete foundations. All this was coordinated by LCDR Martin and his team over in Operations, using plans drawn up by the draftsmen, surveyors and estimators in Engineering. While the work went on, the surveyors ensured things were level and in place. Officers came by periodically to inspect and confer with the chiefs or first class in charge, then return to base to report on progress and problems at the Operations meeting. It all worked, or seemed to.

Seabees work in small teams, often sharing men between companies for larger projects. After muster, teams would climb aboard various vehicles—trucks, personnel and weapon carriers, jeeps—and head off to a job site. They brought water and perhaps lunch with them, along with tools and weapons. They wore hardhats, not helmets, except when going outside the wire. The teams returned to camp each evening for a shower, dinner, a movie or a few beers at the various clubs. A lot of background for the stories I wrote came from the "company clerks." Like me, they were E-4 or E-5s, most with typing skills, who ran the office for the company chief and company commander.

Charlie Company

Pete Peterson was Charlie Company's clerk, the guy in the office who keeps all the paperwork in order. Pete was really a builder, at least that was what the Navy had sent him to school for, but when Chief Otterson found out he could type, he became Charlie Company's clerk.

"In-country," Pete told me, "Charlie and Delta companies shared an office hooch. We're just north of the chow hall, crammed in between the ice plant and the generator shed. Bravo Company has an office hooch next door. Chief Funk, Chief Ruby, and Chief Bragden came on board back in August. Chief Funk and Chief Rude had just left Builders 'A' School in Port Hueneme where they had been instructors—18 of the builders in Charlie have been their students."

In a communication to me, he continued:

> Chief Funk ran things while I kept track of the details. I typed up reports, filed papers, kept the records, answered questions and tried to be useful. Lt. Wells was the OIC for Charlie Company, with Ensign T.W. Bones as his assistant. Nice bunch of guys.
>
> Occasionally, Chief Funk would take me out to one of the projects. So I could get my hand on tools and actually help build something. This helped me keep my Builder's skills up. Chief Funk would sign off on my builder's requirements allowing me to advance in rate to BU2, Second Class Builder (E-5) in 23 months.
>
> The only other time I got out of camp was as part of a security detail on a convoy, or to take the incoming mail down to our detachment in Saigon. When I got to Saigon, I expected to take a few

8. The Battalion

days of R&R, but Chief Rube, who ran the detachment, immediately put me to work with his team remodeling a French villa for the Army's top brass.

Charlie Company built seven 60-foot observation towers on the Chu Lai perimeter for the Army. These were so the Army could watch for VC movement outside the wire. A crew of 12 men poured 250 yards of concrete each day for weeks, creating the bases for the towers. In remote locations, concrete was flown in by Marine HC-53 helicopters, called Jolly Green Giants.

Chief Wade's steel team was on call 24 hours a day, and they often worked late into the night, to repair damage to the Marine's SATS runway. Other steelworkers from Charlie Company built oil storage tanks, aircraft hangers and heliports. Then, in September, men from Charlie worked in 12-hour shifts around the clock to cut out and re-install the center seam on the two-mile concrete runway, all in 20 days. They finished four days ahead of schedule.

Pete shared a Seabee story: "One Sunday afternoon chaplain Lt. Billy Dennis came in with boxes of clothes for the people in the village." A church group in the States had collected and shipped over used clothing with hopes that the Vietnamese people might be able to use them.

That afternoon, Pete shared, some of the 'Bees started going through the boxes and came up with an idea of how to distribute the gifts. About an hour later three jeeps, loaded with Seabees decked out in women's dresses, drove into Tam Ky village. The men drove up and down the streets of the little village, blowing horns and smoking cigars, raising a ruckus. The boxes were distributed amid laughter and a lot of hand shaking and back slapping.

Seabees in drag—it's a Navy tradition! James Mitchener documented the tradition in his book *South Sea Tales*. You can see Seabees in drag in the Broadway musical *South Pacific*, and in the movie adapted from his book.

The Fleet-bee Company

Headquarters occupied a third of the base and included all the support personnel and facilities the construction men needed: the laundry, mess halls for the men and the officers, post office, barbershop, personnel office, paymaster office, supply, base maintenance, transportation.

That wasn't all. Our medical unit

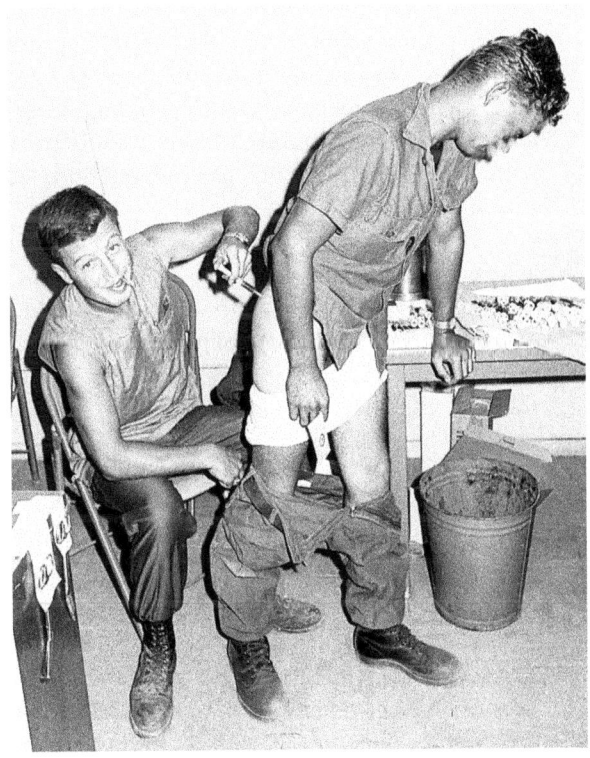

Dennis Smith, HM, a corpsman in the Medical Department, was the lab technician who got to stick needles into a guy's bum when a booster shot was needed.

included nine corpsmen and two doctors, Lt. Jerry Hubbell and dentist Lt. Sam Whisper. Dr. Hubbell, an ObGyn, was serving his reserve time with us. It's just like the Navy to send us an obstetrician-gynecologist, a doctor more experienced in the female body and women's reproductive systems than fixing up Seabees' broken arms, severed fingers, and sunstroke, but he did a fine job.

Dennis Smith, David Bowden and Ed Sarvie were just three of the corpsmen who fixed up the men, stuck needles in bums and doled out pills. I was deeply impressed watching these guys patch up a local Vietnamese kid, wash out someone's wound, sew up a laceration. The kind and compassionate care these corpsmen showed led me to realize that each of us is cut out to do a particular thing. Sticking needles into people, swabbing out a bloody wound, suturing up a laceration—these are not occupations to which I am drawn. But then, writing a story or taking a meaningful photograph is something many other people can't do either. To each his own.

The Men of Seventy-One

There were around 800 officers and enlisted men in Seventy-One. Hard to be accurate as men were leaving, arriving, sent off on TAD, off on detachments, or attending technical schools.

The majority of the officers, somewhere around 22, included lieutenants and lieutenant commanders, with a few newly commissioned ensigns. All but four were civil engineers, with the rest from the fleet. The CO, CDR Richard Coughlin, and the XO, CDR George Brown, were both civil engineers with advanced degrees. Both had shore commands prior to joining Seventy-One, so they had experience with infrastructure, repairs and some new construction, but both were as green as the rest of us when it came to combat duty.

The CO, try as he might to project a tough Marine Commander image, including an ever-present cigar stuffed in his mouth, was just a nice guy. So was the XO. Truly, so were most of the officers, although a few could have used a good kick in the butt, as one of the first class POs (petty officers) said. The vast majority of the men in the outfit were in their mid- to late twenties, as was I. The second and first-class POs were in their thirties, with a few in their forties. We were all "professionals" to one degree or another; we knew how to do what it was we were doing. We had a mission and we didn't need to be yelled at.

The operations officer (S-3), LCDR Roger Martin, was the key officer in the battalion. Next was Engineering, where architects, engineers and draftsmen created the drawings, material lists, and man-power requirements for each project. (More on this later.)

Of the 800 (plus or minus) enlisted, a dozen were chiefs, E-7s, E-8s and E-9s. Most of the battalion was made up of petty officers, E-4 to E-6, most from the construction ranks. Over 80 percent of these rates were IPOs, professional construction workers with various levels of valuable experience who had been recently inducted into the Navy. This program allowed the battalion to hit the ground running when we arrived in Vietnam. Seventy-One was the first Seabee battalion where the majority of the construction ratings were IPOs. "Best bunch of pros I've ever worked with," posted Tuffy Lake to me one day halfway through our deployment. "We couldn't have done what we did without this bunch of professional Seabees."

The XO told me that the IPOs (he used the official designation, DPPOs) not only knew their stuff, they readily adapted to military regimentation, but then the Seabees are not really all that militaristic anyway. When asked, most said they joined the Seabees for the experience of going to the war, but 90 percent said they would not re-enlist (this from an official report). One tour was enough. They complained that the assessment of professional experience was not thorough, that a few E-4s should have been E-5s, and some E-5s should actually have been E-3s.

Finding chiefs with a construction background was not easy; new Seabee outfits were forming Stateside and the demand for advanced rates was fierce. Bringing in chiefs from the fleet was an option. They knew Navy regulations and paperwork, and could run interference with the officers, allowing the more experienced IPOs to get the actual work done.

Those of us in HQ, Administration, were fleet rates, doing the same paper-pushing we'd have been doing on a ship or any naval land base.

The Fighting Seabees

That's the title of the 1944 Hollywood movie starring John Wayne. It's about the formation of the Seabees, the Navy's Mobile Construction Battalions. So, we Seabees are supposed to be able to fight, right? But there were no VC around where we were. We were inside the perimeter, so who did we fight? We wound up fighting each other.

A bunch of guys from the other Seabee battalion up the beach came down for a friendly game of arm wrestling, one-ups-men-ship and drinking. A drunken Seabee from the other battalion elbowed his way in and sat down next to Stapleman at a table full of our men.

"He was tight as a kite," Dick told me the next day. "Wanted to show us how mean and tough he was. He broke a glass on the table and begins to chew on the shards. I guess I must not have been sufficiently impressed for I began to laugh. The drunk didn't like my sense of humor and called me a name. I could see where this was going, so got up and headed for the door. That pissed him off even more. He followed me outside and took a swing. I ducked, he fell to the ground. Before I could get away, he grabbed my leg and bit it. I grabbed his arm in a wrist lock and told him to 'Let go!'"

"His teammates began to gather around, which didn't bode well. With them egging him on, he wasn't going to give in."

"Let go or I'll break your arm," Dick told him.

"'Fuck you,' came the reply, through clenched teeth."

"Once more, let go, then I'll let go." The tension built as a dozen other construction workers were eager for a fight.

"Let go…" Dick said. He didn't.

CRACK!

"I must have snapped his shoulder. You could hear the sound throughout the club." Silence fell immediately.

"You'd better get your buddy out of here," Stapleman told the visitors, their buddy holding his broken arm, now at an alarming angle, to his chest. The visitors gathered up their whimpering buddy and departed.

Nothing ever came of the incident. The sailor broke his arm falling out of the jeep on the way home. At least that's the story that would probably be told.

The Missing Ear

A few weeks after this incident I was walking toward my office after a movie when I happened upon a scuffle near the mess hall. A dozen Seabees were pushing and shoving, yelling encouragement. "Hit him again, for chrissake!" I heard a scream, as one of the crew from Delta Company staggered out of the pig pile, clutching the side of his head.

"He tore it off! My ear!" The Seabee said to me, in surprise. I peered under the cupped hand he was holding to his head. I could see his left ear, still attached, but by only a thin strip of skin. I didn't know the man's name, but I helped him, now in a state of shock or drunkenness, I couldn't tell which, off to sick bay. A corpsman was on duty, and after inspecting the man's wound and cleaning it, he ran to fetch the doctor. I stayed with the Seabee, talked to him about what we'd tell the doctor. We had to get our stories straight.

The doctor arrived and managed to sew the ear back into place, without any sedative. As the doctor taped up the man's head he warned: "This'll hurt like hell in the morning. How did this happen?" No response. No one wanted to get another crew member in trouble. "Lyman, you were there. What happened?"

"Just a scuffle. About a dozen guys pushing and shoving after the movie."

There were similar "scuffles" on our base, and on all the others bases inside the Chu Lai Enclave. The tension had to be relieved somehow. Frustration leads to anger and anger leads to finding any excuse to hit someone. The worst ones were over at the Korean Marines' base. Those guys were serious about fighting.

The man's ear never was right. For weeks it leaked a black fluid from under the bandage. A few weeks later, when the bandage was removed and the wound inspected, it was infected and the ear had to be removed and re-attached, but that was done back in the States.

The Screw-Ups

Every outfit has them—guys who just can't get with the program. They carry grudges; maybe they are angry at their fathers or other authority figures. They refuse to take orders and are bent on getting into trouble to prove they are not to be controlled. They get up to an E-3 rate, screw up, are brought before captain's mast, and are broken back down to SA, E-2. We had two of these guys in our outfit. They never got out of KP duty the entire time we were in 'Nam. They stood on the chow line, throwing mashed potatoes, chipped beef, mixed vegetables onto our trays, as if to say: "Don't like it? Fuck you! What can you do to me?"

These two were creative in the ways they showed their disregard for the service. One noontime, Stapleman and I came through the chow line, sliding our stainless steel trays along, when a foul smell made us gag. It was these two. They grinned as we passed by, holding our noses. "We took off our tee-shirts, pissed on them, then put them back on. Makes the food taste better. Don't you think?"

"Don't drink the Kool-Aid," the other one said. "We dumped two bottles of malaria pills in there. You'll be shitting for a week. Ha, ha, ha."

"Those guys have no self-respect," Stapleman said as we moved to a table.

Norman Albert and Nick Naomi were one week's honey bucket crew. Their official titles: Directors of Camp Sanitation. Each day, they made the rounds of the outdoor privies, dragged out the 50-gallon drums of human waste, poured on gasoline, and set them ablaze.

The Officers of Seventy-One

I always thought all Americans were equal; you know, no caste system as in India, or as in Europe, where the aristocracy "lords" it over the proletariat. Boy, did I get it wrong. The military is a caste system. The officers ruled over us enlisted guys.

I had nothing against officers. I wanted to be one myself, but that didn't work out. So here I was, an enlisted man, a JO3, saluting and "yes Sir-ing" the officers. I knew I could handle it, this kowtowing, as I had only a few more months to deal with it. But it took some getting used to, even though I had a lot of experience in dealing with those who consider themselves "entitled."

Now, being in daily contact with officers, the majority of whom were no better than I, no better educated, nor more of a gentleman than I, I had to swallow my pride and treat the "uniform" (if not the person), with respect. After all, it took an act of Congress to turn these boys into "gentleman," and in some cases there would have been no other way.

I was also a few years older than more than half the officers in our outfit, most of whom had just come out of OCS or ROTC as ensigns. My immediate supervising officer, LTJG Smith, was just 24, while I was 27.

Some enlisted men were intimidated by officers, while others just couldn't handle it—they couldn't stand authority, would rebel and get themselves into deep doo-doo. Maybe these guys never had a father, and if they did, perhaps he wasn't a good father.

How do you get along with authority, while remaining yourself?

I grew up surrounded by wealth and power, rich families who owned summer cottages on "our" lake. The cottage to our left was owned by a dentist whose son was a few months younger than me; his daughter, a few years older. On the other side was an attorney's family, their son, a few months younger than my next brother, Lee. Across the lake there were attractive girls from the families of wealthy CEOs, company presidents, insurance salesmen, plant managers and more doctors and lawyers. There were hundreds of summer cottages surrounding "The Lake." But our lodge was one of the oldest. My father bought it from his dad, who built it before World War I. After the hurricane of 1938, Dad rebuilt the original "camp" into a proper hunting and fishing lodge, using the lumber from downed pine trees. The lodge had four bedrooms, a small bathroom and kitchen and a huge great room, with the dining room at one end and living room at the other. A hand-laid fieldstone fireplace with a half-log mantel occupied half of one wall, while opposite, French doors opened onto a porch facing the lake. The north wall of the great room held racks of fishing rods, at the other end, racks of rifles and shotguns. The remaining walls contained stuffed heads of animals Dad had "bagged."

We were not a wealthy family by any means, but Mom and Dad were the equal, we felt, to anyone on the lake. Dad knew more about the lake, boats, the woods, fishing, and hunting than any other father who had a cottage on the lake. Dad was a great storyteller and public speaker—he was, after all, a traveling salesman. People just listened to my dad. Mom had a natural and insatiable curiosity and was involved in all sorts of clubs, projects and campaigns. We never looked at ourselves, my brothers and I, and especially my mother, as being "less than" any of the wealthy summer folk. Dad and Mom were accepted among the rich and powerful, although we were far from that, and that gave me a sense of equality.

"We have wealth those summer folk enjoy for only two months," Mom would remind us. "We have this lake to ourselves all year round." Then, she'd go on to explain, "Wealth can be measured in more than money." I've never forgotten her wise statement. But Mom did envy the comfortable homes and lifestyles the summer wives had in the cities, with their lavish furniture, drapes and cushions.

Our neighbors arrived just before the Fourth of July, and they left on Labor Day. We had the lake to ourselves the other ten months of the year. The lake became quiet in the fall; flocks of geese flew in on their way south, the leaves turned, the snow fell, the lake froze. We raced our car around on the ice, spinning out of control. Dad chopped holes in the ice to catch fish. We held skating parties for our schoolmates. In the spring we watched the ice go out and the lake fill up with snow melt. The lake was ours; we just loaned it out to the summer folks for a few months each year.

Growing up surrounded by these rich summer people gave me an insight into how I could manage their wealth for my own purpose. If I was nice, helpful, and polite, these wealthy executives would let me take their boats out, and eventually even their daughters. It worked. The idea was the same in the service. I was never intimidated by an officer's rank, although I was respectful, helpful, always doing more than asked or expected. This attitude allowed me to do what I wanted to do in the service.

"Sir, there's a detachment up Da Nang. I'd like to spend a day or two with them and do a story."

"Type up your TAD orders—you know how—and I'll sign them." I got to travel around Vietnam, fly up to Tokyo, join convoys and see a lot more than other guys, even more than most of the officers.

The Officer's Wardroom

There were around two dozen officers in Seventy-One, supposedly overseeing 700 of us enlisted men. Most of our officers were new, just out of OCS. They didn't need to know much, and many of them didn't, as it was the chiefs and the first class POs who actually ran the companies, similar to how the Army relies on its experienced sergeants. But officers could be useful when it came to the chain of command. If you had work orders, R&R or leave requests that needed to go up through channels, that's what the officers do—they could speak to each other. We couldn't.

The more I stayed away from officers, the smoother my life became. As the unit's PR guy and editor of *The Transit*, I had to interact with the CO and XO frequently, as it was my job to make the outfit look good in the eyes of the officers up at Command. I did that, so had pretty much a free hand with what I wrote, photographed and printed. LT Tony Smith, S-2, was the Administration OIC, therefore the PAO officer, and my immediate superior. He allowed me to call him Tony when off the base in civvies. We spent a week together when he and I flew up to Tokyo together, so he, an officer, could negotiate the printing contract for *The Transit*. We shared a room and hung out together for the week, while I put the newspaper together.

On Sunday mornings, even the officers got inspected. Our executive officer (XO), CDR Brown (right), inspects the sidearms of LTCR Martin, Operations; LCDR Patterson, Supply; and LT Dennis, the unit's chaplain.

Tony had been brought up as Quaker, and as such, the killing of people was not in his rule book. How he ever got into the Navy I never learned, but he and I got along, and he read, corrected, and approved everything I wrote.

The Battalion's CO (Commanding Officer) was CDR Richard Coughlin, who went by his middle name, Dan. He was a soft-spoken civil engineer who had graduated from USC and held a master's degree from Purdue. Coughlin spent 14 years in various roles in the Navy's Civil Engineering Service—as instructor in the Civil Engineering School, Operations Officer for Seabee units in the Pacific, and Company Commander with MCB-Three, before being given command of his own Seabee outfit.

There was a lighter side to our CO, one we enlisted men seldom witnessed. The CO and LCDR Roger Martin (Operations) must have gotten into a bottle of Jack Daniels one evening, because they ended up producing a compendium of dozens of Coughlinese terms and their definitions, complete with appropriate (and inappropriate) double entendres and innuendos, in order to clarify for the battalion at large the deeper meaning of the CO's ramblings. (I got this from the CO's son, Ted Coughlin, in recent years and share a few of the witticisms here.)

Recuss—to orally ponder a matter of great significance, or insignificance, at great length in unison with the CO, until all in attendance have succumbed to attrition or dormancy, and the original agenda has long been forgotten.

Simonize Our Watches—to make one's chronometer conspicuous in splendor and beauty by constant polishing. In actuality, the term is used by our "Spit and Polish" CO as a command to synchronize, with great effort, the grooming of the sand throughout the camp in anticipation of a visiting Admiral.

CDR Coughlin, our CO (commanding officer), indicates a location where one of our detachments would be heading. When I took this picture, he told me to make sure the map was out of focus, as the destination was secret.

Oooh Yeah!—A jargonish, unliterary vulgar sigh, connoting tacit and probably delightful approval at the sound or sight of some indisputable pleasantries. Has utilitarian application over a wide range of subject matter, from reacting to another successful project completion, to the manifestation of one's excitation upon visually and or manually inspection of a titillating prospective morsel of feminine accomplishment.

Outstanding—an astronomic level of tediously developed competency and/or condition which is extremely difficult if not impossible to obtain, but which most everything and everybody is in this battalion, except the Supply Department.

Out-Damn-Standing—a judgment reserved only for superhuman accomplishments; therefore, seldom used because of the lack of super-humans in this battalion. Has, on occasion, been used as an exhaust for long dormant delirium upon the appearance in camp of some irresistible effeminate stimulus.

Troll—a transitive verb denoting a sporting procedure for fishing after 2100 hours. A slow rising lure is particularly effective in Western specific areas, if folding green is added to the bait. But inevitably, should the hook becomes engaged in the troller's mouth and he is pulled along unmercifully by species known to be as much as 36-inches by 24 × 36, until his yen for fishing is exhausted. For maximum effect, should be repeated in the same locale for the same fish, unless the Bamboo telegraph makes it impossible to take anything but a $4 catch.

The CO passed away in 2012. I have been in contact with his son, Ted, whose remembrance of his father can be found in the Appendix.

The XO (Executive Officer), CDR George Brown, was a graduate in civil engineering from Lafayette College. During high school he'd entered the Naval Reserves as an enlisted

The Executive Officer, CDR George Brown.

man, then upon graduation from college he received his line officer commission in the Reserves and was assigned to the Salvage Divers School in Bayonne, New Jersey. His career included assistant operations officer for the Seabees in the Atlantic Fleet and head of the Management Department for the Caribbean Division of Naval Engineering Command, before being assigned to Seventy-One. CDR Brown passed away in 1971. I have been in touch with his daughter, Cheryl Brown, and her remembrance of her father can be found in the Appendix.

The CO, XO, and all the officers were all in the same boat as the rest of us. This was to be their first assignment to combat duty. (Please forgive me, I have little recollection of the rest of our officer corps.)

The Battalion's Sports Report

There was very little time for recreation or sports in this man's war, except on Sundays. But boys will always find time to throw, kick, pitch, or toss a ball around. Sports, or the illusion of sports, filtered down to us at Camp Shields on the beach in Chu Lai.

One of the officers, LCDR Parson, could be found jogging around the camp perimeter in the evenings, chased, and occasionally passed, by Engineer Assistant Zupon. Twenty laps around the base added up to a few miles, and in this heat, that was enough.

A firing range opened near the beach and a dozen or more 'Bees could be heard out there popping off their M14s and .45 Colts, shooting at No. 10 tomato juice cans. This not only improved marksmanship, which in the war zone might come in handy, it also relieved tension, stress and the frustration of military life. I used the range to test fire my .45 pistol, but found I was deaf for two days afterward. How the men in the bush managed with all the firing going on is beyond me. Must have been even worse for the men in Artillery, firing off those 105s.

Charlie Company built a swim float and it was anchored out beyond the break. Our special services officer and his chief bought a few surfboards, but by the time they got here, there was very little surf. Then, when the monsoons approached, the surf was too dangerous and the beach was closed. On Sundays, Dive Chief Wade from UCT and his assistant Bill Johnson took those of us who could swim up to the reefs off Rosemary Point, so we could snorkel and dive among the coral and fishes.

The hoopsters from Seventy-One and our softball teams managed to practice on a few evenings, with an occasional game on Sundays with the other Seabee outfit, or a Marine outfit up the beach, but I'll let Wally Skop tell the story.

Wally, more affectionately referred to by his drinking buddies as "Scuzzy," was a yeoman third, riding a desk in Admin. He had become our battalion's sports reporter. I got him to sit down each month and pen a column for the back page of *The Transit*. He turned out to be a pretty good writer, even if some of his reports were for imaginary contests or wound up poking fun at officers and enlisted alike, but what he wrote was always interesting reading, if irreverent.

Take Me Out to the Ball Game
by Wally Skop, YN3

In June, Seventy-One's Softball Team had its first practice on the beach. The boys seemed to have impressed their Coach LTJG Conroy, an all-American baseball player while attending University of

Wally Skop (left) and I hung out a lot. We called him "Skuzzy," a wise-cracking kid from upstate New York. I got him to write the monthly sports column.

Rhode Island. This first get-together may have been the first time in years any of these players had swung a bat or thrown a ball. Coach Conroy must had called on some voodoo for with only two days of practice a game with MCB-8 was scheduled for June 11.

This is a hustling team, just the way their Coach wants it. The infield, although small, is very quick with no trouble completing a fast double-play. Hitting seems to pose a problem, but after a few more swings at a good fastball the team's timing should sharpen and they will have no trouble getting men on base. Coach Conroy seems to be the kind coach that expects the best from his men, and they seem to be very willing to give him just that.

When we play MCB-8 it will be on their Laterite field up at Rose Mary Point. So, pack up a case of cold Bud and be there. We can use all the vocal support we can muster.

Seventy-One did lose their first game to MCB Eight, 5 to 2.

The Nose Broom Competition
by Wally Skop, YN3

In other morale building activities: the July edition of The Transit announced the Battalion's first mustache growing contest. The competition, which included mustaches from all companies, including the officers, was to culminate on Labor Day. The winners were to be chosen from a panel of female nurse-judges from the hospital up the beach. The winner to get a free trip to Okinawa as a representative of Special Services to bring back razor blades. The CO will present the winner with his own "mustache cup" suitably inscribed, and three nights of free drinks at an appropriate club.

"The Winner Is!" CM Schroeder (white t-shirt) won the Mustache Contest during the final round of judging. Three ladies from Task Force Oregon, just up the beach, were judges: Miss Rosemary (Cooky) Cook, from Great Falls, Montana; Gail Allen from Georgia; and Sally Kalt from Milwaukee. More than 20 Seabees entered the contest. Runner-ups were CMA3 Chet Bartko (far right) and EO2 Jerry Monetecupo. Storekeeper Sellers (center) won "Most Appropriate" award.

From the September 22 edition of *The Transit*:

The Inter-Company Basketball League
by Wally Skop, YN3

The inter-Company basketball league, which flourished for the past two months has finally come to a close this past week. In the last regularly scheduled game of the second half, Headquarters Company defeated Alpha Company. Perhaps the most exciting and best played game since the start of the league back in July. Both teams were undefeated going into this game, and the winner would find themselves sitting on top of the league with the second half league title.

As it turned out HQ jumped to an early lead in the first quarter and maintained that lead throughout the game, standing up to some persistent rallies by the Mechanics of Alpha Company. Gusty winds swept across the court throughout the game resulting in passes and shots that fell short of their mark for nearly the whole game. Alpha Company was never really out of the game, although they did lose by 13 points.

Tom Wyckoff, who was held scoreless for three quarters began to click in the last quarter as Alpha Company began to cut away at the early lead HQ had established. Tom Reinfuss played exceptionally well for the Mechanics, but a very close defensive game by Dave McMinn of HQ prevented Reinfuss from using his big height advantage. This was an exceptionally close game with very few fouls committed during the entire game, except at one point in the third quarter, Tom Wyckoff tried to take a bite off the finger of an HQ player, that did raise a little objection from the victim. It was all-out team effort by headquarters that took them on the road to victory the second half title.

Jim Maxwell and Dick Russ provided most of the offense of thrust for HQ, with McMinn superb in controlling the height advantage of Reinfuss, who was Alpha's most consistent score in previous games. Tony Ferro worked the ball well from his guard position and set up many key plays for the big man under the net.

Alpha Company began to press hard during the second half, but Ferro had a little trouble getting the ball down the court. A cheer went up from the supporters of HQ when they noticed Ferro actually bending over fighting for a loose ball. This was truly an exceptionally fun game to watch, and both teams were in the best condition for it. This game marked the ninth consecutive win for HQ, who lost only one game since beginning of the league competition.

In the coming weeks there will be a playoff between HQ, Charlie Company and our Officers, to determine the winner of the first-half competition which ended in a three-way tie for those three teams.

Hedging Your Bets
by Wally Skop, YN3

Some of the officers have found a new source of investment. It appears that investing a few of their MPCs (Military Payment Certificate) in Seventy-One's teams, before each game is a sure profit-maker, perhaps as good as holding shares of IBM.

While there were no dancing cheerleaders during half-time in recent basketball games, we were entertained as LCDR Martin danced back and forth over the court, placing bets and collecting his winnings; all this he did without a work-order.

Track and Field
by Wally Skop, YN3

Among the other sporting events we enjoyed on our deployment, there was that 100-yard dash that took place during breakfast one morning in August. Our friendly Marine aviators next door decided to use the MSR (Main Supply Route) for bombing practice. An A4 jettisoned a 500-pound bomb on take off, tearing a hole in the road adjacent to our camp entrance. The chow hall entrance took on the appearance of a well kept track meet as 50 odd Seabees shot out of the door running like hell to the nearest mortar pit, thinking we were under attack.

A Rash Idea
by Wally Skop, YN3

Our own Dr. Hubbell is considering a heat rash contest to be held during our next USO Show. Judges will include nurses, this time from the hospital up at China Beach. Categories will include, Best Looking Rash, Biggest Bumps, Deepest Color. The champion will be determined on the Most Bumps per Square Inch. Since the judges will be female, only heat rash on the upper part of the torso will be displayed. The prizes will include: a month's supply of cornstarch, donated by CS1 Leveski; one wire brush compliments of LT Clay from Bravo Company. The champ will also receive a ten-day TAD to Sweden with Hospital Man Finley to bring back supplies.

So start breeding your heat rash now. If you don't have one, all you have to do is laugh at the guy next to you lying on his rack scratching like the devil.

Chapter 9

The 'Bees Get to Work

It All Starts with Engineering

I learned early on that there was one place on our base where I could find out what was going to happen before it happened—the Engineering Department. Their Quonset hut was just a few away from my plywood office hooch. The first class PO there was EA1 Tuffy Lake, and I knew I'd always get a story out of him.

"In some battalions, Engineering takes a back seat to Operations. Not here," said Tuffy, "not in this outfit." He was explaining how "his" Engineering Department worked.

First Class Engineer's Assistant (EA1) Tuffy Lake ran the Engineering Department.

I was leaning on a drafting table in the Engineers' Quonset hut, scribbling down notes from his explanation. "LTJG Powers, the OIC here, and I have come up with this Total Engineering Concept—it's more like how a civil construction company works." LTJG Stephen Powers (who until recently had been Ensign Powers) was a recent college grad, but was now a Naval civil engineering officer. He had little field experience in construction, though; he left that up to Tuffy.

"We'll make a good Seabee officer out of Powers before we leave 'Nam," Tuffy added. "It's here that any new plans and job orders are vetted, drawn up, budgeted, planned, material lists generated, and construction teams assigned."

I joined Tuffy almost weekly for a jeep ride to photograph job sites, so I knew some of his story. Tuffy (his real name was Francis) had been a fire control technician on a destroyer during the Korean War. After that "conflict" (as some term it), Tuffy moved to Alaska to conduct surveys and build roads. When this war came along, he re-upped. With his military history and construction experience, the Navy recruiters promised him he'd be welcomed back as a chief in the Seabees, but that fell through, and first class rating was what he got. This pissed him off, but here in Seventy-One, he did the job of a chief anyway.

"I told LTJG Powers we needed a Chief in here to do what I don't want to do, to do what Chiefs do; paperwork, inspections, running the office and personnel. We got one, but he was close to worthless. Must have been kicked upstairs at one point, so Powers and I got him moved over to Special Services, handing out baseball gloves and basketballs." Tuffy pulled no punches.

We'd been in 'Nam for three months and it was time I explained to our readers how this battalion worked. Since Tuffy knew every aspect of construction, as well as how a military battalion worked, officially and actually (there is a difference), I asked him to explain how Engineering fit into the organizations; to explain the chain of command.

"Orders come down from 32nd Naval Construction Regiment in Da Nang," he said. "Regiment oversees five Seabee outfits in I CORPS. MCB-74 and 9 are up in Da Nang; here in Chu Lai MCB-6 will soon be replaced by 8, then there's us. There are more battalions up in Hue—Phu Bai, Dong Tam, and Quang Tri." By that summer of 1967, there were more than 4,000 Seabees in just this northern part of South Vietnam, with more battalions in the south, who like us were building bases, airstrips, landing facilities, hospitals, and headquarters for the brass. We were building a war machine to rival World War II.

"Yes, but what do you do here?" I asked. "I mean what do all these people do here?" Tuffy's team included field surveyors, architects, draftsmen and engineers. Behind us,

Seventy-One's crews linked together corrugated steel planks to form a large heliport for the Army. Our officers, including the project OIC (left) and two chiefs, confer over plans with the CO (cigar) and XO (right).

on sloped drawing tables, draftsmen were bent over T-squares and triangles drawing up the plans for a series of barracks for some new unit arriving in a week.

"Engineering plays an important role from the very beginning of any project. At least in this outfit it does," Tuffy explained. "Even while plans are still being formed, we conduct research, scout locations, find out what problems we may encounter. We source materials, take soil samples, estimate cost and manpower needs, consider transportation and security issues. From this information, the architects and engineers, estimators and draftsman can provide Operations and the construction companies with bulletproof plans and drawings."

Imagine me busy scribbling away on a yellow lined legal pad, using my own version of shorthand to get what Tuffy is explaining. My mother was a secretary in the 1920s, and had showed me the shorthand she was taught for taking dictation. I never thought I would ever need that skill, so I didn't bother to take her seriously. It would have come in handy now, as my self-invented method was not very effective. I was lucky to get enough down on my notepad to reconstruct the conversation later at my typewriter. Tuffy rambled on. I scribbled.

"The first of our men on a job site are the surveyors. They take elevations and create a contour map of the site. From this the engineers here in the office can plan for drainage, placement of the building, walkways, roads." One of those surveyors, Bob Wagnor, was a member of my drinking team. He was a graduate engineer who elected to enlist rather than go to OCS and become an officer. As an enlisted man, he'd only have to serve two, not four, years. Bob was an IPO EA3, one of the team leaders out in the field with a transit, leveling rods and his notebook, overseeing the grading of a site, staking out building foundations, roads, ditches and culverts.

I had spent two and a half years as a mechanical engineering student in college in Springfield, Massachusetts, trying to master drafting, bridge truss systems, fluid dynamics, and thermodynamics. It was that last course that told me I was not going to be an engineer. I transferred to BU to study journalism. But those years with a slide rule (this was long before computers and calculators) gave me a deep appreciation of what engineers do and how they do it. Studying engineering also gave me an understanding of how problems are solved, how to think logically. I also learned that engineers are different people from mechanics. Someone told me an engineer may know why a machine stops working, but the mechanic knows just where to give it a whack with a hammer to get it running again.

"Before the crews start on a project they know how much soil they'll need to move." Tuffy was still explaining stuff. "How much crushed rock to bring in, water availability, storm and water drainage, supply and material requirements, manpower, electrical power needed, roads built to the site, distance from camp, and security necessary to protect the job site. Before the crews begin they know what they're in for." Tuffy was serious about his job.

During actual construction, Tuffy and LTJG Powers visited each job site, occasionally with me tagging along. Tuffy and Powers checked in with the OIC or the chief of the project, and I'd shoot photographs. Tuffy took samples of the concrete, soil, asphalt and building materials for testing. "We do a lot of testing right here in this office," Tuffy continued. "We remain in contact with the surveying teams, we brief personnel here in planning and estimating on progress, all to ensure quality control." He was very proud of the work his team was doing. During the daily operation meeting, when all department officers were present, Tuffy was the only enlisted man in attendance. LTJG Powers and CDR

Martin, the operations officer, insisted. "If any one of the officers has a question about any one of our projects," Powers told me later, "Tuffy will know the answer."

The issue of quality control came up time and again, as it was becoming one of Seventy-One's missions to be known for quality-built projects. When I interviewed LTJG Powers later he said, "We are lucky to have Tuffy on board. He not only knows construction, but he knows how to run this department." He went on to say that Tuffy was also a pleasant guy to work with and that since the skipper insisted on quality control, that started right there with the Engineering Department. "We ensure each project assigned to us by Regiment fits into the overall Chu Lai plan and landscape. Every project we take on must fit into the drainage system inside the base."

There I had it—thanks to Tuffy, another story for *The Transit*.

The Quang Ngai Express

It was a week after we had landed in Chu Lai and the battalion was getting busy.

I was in the Operations hut one morning with a collection of officers, chiefs and key enlisted first class. LTJG Powers and EA1 Lake were there from Engineering. LCDR Roger Martin, the Operations OIC (S-3), was outlining an upcoming project Seventy-One had been given by the regiment in Da Nang. "A detachment of 27 of our Seabees will be spending most of the summer in Quang Ngai," he began. "That's a provincial capital 30 miles south of here. They'll be building a complete camp for the ARVN [The Army of the Republic of Vietnam]."

"This project had been in the planning since our Advance Team arrived here a month ago," said LTJG Powers.

"There are five separate components to this project," Tuffy added, unrolling a site plan on the table. "This cantonment, or garrison, is for the ARVN and will include 22 steel buildings for the Fourth Battalion, Fourth Regiment, Second ARVN division, with a completion date of mid–August. To this has been added two more steel buildings for the Second Army Division QM Repair Facility to be completed by mid–July. There is to be another 30 of these steel buildings for additional battalions of the Vietnamese Army." He continued, "These buildings will provide barracks, mess hall, repair shops, reinforced bunkers and a HQ for the MACV Advisory Team who will work with the ARVN." Combat operations were ramping up in Quang Ngai Province and the ARVN were taking on most combat roles, but we had to build their garrison.

"These steel buildings come prefabricated," LTJG Powers added. "They will be shipped here to Chu Lai from Da Nang, then trucked to Quang Ngai by convoy. There will be a convoy heading south every week to re-supply the detachment."

"LTJG Ed Rüdiger will be the OIC," Martin added. "He'll have 27 enlisted men in his detachment, departing April 15—three days from now. They'll take their equipment, tools, personal gear and materials," said Martin, continuing, "'Bell' Bailie, First Class Equipment Operator, will be in charge of the earth moving; Chief Mitchell and First Class Builder Knight will be handling the concrete."

LCDR Martin continued, "The team will have to fend for yourselves down there," he said. "Set up tents and a latrine. You'll have to man your own perimeters as the ARNV are still pretty thin there. We'll provision you weekly when we convoy in the building materials. We are sending along a Medic and a mess cook together with a field kitchen.

Recently advanced LT Ed Rüdiger (front row, third from left) was pulled off the Quang Ngai Detachment in July to lead the new Seabee Team 7101. They flew back to Davisville for more training then re-deployed to nastier spots.

You'll have to find a source of drinking water. There's a river nearby but that water should be used only for making concrete. Maybe a shower as well."

A convoy of a dozen trucks, carrying earth-moving equipment, materials, supplies and men, were loaded, and early on the morning of April 15 the detachment boarded the trucks. A dozen volunteer Seabees came along to provide added firepower in case of attacks. LTJG Rüdiger and one of the chiefs led off with a jeep.

One of our older Seabees, John Murphy, EO1, and I joined the convoy to Quang Ngai to do a story on the detachment. Before enlisting in the Seabees, at the age of 50-something, Murphy had been running his own construction company, building roads for the Catholic church in Central America. He'd run into trouble with a larger construction company who didn't appreciate Murphy's competition, and ran him out of town. When this war came along Murphy enlisted in the Navy's DPPO program and was accepted as a first class equipment operator. He had more practical experience in running a construction company than any officer, but he wasn't interested in either management or driving a dozer. He came to Vietnam to help the Vietnamese rebuild what the war was demolishing. He spent his entire deployment working with the local Vietnamese out in the villages, engaged in "Civic Action" projects. At the end of World War II, Murphy was an Army reporter for *YANK* magazine, and I was fortunate to get him to write a few stories for *The Transit*.

On this convoy, John rode with the lead driver, Road-Master John Roche, while I sat by the tailgate in the back of a troop transport six-by with ten other Seabees, volunteers who came along to provide protection. While I was taking photographs from the truck body, John was taking notes for a story he'd later write for *The Transit*. Here's his story.

9. The 'Bees Get to Work

Hess and Reedy (left), along with four other desk jockeys, fill up the back of a six-by truck, providing dubious security for the convoy in case of an ambush. They shot more film than ammo.

What's in a Laugh?
By John Murphy, EO1

"Rear Echelon Commandos," someone jibed. But nobody grabs the bait as the sound of the mortar shell cut the thick morning air of the nearby valley.

Maybe it was the still fresh scars from the latest VC mortar attack on Highway One, or maybe just the heat and the choking red dust. The "Roadrunners" have already been pounding through this miserable stuff for a couple of hours—a Seabee supply convoy from Chu Lai to Quang Ngai, 30 hot, nervous miles to the South.

Road-Master John Roche, First Class Equipment Operator from North Kingston, Rhode Island smiles as he turns to the new shotgun rider beside him.

"Nice country ... mind if I sing?" he asks, rhetorically, planning to sing anyway.

The "Roadrunners" are mostly new Seabees in Seventy-One, youngsters whose civilian occupations qualified them for the Navy's DPPO program last spring. Roque and a handful of others are the exception. At 30, Roque is an old timer, and a career man, been in the Seabees for more than 10 years, but like most of us coming to Vietnam, war for him is a totally new experience.

The bluff and wisecracking that made up conversation around the battalion a month ago as they prepare to leave the states is in bad taste now.

For these roads, bridges, bunkers and hut builders, this is a war of nerves and sweaty, thankless hard work is punctuated by the mortars, mines and snipers.

The convoy, called "The Quang Ngai Express," is the only physical link between battalion's base camp in Chu Lai and the 28 Seabee construction crew in Quang Ngai, 30 miles away.

That the enemy knows The Express will be passing is taken for granted. In fact, seasoned combat troops are making book on how long Charlie will wait before hitting the convoy and job site—and even the greenest "Roadrunners" knows all this better than anyone in the front office could tell them.

Top: The huge trucks from Seventy-One crept through small villages and hamlets as the convoy made its way to Quang Ngai. *Bottom:* A contrast in transportation—the Seabees' mammoth six-bys kick up dust and make a lot of noise, while the Vietnamese carry on with more traditional means of transportation.

Roche, whose pert, red-haired wife, Beverly, sat up with him until 2 a.m. the night he made his departure to Vietnam, has a quiet way of reassuring his new shotguns on each trip.

One of the younger drivers, third class equipment operator Mike Manencia of Aberdeen, Washington says: "Roche doesn't talk much, but you know he doesn't miss much either. He's quick, and everybody who has been around here at all will tell you that on this job there's the quick and the dead."

Every week or so the 8- to 10-vehicle Quang Ngai Express rolls out of Camp Shields carrying just about everything needed to keep Seventy-One's Quang Ngai Detachment moving at the Vietnamese Ranger camp they are building.

As a convoy grinds its way past the Korean Marine security unit about halfway out, the "Roadrunners" are on their own in an area where the VC still move freely. Each time the Seabee truck passes, one of the Long Tom field gun fires in salute.

Reactions don't very much. Instinctively, the shotgun rider twists in his seat during the big blue muzzle flash almost before the sound is heard, the Road-Master sings a little louder.

Nobody in the convoy is thinking rear echelon now. There's no more need for feeble jokes. Everyone laughs, even if sometimes silently, to himself.

This Photographer Tags Along

The road trip to Quang Ngai is not a pleasant ride, but it did get me and the volunteers out of camp for a day, into the Vietnamese countryside, where we got see the people we were supposed to be protecting.

I made photographs as we drove along Highway One, a dirt highway that stretches from the DMZ all the way to Saigon. The road gets "swept" each morning by Army or Marine EOD (Explosive Ordnance Disposal) teams for mines the Viet Cong placed during the night.

We lumbered down the road in a cloud of dust, through hamlets and villages, the kids running alongside, shouting "Seabee numba one!"

Out into the countryside, we sped up, only slightly. Rice paddies spread out on both sides, farmers plowing the wet soil with pairs of oxen, and two Vietnamese were hoisting water from the irrigation ditches into the paddies, the way their ancestors had done for hundreds of years.

The convoy took a detour around a recently demolished bridge, or crater, where a road mine was detonated in place. Later in the day, a team of Vietnamese would repair the crater, but the bridge would need a team of Seabees or Marine Engineers to fix it.

It was mid–April, and we were into the dry season. It would be dry all summer, they told us. The rains, the monsoons, would come just about the time we head back to Davisville, in early November. MCB-40 would take over Camp Shields; they would be the ones to deal with the mud and ruts on this highway. Right now, all we had to do was eat the dust from the trucks ahead.

As we neared Quang Ngai, the roadside became crowded with buildings. There were schools, with hundreds of kids in formation, in outdoor classrooms. Traffic on the highway increased. Small trucks, vintage French Citroens, Deux Chevrons, Vespas, no-brand motorbikes, and foot-powered bikes crowded the road, along with pedestrians by the score. Shops, stores, restaurants, repair shops crowded in, our fleet of huge trucks slowed to a crawl, negotiating through the streets of Quang Ngai.

We arrived at a wide-open camp site on the far side of the city. The trip had taken us five hours. The trucks lined up under LTJG Ed Rüdiger's directions, and the Seabee security team piled out. Lunch would have to wait as everyone began unloading the trucks. The Road-Master needed to get back on the road by 14:00, in time to get us back to base before darkness.

Lumber, tools, a portable concrete mixer and bags of cement were off-loaded, along with a road grader and dozer. Tents, bedding, sea bags, cooking equipment, boxes of C-rations and canned goods were stacked. There was a water buffalo, a portable 300-gallon water tank that would provide the detachment with water for drinking, cooking and concrete-making. If there was any water left, a sponge shower could be had.

The off-loading went quickly, as the 27 men on detachment and the security team formed a bucket-brigade to shift boxes into a hastily constructed tent.

The convoy heads back to Chu Lai, trucks now empty, passing through the city of Quang Ngai, its streets crowded with life and commerce, despite a war nearby.

It was C-rations for lunch as we filled up our water canteens with very warm water from the water buffalo, climbed back onto the trucks, and began to thread our way through the streets of Quang Ngai, heading north.

There would be another convoy to Quang Ngai the next week.

BOOM! Construction Goes On

A few weeks later, Murphy spent a few nights with the Quang Ngai detachment, to file the following story for *The Transit*.

Seabees Built While the War Goes On
By John Murphy, EO1

Thick dust boils up over a Seabee road grader as it nears the barbwire line called "The Fence."

At seven in the morning, the sun already high, the breeze hot and humid. Rarely visible from the operator's seat are the red-yellow flashes from the South Vietnamese field gun 50 yards to the right. Hits from the heavy rounds echo back a second later as the rounds pound into the tree line across the rice patty.

The sound of small arms fire coming from up a palm and fern grove 50 yards to the left all this sound is lost in the roar of the big machine's engine.

The ARVN infantry platoon has made contact with the Viet Cong company-size guerrilla force half a mile outside the South Vietnamese perimeter. Pinned down momentarily by VC mortar and automatic weapons, the ARVN platoon leader has called down military artillery support. A second platoon sweeps every hiding place between the fence line and the main action area for VC infiltrators.

9. The 'Bees Get to Work

Just inside the fence, a road grader, a bulldozer and a concrete mixer are surrounded by shirtless, sweating Seabees conducting business as usual. A few yards further back, a cluster of their buddies swarm over the steel and timber buildings being enclosed with sheets of blistering hot metal roofing.

Between artillery rounds, the water truck arrives from the river, joined by a dump truck loaded with gravel to start today's concrete pour. Another barracks floor slab will be in place before C-Rats at noon.

And the war—Quang Ngai style—goes on.

The men of Seventy-One's Quang Ngai detachment have been labeled "—30—" (a newsman's symbol indicating the end of the story) by a journalist who stayed just long enough to establish that while there is a shooting war going on under their noses, these Seabees see their daily construction mission as the only thing worth talking about.

The detachment's OIC is an Ivy League running guard named Ed Rüdiger, a new Lieutenant (JG) in the Navy Civil Engineer Corps. His cool, among all this noise, comes at least in part from living amid the subway and skyscrapers of Manhattan. He's the man the crew formally calls "Mister" and privately calls "Boss." Like many who come to Vietnam these days, he was new at this war business for several hours. Then, the first VC mortar shells began exploding on the air strip in Chu Lai, flanking Seventy-One's base camp; the place this crew speaks of nostalgically is "the big world outside."

In the woods, beyond a rice paddy, an explosion rocks the work site.

A.J. Thompson, Builder Second Class, and a regular on the volunteer local Chapel building detail, says he sometimes misses seeing his buddies back "in town." Then conversation turns to a probable completion date for the Quang Ngai project and he is filled with misgivings about disbanding this Detachment, being lost in the shuffle, back in Chu Lai, amid 800 other Seabees.

The project at Quang Ngai, urgently needed by ARVN troops, who were still sleeping under ponchos and eating next to their fighting holes, is directly dependent on supplies sent by convoy from Chu Lai, through an area the VC continue to harass civilians and military traffic. In fact, this urgency was highlighted a few weeks ago when Seventy-One's supply people enlisted the big Marine Corps Sea Knight helicopter to airlift four tons of cement into the World War II Japanese-built airstrip adjacent to the job site, by-passing the convoy route.

Top: A grader levels the work site, as a firefight goes on nearby. *Bottom:* The barracks for the ARVN Regiment are being assembled on site, as artillery can he heard, and seen, in the hills beyond. The team created an entire camp for the Army of the Republic of Vietnam (RVN) on the edge of Quang Ngai.

Part of the U.S. assistance to the Republic of Vietnam Armed Forces buildup, this project covers a 10,000 square feet area between the outer and inner perimeter of the existing ARVN compound. When completed in August, the new camp will contain 23 buildings, an electric power plant, and running water.

For G.W. "Bell" Bailie, First Class Equipment Operator in charge of the earth moving on the job,

Builders Mollett and Childs frame up forms for a barracks foundation. Later, concrete will be carted from the mixer to the foundation in wheelbarrows.

the Quang Ngai experience is a bonanza. A veteran of 15 years with the Seabees, from Grand Turk to Antarctic, he's reputed to be the battalion's "Sea Story Champ." He figures this deployment will only add to his supply of tall tales.

Like his counterpart, First Class Builder C.B. Knight, and their leader Chief Mitchell, Bailie sees the war almost exclusively in terms of rock and earth moved, concrete poured, buildings completed, and man-hours expanded. However "hairy" it made be to anyone else, this is simply the construction business to the older men and their crew.

They seldom get any closer to editorializing their endeavors than to coin nicknames for everyone who comes on the job. For example, a pair of Third Class Equipment Operators, R.J. Haley and E.C. Perry, answer up to "hinge pin," a label intended to reflect considerable praise on the two youngsters who are a day ahead on virtually every volunteer duty roster.

The urge to make friends with the Vietnamese around them runs deep within the Seabees. That they have succeeded is evident. Whenever they traveled the streets of Quang Ngai, where the people have been at war for as long as most can remember, they get waves and shouts of greetings. As they rumble in and out from the work site, the Seabees wave back. Friendly smiles flicker across wrinkled faces, and children run to street edges to return the waves and shout "Seabee number one!"

At nights in their tents just below the ridge crest, guarded by Vietnamese soldiers, who look directly down the enemy's barrels, the Seabees shoptalk finally gives way to letter-writing, battalion news, and thoughts of that another planet, known as The Real World, about which they rarely talk.

Learning to Drive a Dozer ... at Night!

"Lyman, you doing anything?"

It was Stapleman, my EO3 buddy, the one who went on Cinderella Liberty. He was back in the saddle again, operating a D8, the largest dozer Caterpillar made then. It was past midnight, and I'd wandered into the mess hall after wrapping up film processing in the darkroom.

"Why?" I asked. "You got something interesting going on?" Dick and five other heavy equipment operators were taking a mid-shift break and getting chow. I sat down. "It's past midnight. I'm heading to bed."

"Go get your greens on and bring your helmet and flak jacket. I'm going to show you rear echelon flakes how we Seabees do our thing. I'm going to teach you how to operate a dozer." Dick and his crew were working the night shift at a laterite pit, providing material for an Army Cavalry heliport we were building out on Rosemary Point. The project was on a fast track; we had only a few weeks to complete this project before an Army Cavalry division was to arrive in Chu Lai.

"I'll wait right here until you get back," he said. I ran over to my office, climbed out of my shorts and tee-shirt and into my greens, grabbed my sidearm, ammo belt, helmet and flak jacket and returned. It was too dark for pictures, so I left the camera behind.

The Army was moving into the Chu Lai Enclave, replacing the Marines who had held the base for almost a year. Along with the Army came its modern-day version of the cavalry—Roger's Rangers; Army Hueys. These stallions of the sky needed landing sites and fueling and maintenance facilities. Our outfit got the assignment to build these in the last weeks of April. The completion date for the helipads, roads, barracks, mess hall and fueling area was set for May 24. Work began on May 8, then the Naval Construction Regiment in Da Nang updated the completion date to May 15.

"They're nuts," one of the EOs commented. "We'll be lucky to meet the original deadline." Nevertheless, the Seabees went to work around the clock. Our crews were augmented by more earth-moving equipment and drivers from nearby MCB-Eight. Crews from both units worked 24 hours a day.

Chu Lai was all sand. You can't build roads, runways, or helipads on sand. A subsurface of something stable was needed, and that's where the laterite, a red soil full of iron deposits, came in. It compacts as hard as a rock. The Seabees found what they needed, but it was in the foothills, a mile or more outside the barbed wire perimeter, in VC country. We had to provide our own security for the site, with lights and Seabees on guard duty all night. To reduce the hauling time for the earthmovers, we got permission to cut another access gate in the base perimeter. A Marine unit guarded this impromptu gate.

Stapleman and I rode out to the laterite pit, a few miles outside the perimeter, right in the middle of VC country. Rocket flares floating down on parachutes and floodlights above the pit illuminated a hillside of red earth, part of it carved away. A squad of Seabees carrying rifles were on guard duty on the hill around the pit so work could continue 24 hours a day. The men climbed aboard their respective machines—dozers, dump trucks, front-end loaders and huge self-propelled earth-moving scrapers. The scrapers could scoop up tons of red laterite soil into their bellies, close the belly, transport the load to a construction site, and dump the load. The dump trucks needed to be loaded by front-end loaders. Dick and I climbed aboard his dozer and fired it up, diesel smoke spewing from the stack.

"Your job is to scrape up piles of this stuff so the front-end loaders can fill the dump trucks," Dick instructed over the roar of the diesel engine. "Then, when a scraper comes along, you come up from behind and push him along as he fills his belly." A Seabee chief was there with a flashlight, directing the flow of trucks, scrapers and dozers.

Dick sat in the driver's seat while I perched on the seat back, holding on tight. Dick maneuvered the dozer, adjusted the blade, lowered the three huge tangs, or rippers, at the rear of the D8. These loosen the hard laterite—a rich red soil that provided excellent base material for the helipads. Back and forth—real easy, right?

"Here, take the controls," Dick directed, as we swapped places. Sitting in the driver's seat, I was faced with a wall of levers and pedals. "That lever is for left, that one is for right, throttle is there, blade control ... there. Oh, yes ... that's the brake, and the shift." Off we went, jerking along as the blade dug in, only to come free as the dozer hobby-horsed across the uneven terrain. I took a few passes before Dick suggested I'd had enough for my first lesson. We switched seats. The trouble was, I had no idea what I was doing, and Dick was having fun at my expense. He would lord that night over me at the bar for the rest of our deployment.

A scraper came alongside, its belly open, drinking in mounds of the red laterite that Dick had recently loosened. Dick came up from behind the scraper, with the dozer blade against the push plate on the rear of the scraper. With the dozer pushing, the scraper moved ahead, filling the body, then it closed hydraulically and headed off to the job site. Another scraper was right behind, and Dick had to go to work. He flagged down the scraper driver and told me to scoot over and ride along on the other vehicle.

I climbed aboard the green machine and sat on the engine cover, next to the exhaust stack. The operator, Wade, a 20-year-old EO3, gave me a wink and slipped the scraper into low gear. The noise of the engine was too loud for conversation—and words were not needed. I knew most of the EOs in Alpha Company and my presence was not out of the ordinary, as I often accompanied a convoy or was seen photographing project sites.

These mammoth CAT scrapers, or earthmovers, needed to be pushed from behind by a dozer as they struggled to scoop up soil. The outfit received two more powerful earthmovers later in our deployment, and with a second engine driving the rear wheels they could work without assistance, but the lack of spare parts kept them in the shop most of the time.

The engine screamed as Wade began going through the 12 gears, getting the mammoth earthmover up to speed. We left the lights of the pit, waved to the guard at the entrance and headed into the night. With no springs or shock absorbers, the 20-foot high earthmover lurched down the dirt road, dust and gravel streaming off the huge flotation tires.

Wade was dressed in just his green pants and boots, no tee-shirt under his flak jacket—it was too hot for that. He had his service rifle and helmet on the seat beside him. Not wearing a helmet? Then I realized why—the rough ride with a heavy steel pot on your head would be too much for anyone's neck. Down the dark highway we rumbled, the lights on Wade's scraper illuminating the dust of the scraper just ahead.

The giant earthmover thundered along over the heavily potholed Highway One, still a few miles outside the protected parameter. Wade gripped the steering wheel, I held on to the engine cover. He slowed the rig as an empty scraper, returning to the pit, lurched into the ditch along the side of the road, allowing us to pass. Wade slipped his monster into low range, the scraper's diesel screaming as we picked up speed. A few minutes later we slowed again and passed through the barbed wire perimeter gate, past the security guard, back into safer ground. Three flares hung in the black sky, casting their red light over the flat sands of the Chu Lai base.

The Army heliport, at the north end of the enclave, by Rosemary Point, was lit up with portable floodlights. The place was a hive of activity. Earthmovers and dump trucks were depositing loads of laterite, dozers were pushing the soil around, graders then smoothing and leveling the laterite.

Two heli landing pads, laid out in the shape of a cross, were ready for the steel matting. There were to be 55 ready pads in all, each 24 × 24 feet, in two different locations. In addition, crews were building a 90-foot-wide access road, 1,000 feet long, tying in the new Army heliport with the rest of the Chu Lai base. Steelworkers from Charlie and Delta companies were laying down and locking together aluminum planks, creating dozens of maintenance pads.

I dropped off the earthmover as it finished its dump. It headed back out to the pit and I joined the engineers and surveyors who were overseeing the project. With their transits and tape measures they were ensuring that the depth of the laterite was adequate and that the slope of the pads would provide adequate drainage when the monsoons arrived. Around 3 a.m., I caught a ride back to camp with one of the chiefs and went to bed. I skipped morning muster and slept in. I told the XO I spent the entire night getting a great story. It appeared on the front page of the first edition of *The Transit* published in Vietnam.

As the completion date neared, crews from Seventy-One and Eight finished shifting, moving, and leveling 80,000 yards of sand and 40,000 cubic yards of laterite. The equipment operators took their machines back to base. It was now up to the steel workers to lay down the remaining 300,000 square feet of aluminum matting—enough matting to cover 16 football fields.

By Sunday, May 14, the Seabees had done what the Army Engineers predicted couldn't be done. We'd finished the heliport on time. Marine GEN Walt said we would—and we did. That next day, at 12:30 p.m., Monday, May 15, with tools, materials and construction vehicles still scattered around the job site, Navy Captain Miller and project officers LTJG Cameron and Jay Conroy of Seventy-One ceremoniously placed the last mat. A cheer went up from the 200 men from Alpha, Charlie and Delta companies who had devoted so much to the project.

Acres and acres of inter-connected corrugated steel planks covered the hillside on Rosemary Point. The planks were laid down on a foundation of crushed stone and laterite. These differed from the aluminum and steel planks used at the SATS runway, as they took less of a pounding when the choppers set down.

During World War II, the Seabees built roads and airstrips on the islands of the Pacific, winning the praise and admiration of all the services for their ability to get the job done. That same "Can Do" attitude was here that day, when the Seabees of Seventy-One and Eight honored that strange desire to push through and prove they can do what others say they can't do … they completed the job on time.

The Stone Men of Seventy-One

Dust rose from under the clatter of the compressed air drills biting deep into solid rock at the top of the ridge. I was sitting in a jeep with LT Robert Sharp, OIC of our rock and stone operations, breathing in the dust. I was tagging along on the lieutenant's morning inspection rounds—XO's orders. He wanted me to photograph and write a story about the fine work this bunch of Seabees from Alpha Company were doing. I covered my camera with a chamois cloth to keep the dust off the lens. Along with dust, the air was filled with the sound of heavy machinery, and the occasional explosion as dynamite carved away another section of the rock cliff.

We had just pulled into our first inspection stop—the Seabee rock quarry—two miles outside the Chu Lai perimeter, in the foothills of the highlands that rose in the west. There was no ignoring the feeling that we were being watched by the VC living in the mountains just beyond.

"How many of our men are here?" I asked the lieutenant. "There must be a dozen or more."

"The quarry boss here is Master Equipment Chief Sturges," the lieutenant said. "He has a crew of over 50 of our Seabees from Alpha Company. About half his stone crew is here, the rest operate Old Flintstone, the rock crusher, and the asphalt plant." Sharp waved to a first class, who had been directing lines of trucks arriving and departing. The

The quarry face: LT Robert Sharp and Master Equipment Chief Sturges (far right) chat as a crew works to repair the ancient shovel. The larger blocks of granite in the foreground would be reduced using hand-held drills before being loaded for transport to the crusher.

PO traipsed over, covered in dust and wearing sunglasses, an open flak jacket and a hard hat instead of a steel helmet.

"EO1 Norman is in charge of the day crew here," Sharp said. "The night shift is run by EO1 Ashland. We operate this quarry 24 hours a day," he added. "Our guys blast and move tons of granite into those waiting trucks bound for the rock crusher plant."

I knew some of these Seabees—some were lifers or veterans of prior service, but most were seasoned professional stone-men who'd left civilian life to join the Seabee IPO program in the previous year.

"Is there any chance of the quarry being attacked?" I asked. After all, we were a few miles outside the perimeter.

"See those Marines and a few of our Seabees up there on the cliff?" he said. "They are armed with rifles and grenade launchers. They have deployed Claymore mines all around the quarry. They patrol the cliff, day and night."

The first class and the lieutenant were now in deep conversation, so I got out of the jeep to photograph the operation. Air compressor drills bored holes into the cliff top, creating a lot of noise and dust. Into this long line of holes went sticks of dynamite, wired together so they all went off the same time, carving away a wall of broken granite.

Two dozers, D8s, pushed and scraped loose boulders and rock into piles for a mammoth shovel and a few front-end loaders to scoop up, loading the waiting bodies of huge Euclid trucks—each piece of equipment driven by a shirtless, sweating, dust-covered Seabee from Seventy-One.

I saw a group of Vietnamese, dressed in black with conical reed hats, off to one side smashing rocks into brick-sized pieces with sledgehammers, the same way they've done it for centuries. I made a few photographs, then returned to the jeep where the lieutenant introduced me to another EO2. "Carnahan here runs the drilling and blasting day crew for a 12-hour shift. EO1 Sadler handles the night shift. Between the two crews, they use over 40,000 pounds of dynamite each month, reducing the cliff to rubble, capable of transport."

"Can anyone tell me why there are Vietnamese working here with such primitive tools?" I asked.

"Petty Officer Carnahan thought it would be a good idea to have the Vietnamese locals involved," the lieutenant said, as Carnahan flashed a broad smile. "The quarry is actually owned by a local Vietnamese woman."

"It's not necessarily to increase production," Carnahan explained. "It's a way to give the locals an income source. You know—'Civic Action'—make them feel part of the process. Besides, they are producing nice uniform stone bricks for cosmetic work along the walkways on base."

"The CO gave his blessing and Carnahan hired a dozen Vietnamese rock pounders," explained the lieutenant. We climbed into the jeep and I returned my camera to my bag and held on as we bumped out of the quarry.

A local laborer could earn American dollars for breaking up large stones into the size of bricks for landscaping projects.

"What's that siren mean?" I asked. "Are we being attacked?" A siren wailed three times.

"It's the blast warning. They are about to set off a string of dynamite."

BOOM!

A cloud of dust enveloped the cliff face behind us, as tons of broken granite slid down into a pile at the bottom.

The Viet Cong Helped Our Operation

As we exited the quarry, we had to wait for a gap in the traffic on Highway One, so the lieutenant told a story. "Not all of the dynamite we use comes from the States," Sharp

"Fire in the hole!" Composition C, commandeered off a VC trawler, goes off, carving away another section of the quarry face.

told me. "A few weeks ago, a Navy swift boat captured a Communist trawler just offshore from Rosemary Point. The crew uncovered over 10,000 pounds of explosives, small arms, munitions, mortar rounds, rockets and military supplies bound for the guerrilla forces in Quang Ngai Province. I took the opportunity to relieve the sailors of the confiscated explosives, and had my men move 72 boxes of composition C-4 to the rock quarry."

"We use an average of 500 pounds of C-4 daily in blasting operations," he continued. "The boys found the Viet Cong gift more than useful. Quarry boss, Master Chief Sturges, told me the stuff has a little better kick than the dynamite we've been using, but it leaves a black dust over everything. When I asked if his blasting crew liked working with the captured C-4, Sturges replied, 'They'd rather be the ones setting this stuff off than letting Charlie do it.'"

"Where did the VC get all that stuff?" I asked.

"The ammunition and small arms are Chinese, the rockets are Russian, but the boxes of C-4 contained instructions … in French, leading us to assume the C-4 must have been stolen long ago when the French were here in Vietnam. Some of the boxes showed signs of dry rot," he added.

"Seventy-One's rock quarry operation," Sharp boasted, "is the second largest in South Vietnam. We produce over 40,000 cubic yards of loose rock for Marines, Army, Air Force and Seabee construction projects all over the Chu Lai Enclave."

The lieutenant found a gap in the stream of military trucks, bikes, motorcycles, Vespas and gunned the jeep into a slot.

"That's a lot of rock your guys are blasting up there," I added.

"We need all we can get. The list of repairs and building projects is long. Roads are a priority." I was experiencing what he was talking about as the jeep swerved around potholes and bounced over ruts. "The Army wants as much of this highway paved as we can muster. Right now, this a dirt highway, if you can call this road a highway. It's too easy for the VC to plant mines in dirt roads. If we pave it, the VC can't dig a hole to plant their mines."

We left the highway and entered the perimeter road, following the dust of a Euclid full of granite boulders and rock. Back on paved surface, the dust disappeared and the ride smoothed out.

"When the monsoons arrive this fall, that road back there will be muddy and slick as a greased frying pan. It'd be hard for our heavy trucks and other military vehicles to move."

LT Sharp's job each morning was to make the rounds of the various sites and plants his crew managed and ran. The quarry, the rock crusher, the asphalt and concrete plants were all on the list. Then, each afternoon, the officers, chief POs and company commanders gathered to bring Operations, the CO and XO, and each other, up to speed on where the various projects stood, share progress and delays, discuss the need for more materials, manpower and equipment. Each department head reported in, everyone made notes and responded with offers to help, loaning manpower, expertise, or insight into the construction process to speed things along.

The lieutenant made a long drive around the end of the SAC runway, past the munitions bunkers, following the truck ahead to the rock crusher.

Old Flintstone, Still Running After All These Years

It was to the rock crusher that the boulders the size of refrigerators, along with smaller stones and chunks of granite, were delivered and broken down into various sizes.

"Old Flintstone, is what her crew calls her," LT Sharp said, over the noise of the jeep. "She's 15 years old. She's seen Naval service from Alaska to the Philippines. She's been operating for more years than most of her Seabee crew. She's here now in Vietnam, still operating, although just barely. Crushing hard granite can be tough on the old girl," added Sharp.

Here too, the air was full of dust and noise—the operators wore flight-line earmuffs to deaden the machine's thunder.

EO2 Ingraham, who operated a rock crusher in civilian life, opens the "chute" of Old Flintstone, as another load of stone from the quarry is dumped into the waiting jaws of this mammoth machine.

"The old gal and her crew," Sharp attempted to explain over the noise, "produce crushed rock of varying sizes and gravel for runway foundations, roadbeds, parking lots, building foundations, along with aggregate for Seventy-One's concrete and asphalt plants."

We watched as a steady stream of boulder-filled dump trucks arrived from the quarry, backed up to this three-story steel monster and dumped their loads into a waiting hopper, then drove off, returning to the quarry for another load. A steel conveyor in the bottom of the hopper moved the stone into the vibrating and jumping jaws of the crusher, tossing the stones against each other, breaking off chunks that fell further down inside the funnel-like jaws to be smashed and ground into even smaller pieces. The crew watched the boulders jumping around between the jaws, minding this monster, controlling the speed and aggressiveness as the jaws clatter, chewing up boulders, reducing them to bite-size pieces.

The crushed stone then traveled over a system of vibrating shakers and conveyor belts, sorting the material by size, transporting them to mountains of stored rock and gravel by size.

"Old Flintstone's crew turns out cubic yard after yard of crushed rock—more than any other rock crusher in Vietnam."

Front-end loaders filled trucks with specific size rock or aggregate bound for work sites or other plants run by Seventy-One crews—the asphalt and cement plants.

"Seventy-One operates more big-dollar machineries than any other similar outfit in-country," the lieutenant boasted, as we headed off toward the "hot batch" asphalt plant nearby. LT Sharp's second, LTJG J.F. Conroy, was waiting for us at another towering, smoke-belching plant.

The asphalt plant, belching smoke, heats up gooey black tar then mixes it with sand and gravel for paving roads throughout the enclave as well as Highway One outside the perimeter.

"Chief Napier and his squad from Seventy-One's Alpha Company are currently going through a process of quality control," LTJG Conroy explained when we arrived. "They are washing the supply of aggregate to eliminate dirt and dust before it goes into the final mix. Dust hinders the binding of asphalt to the gravel, resulting in an inferior mix."

Conroy explained the process that goes on inside a huge rotating drum. "We heat up sticky, black tar, which comes in those drums," he pointed to rows of pallets, each stacked with 55-gallon drums of tar. "Those conveyor belts feed aggregate from the rock crusher into the top of that large hopper, a furnace below heats up the tar [asphalt] melting it, the two are combined in a mix tank, then fed into waiting trucks, still hot."

I photographed the plant, with its five-story smokestack, and the surrounding 30-foot-high mounds of aggregate. Photographing the construction process and projects my outfit was doing was difficult for my small-town New England mind

Sand, gravel and bags of cement are mixed in this tower, water is added, and the slurry fed into a waiting truck for delivery to building foundation sites.

to comprehend. The enclave was larger than the Newport base back in Rhode Island, or Quonset and Davisville combined. The military, I was beginning to realize, is another world. Most civilians had no idea of its scope, or its size.

"One more plant to visit," Sharpe said as he got into the jeep, shifting into first to head off to the cement plant. BU1 Fielding was the plant manager there and he was expecting us.

"When Seventy-One arrived in Vietnam in April," Fielding explained as I took notes, "RMK-BRJ [contractor Raymond-Morrison-Knudson], a huge American construction consortium, under contract to the United States Navy, was building infrastructure here in Vietnam. It was getting too hot and too dangerous for the civilians, so they left, turning over the operation of the quarry, the concrete and asphalt batch plants, and all of their projects, to the Seabees," Fielding said. I thought perhaps the civilians were just too well paid and the Navy could get the job done for a whole lot less by bringing in the Seabees. After all, we worked for a fraction of what civilian construction workers were paid.

"The three machines we operate are valued at more than $4 million," he said, "including transportation to and set-up in Chu Lai. The asphalt plant is a modern 200-ton per hour complex, larger even than most plants stateside."

"We have a maximum daily capacity of 1,800 cubic yards of premixed concrete a day," Fielding went on. "We could produce more, but our operation is limited by the small number of cement trucks we have."

As with the asphalt plant, conveyor belts carried sand, gravel and dry cement to the top of the mixing drum. Water from storage tanks was fed in as the tank turned and paddles inside tumbled the ingredients into a material the consistency of putty. Cement trucks lined up under the plant, each was loaded with wet concrete, and left for the job site.

The lieutenant and I, covered in dust that was now cemented to our sweat-soaked fatigues, climbed back into the jeep and headed back to Camp Shields—me for messhall lunch and the lieutenant for lunch with his fellow officers. We left the cement plant, following a mixer truck heading for a hospital project our Seabees were building for the Army up by Rosemary Point. I had a roll and a half of photographs and a few pages of notes.

Building Powers' Observation Towers

The Army wanted seven of these 60-foot observation towers to be built, to keep an eye on the land outside the wire. Two of these had to be built off-site and ferried into place by helicopter.

"We'll be building a series of seven observation towers along the perimeter," the XO was telling me. He suggested, "This is something you should be covering." The XO's story suggestions ... I considered them to actually be orders.

Usually, my first job each morning was to find out what was going on within the battalion, what projects were underway, coming up, or nearing completion. I'd check in with Tuffy Lake— the first class engineering assistant— who knew what was happening, or what was about to. No one knew more than Tuffy about what was being planned, built, or fixed. But the XO—in fact, every officer—had a pet project they wanted to see covered in the next issue of *The Transit*. Some of the projects were inside the perimeter, while others were a day's drive or a chopper ride away. If nearby, I'd request a jeep and driver, usually my buddy Stapleman, if he wasn't off driving a dozer. We'd drive to a job site where I'd chat with the project officer or chief, find out what was happening and where I could stand to take a picture or two. I might find myself riding on a dozer, hoisted into the air by a crane to get a bird's eye view, or waiting until the dust settled. As I've said, the men had gotten used to me by now and not only tolerated my presence but were eager to get their picture and their project in the paper. When a photograph or their name appeared in *The Transit* I'd made a friend. Handing out 8 × 10 prints I'd made in the darkroom to the chiefs and officers won me permission to get the shots I wanted. Also, being a photographer gets you into places others are denied: behind police barracks, backstage at a concert, or on a construction site in Vietnam.

Today's assignment sounded exciting. "They're going to be using helicopters to set the concrete bases," the XO added. "Some of the towers are located in inaccessible places. We'll build a few towers here, then deliver them by flying crane. Should make for some interesting photographs. LTJG Powers is in charge. Coordinate with him, and take Widmark with you." Tom Widmark was the unit's photography assistant. He was a really an EO3 who had been coerced by the CO into moving from Alpha over to Headquarters Company. We did have a first class photographer's mate on board—Knupp—who, Tuffy Lake told me, had a fear of flying and would not go up in a helicopter to make aerial images, so Tom wound up taking and processing most of the construction progress pictures.

First Class Knupp did train Tom in his role as a Seabee photographer, including aerial surveillance, portraits of officers and enlisted men, project progression photos, the stuff any commercial photographer would be called on to do in civilian life.

While Tom was photographing the job sites, providing progress images to be included in Operations' reports to regiment, my photography had another purpose altogether. I photographed the men working, in order to illustrate my stories. Tom and I used the same equipment; we just saw things differently. He and I shared the darkroom, which I'll talk about later.

The order for the towers had come down from regiment headquarters in Da Nang: The Army, now guarding the Chu Lai complex, wanted seven 60-foot towers placed along the perimeter. These towers had proven useful in spotting Charlie's movements up near the DMZ—so the Army wanted them here. Each tower was fitted with a top deck, surrounded by sandbags to protect the observers on duty from snipers, and with a tin roof overhead. They were designed to stand even with one leg shot away. The access ladder to the top deck was inside a corrugated steel conduit, to shield the guards climbing up and down.

Five of the seven towers were straightforward projects, their locations accessible by truck, so the tower bases and the towers themselves were constructed on site, the towers themselves raised into place with Seventy-One's crane.

Towers 6 and 7 were another story. Tower 6, overlooking the Tra Bong River, was so far off in the bush, trucks could not deliver building materials; Tower 7 was on the top of Signal Hill, which only a mountain goat, or a Marine, could climb. What to do?

The operations officer, Naval Civil Engineer LCDR Martin, made a few phone calls, first to the Army and then to the U.S. Marines.

"Could we borrow a helicopter or two?" he asked each. "Ouch!" he said when he was told the price—$1,600 an hour. "I need to ferry buckets of wet concrete to inaccessible locations for *your* observation towers, then fly in the towers themselves." He got an okay, and a schedule was arranged.

A Jolly Green Giant, or "Hook," drops off two tons of wet concrete in a jet engine case, as a Seabee scrambles away from the dust of the downdraft.

Widmark and I hitched a ride out the top of Signal Hill one morning, just as a huge Marine helicopter, a Sikorsky CH-3 called "The Jolly Green Giant," was approaching the construction site. Dangling below the chopper's belly was what had once been a huge jet engine shipping container, which was now filled with two tons of wet concrete. The chopper hovered over the crest of the hill, its downdraft kicking up clouds of red dust into the hot morning air. The Seabee crew, 13 guys, scrambled to untie the harness connecting the chopper to the crate of concrete. One Seabee, his face streaked with sweat and dust, gave the "all clear" signal, two thumbs up, and the bird began to slowly pull away from the hill. The downdraft from the copter's rotors blew over a sandbag bunker, knocked down a radio mast, and destroyed one of the Army's plywood huts. The dust covered Widmark and me and got into my camera bag and into my camera.

The chopper circled the hilltop once then headed north, back to Chu Lai to return with another batch of concrete. The Marine chopper, from MAG 16 in Da Nang, had one of our Seabees on board to coordinate the exercise. In all, the chopper ferried eight loads of premixed concrete 11 miles to the top of Signal Hill that day.

The chopper and the swirling dust gone, the Seabees began manhandling the wet

The chopper out of the way, the men from Charlie Company set up a bucket brigade to fill the waiting foundation forms with the wet cement.

concrete, via bucket brigade, into waiting forms. Once the forms had set, these bases would support the massive 60-foot observation towers.

While building Tower 6 near the village of Tan Ka, the crew enlisted the local kids into helping with the bucket brigade, returning the empty pails back to the container. Slave labor, you say? No, the kids were overjoyed to help the big American guys, and in return got candy bars and cans of C-rations.

Towers for 6 and 7 were built and erected off-site, near our base, by Charlie Company. When the time came, the completed structures were airlifted out to the work site and gently set in place. For this final phase of our "Powers' Towers" project we needed a really big helicopter. The Army sent us a "Flying Crane," a huge dragonfly-shaped heli, one of four in South Vietnam. The deployment of Tower 7 atop Signal Hill went according to plan. Tower 6, on the Tra Bong River, overlooking the hamlet of Tan Ka, was another story. The Flying Crane picked up the completed tower, but before it got to the site, it

1943   U.S. NAVAL MOBILE CONSTRUCTION BATTALION 71   1967

Vol. 1 No. 4 — (Family Gram) — THE TRANSIT — July 20, 1967

THE FACE OF VIETNAM

The face of Vietnam — It has seen a long cruel life. This 93-year-old Vietnamese gentleman has seen his country torn apart by political strife and the war machines of invading armies. Indo-China has never known the peace of other nations, only the struggle of outsiders to conquer the rich productive farm lands that edge the South China Sea. Yet these Vietnamese persist — they are here, with their families, their farms, and their hamlets — the people and the land are one. Invaders come and go, time is slow for this country, patience is a way of life, they wait — soon this invader and his terror from the North will go too, soon they will rest from the fear that has gripped the Vietnamese for over one hundred years.

Seabees and Marines
BUILD ARMY TOWERS

CHU LAI, REPUBLIC OF VIETNAM—Seabee construction crews and a Marine "Jolly Green Giant" helicopter teamed up this week to build a pair of observation towers for the Army's 196th Infantry near Chu Lai.

A huge green Marine CH-53A helicopter hovered over the crest of Signal Hill, its down-draft kicking clouds of red dust into the hot morning air. Beneath the hovering craft a team of 13 Navy Seabees scrambled to undo the harness that connected the 'copter to their "bucket" of concrete. One Seabee, his face streaked with sweat and grime, gave the "all clear" —and up thrust thumb—and the bird moved slowly away from the hill leaving the 'bees to man-handle two tons of concrete into waiting forms—forms that would support a massive 60-foot observation tower.

Dust still swirling around the mountain top, the Seabees set up a "bucket brigade", trans-
(Continued on Page 4)

A hovering Marine CH 53 A, the "Jolly Green Giant" kicks up dust on top of Signal Hill as Two Seabees work to undo the harness connecting the concrete bucket to the 'copter. The terrific down-draft created by the craft, blew down sandbag bunkers, radio masts and the three Army personel's plywood quarters during the ferrying operations.

Calling America
MARS TO OPEN

"Camp Shields, Vietnam calling America!" Seabees at MCB 71's Vietnam Camp Shields will soon be talking person-to-person with their families back in the States. The MARS (Military Affiliated Radio System) will go into operation by the first of August, according to Second Class Builder Tom Hyams, Special Services official. The "ham" radio station, licensed for unofficial battalion use by the Chief-of-Naval-Operations, will be used nightly by MCB 71 Seabees to place radiophone patches back home.

Licensed as NOEFU, the MARS unit here at Camp Shields will share the air with all other Vietnam based Seabee battalions on a 2 to 3 night-a-week schedule. Operating nights, 2200 to 0300 (roughly 10 am to 3 pm Eastern Daylight Savings Time), the service will be on a "first-come first-service" bases, regardless of rate or rank.

Calls placed through to State-side families will originate from the "gate-way" station in Port Hueneme, California. After receiving the Vietnam MARS operators's list of calls, the gateway operator turns the numbers over to a telephone operator for placing and the fun begins. The telephone operator will alert the respective families that a call from Vietnam can be expected within hours, then as each call is completed the next family on the list is "hooked up". The time limit for all calls will be 3 minutes, with the State-side receiver paying the telephone charges from Port Hueneme, California.

Funds for the radio facility were supplied by the 30thNCR's Monthly Recreation allotment and handled through MCB 71's Special Services.

Families receiving calls from a MARS station in Vietnam must use the radio operator's jargon and finish each statement with "over" before the other party can reply. There is a small time delay of a second caused by the 18,000 miles, so take your time — it's been a long time since that Seabee has heard your voice.

MCB 71 SAFEST IN RVN

CAMP SHIELDS, RVN—Another record was broken recently, when MCB 71 became the safest Seabee battalion on deployment in Vietnam. The Battalion passed the three month mark without one "time lost accident" on the books—a record for starting a deployment.

The first weeks, and months that a unit deploys to a new location are usually the most accident prone. New environments, new methods and "getting use" to things account for the accident rate, but not so MCB 71. The first three months in Vietnam for the Battalion proved "time lost accident" free. A record not only to be proud of, but one that needs building.

Safety Officer Lieutenant-Commander Roger Martin, attributed the first three months of lost time accident free days to the strenuous activity of Safety Chief Suppo and the vigorous safety program instituted by the command back in Davisville. He went on to point out that the "record" was due, in large part, to the efforts of each Seabee in Camp and on the projects. Reporting of un-safe conditions, work hazards and possible danger areas and methods, have saved the Battalion much time, and avoided needless injuries.

Bernie Nowakowski SN, assistant to the Battalion's Safety Chief, puts up the "Big 90" on the Seabee's Safety Board at Camp Shields. The board is an added reminder to the men of the safety program that is constantly under way.

The July 1967 edition of *The Transit* carried a front-page story on "Powers' Towers."

ran into a rain shower. As the chopper attempted to place the tower on its foundation, dust blown up from the chopper's rotors got mixed up with the rain, creating a wall of airborne mud. Visibility went to zero, so the pilot had to jettison his cargo, short of its concrete base, smashing the tower into pieces. The carpenters from Charlie Company built a replacement.

In all, Charlie spent five weeks on the seven towers, most of that time waiting for a chopper. This operation was the first time a Marine Jolly Green Giant had been used to ferry concrete in jet engine packing crates.

The Seabee engineers were great problem solvers, able to adapt to the conditions, the equipment and materials available. In Vietnam, with a war going on around us, that presented an additional challenge. The officers, chiefs and petty officers, those with commercial construction experience, all shared the same philosophy: Bring the job in on time and under budget.

"That's one place I'd not like to spend the night," my buddy Skop observed, studying the platform on top of Tower 3. "You are a sitting duck up there." True, the towers did take small-arms fire, and the occasional mortar round would attempt to knock one over, but the towers were still there when we left Vietnam.

Each tower, its concrete base and site prep time cost more than $10,000; that's $70,000, plus the helicopter bill. This war was getting expensive. Even with two Seabee battalions, plus an Army construction brigade, it was hard to keep up with requests from the Marines and the other forces—American, Korean and Vietnamese—for more and more facilities. More battalions were arriving every week, and only a few were leaving. There were more than 60,000 servicemen within the Chu Lai compound, in twenty different units, in 1967.

Photography in the Combat Zone

Photography in this hot, dusty, humid place had its challenges. First, the dust got into everything; on lenses, inside the cameras, onto the film. The heat cooked my black body cameras and overheated the film. Then there was the darkroom—one of the few air-conditioned spaces on our base, but the water that came into the lab was over 90 degrees. Film needs to be processed and washed at 72 degrees. If the chemistry is too warm it increases the grain, called reticulation; it ruins the tones in the negative.

I found a way to bring down the water to a manageable temperature. Each evening, upon leaving the darkroom, I'd fill the 10-gallon Arkay rotary print washing with water and let it sit overnight in the air-conditioned space. By morning, I had water near 72 degrees. When we first used the space, we were getting small scratches in our negatives. We discovered it was from fine sand in the incoming water. A filter fixed that.

By mid-summer, I'd shot more than 50 rolls of film. Each roll contains 36 frames—that's close to 1,800 images. The Navy was supposed to provide me with a camera and film, but I didn't like their equipment, so I bought and used my own. I even provided my own film. I wanted to own what I shot, and not give it to the Navy, but this became a problem. The XO kept telling me, "The photography department up at regiment wants your negatives." I knew they'd look at the film, and if it wasn't a photo of a construction site, they'd throw my film away. "Just give them something. Give them negatives you don't want," CDR Brown said.

So I did. Some of my good images went along with the rolls of construction site photos, but I came home with more than 60 rolls of 35mm TriX film, along with 20 rolls of medium format film. Photographers, like authors, artists, even inventors, are protective of their copyrights, their intellectual property. I was and still am.

We Got Ourselves Another Convoy...

"We have a convoy heading to Quang Ngai, Lyman." I was standing before the XO in his office in late July. "We've been tasked with trucking four huge metal tanks down to a sugar refinery run by the South Vietnamese government. It'll take all day. This something you want to cover?"

"A convoy is always a good story," I replied. "When do we leave?"

"It'll take a few days to organize the personnel," he said. "The tanks are being shipped to the Sand Ramp from Da Nang. They are supposed to arrive tomorrow. It'll take most of the night to transfer the steel tanks from a barge to the low-beds. Get ready. I'll assign you to ride shotgun for Ensign Johnson, who will ram-rod the convoy." I knew Bernie Johnson, a 25-year-old ensign from Gainesville, Florida. Fresh out of OCS, he'd already led a dozen of these convoys to Quang Ngai, and knew what to expect. We were to transport three 22-ton tanks and a 40-ton tank, all of which had been manufactured in Japan, shipped to Da Nang, then transported to the Chu Lai Sand Ramp. Our job was to get the tanks to Quang Ngai. This was more of a civil action mission than military.

Every week or so, a convoy from Seventy-One headed to Quang Ngai to re-provision our 30-man detachment there. Each convoy needed a squad of our guys to come along as protection. A lot of the Admin 'Bees volunteered, just to get out of the office.

The convoy to Quang Ngai was a 35-mile drive down Highway One, a rough dirt road through unprotected country, through villages and hamlets, farmlands and wide-open countryside. I'd made the trip a couple of times, as it was a great way to see Vietnam and make photographs.

I was up before daybreak, waiting, when Ensign Johnson drove up in his World War II–era jeep. I climbed in with my rifle and camera bag, my .45 in its holster, canteen and ammo pack on my belt, my helmet on my head. I was all set. We drove through the Chu Lai Enclave to the Sand Ramp where four of our low-bed semis were lined up. During the night, a crane had transferred the tanks, one by one, from the LSTs to the trucks. Our 'Bees were strapping them down with webbing when we arrived. We were ready to roll as the sun came up. Beside the four flatbeds, there were two six-bys with a squad in each to provide security on the trip, and a wrecker in case of a breakdown.

A radio, hanging by it strap on the jeep's dash, squawked, "All clear to Binh Son." It was an Army EOD team up ahead which had just finished sweeping the highway for mines. We pulled out of the loading area, the jeep in front, a six-by with driver, shotgun and five men in the truck body next, followed by the four flatbeds. Bringing up the rear was a large wrecker along with the second six-by with more Seabees, rifles between their legs, cases of C-rations and carboys of water on the floor.

Highway One snakes 600 miles from Hue to Saigon, much of it unpaved and dusty. By 8 a.m., the road ahead was lost in a haze of dust, as civilians and military traffic began to build up. Jeeps, personnel carriers and construction vehicles were crowded in among bikes, Vespas, ancient cars and small Toyota pickup trucks. We passed three-wheel Vespas, and

Top: **Ensign Bernie Johnson, a 25-year old civil engineer from Gainesville, Florida (seated), chats with the road-master (far right) and fellow officers prior to departing on yet another convoy through VC country.** *Bottom:* **Our convoy rolls past villagers pulling fishing nets from a pond, with kids, as usual, getting in the way.**

Lambrettas (tiny trucks) heading north, stuffed to overflowing with families, crates of chickens, bales of hay. We squeezed through villages, our trucks and tanks filling the narrow street.

In our tiny jeep, Ensign Johnson was able to scoot back and forth along the convoy as it labored along Highway One. This allowed me to photograph different parts of the convoy as it passed by green fields, men plowing rice patties with oxen, men and women transferring water from a stream into their rice paddy, using a sling bucket system, women washing clothes by the side of a river and kids jumping off a bombed-out bridge into brown rivers.

It was slow going. The ensign would shoot ahead to clear traffic through a hamlet for the trucks to pass. The tanks and trucks took up almost the entire roadway. Passing under phone and communication lines, the shot gunners hopped up on top of the tanks to walk the wires overhead. The convoy rolled at a snail's pace through the small roadside villages of Noch Mon, Binh Son, Son Tihn and into Quang Ngai. We skirted demolished bridges, and wires and palm trees were pushed aside. Progress was slow, often no more than six miles an hour. Other traffic was halted as the convoy passed. Kids ran to the edge of the road to wave and watch the huge trucks pass.

Despite the breeze as we moved along Highway One, the sweat poured down my neck, soaking my clothes. There was an ever-present, nagging feeling we'd be ambushed, hit a road mine, or that a sniper would pick off one of us. Nevertheless, I was in my element. I imagined myself a *National Geographic* photographer assigned to document Third World agriculture and society. The farmers had no tractors, no implements, just muscle, patience and animal power. My next concern: did I bring enough film?

It took the convoy six hours of tedious driving, and we arrived at the sugar mill site just after noon—only to find that the 100-ton-capacity floating crane that had been dispatched from Da Nang to lift the tanks off the flatbeds was stuck 15 miles downriver. Ensign Johnson, two chiefs and the drivers huddled with the Vietnamese civilians. The low-beds needed to be unloaded, turned around and the convoy headed back as soon as possible. No one wanted to be driving Highway One at night.

The men came up with the idea of rolling the tanks off the trucks. We found a ramp near the site of sugar mill, level with the truck beds. One by one, the trucks rolled up to the improvised ramp, and the convoy's wrecker, dug in opposite the trucks, ran a cable to the opposite side of each tank. With its powerful winch, the wrecker rolled the four tanks off the beds and onto the riverbank.

Slowly passing through villages gave us a view of Vietnamese life we did not see inside our protected enclave back in Chu Lai.

9. The 'Bees Get to Work

1943   U.S. NAVAL MOBILE CONSTRUCTION BATTALION 71   1967
CHU LAI, RVN
Vol. 1 No. 5 (Family Gram)   August 24, 1967

VIETNAM SWIM BREAK

CHU LAI, SOUTH VIETNAM—Forced to take a cooling dip in a Vietnamese stream by temperatures that reached into the 130's, Seabee Leo Braunby, from the Lake George region of New York State, escapes the heat as he takes a break from a current construction project under the scorching sun of Chu Lai, South Vietnam. Accompanying him in his "swim-break" is his huge Euclid TS-24 Earth Scraper. The two were moving earth near the site of the Army's Huey Helipad in Chu Lai.

30 Go To Binh Son

BINH SON, SOUTH VIETNAM—The third Seabee Detail from MCB 71 has left Camp Shields, Chu Lai for a two month project for the Republic of Korea Marines in nearby Binh Son.

Chief George Gierloff, under Navy Lieutenant (jg) Jack Wilkinson of Delta Company, has taken thirty men to the town of Binh Son, fifteen miles south of Chu Lai on Route ONE. The detail, comprised of Delta Company builders and a number of Bravo Company utilitymen, will remain at the Binh Son location, eating, sleeping and working with the Korean Marines during the 9-week project. One cook, CS1 Sievert, of MCB 71's award-winning galley, will accompany the team, providing the men with chow. Navy Hospital Corpsman, Dick Roberts, will be along as the unit's "medic".

The project, calling for more than seven buildings, will include a 3-ward hospital. Materials; concrete and wood, will have to be convoyed south to Binh Son throughout the detail's stay.

Seventy-One has deployed, at present, a 30-man detail to Quang Ngai building for the ARVN's a fifteen-man detail near Saigon, in the Delta region, constructing facilities for the Navy's Sea Hawk Attack Helicopters. Plans are still in the formation stages for sending still another detail to Duc Pho — seventy-miles south of Chu Lai.

Heavy Work Load Ahead
SEABEES BUCKLE DOWN

CHU LAI, SOUTH VIETNAM—"This is what we've been waiting for!" stated MCB 71's Commanding Officer Commander R. D. Coughlin. "We've now enough to keep us more than busy for the rest of the deployment."

And enough work to keep the entire battalion working 'round the clock for three months was received recently from Seventy-One's operational commander, the 30th Naval Construction Regiment in DaNang.

71 Carts 47-Ton Tanks South To Quang Ngai

CHU LAI, SOUTH VIETNAM—Four huge steel tanks bound for a sugar plant in the capital city of Quang Ngai, South Vietnam lay on a barge at the Sand Ramp in Chu Lai. They had just made the six-hundred mile water trek from Saigon. Seabee equipment operators and truck drivers were laboring throughout the night swinging the tanks into place on the flat beds of four 60-ton tractor-trailers. A hard, nerve-racking 35-mile haul lay ahead for the four drivers and their "shot-gun" guards—35 miles of rough road, through Viet Cong territory.

The U.S. Third Marine Amphibious Force in Da Nang had requested Navy Seabee Battalion MCB 71, in Chu Lai to provide heavy-equipment trucks and experienced drivers for the hauling of four large evaporators, south, to the city of Quang Ngai. The tanks, fabricated in Japan were destined for a sugar refinery under construction by Vietnamese civilians and the ARVNs (Army of the Republic of Vietnam). Seabees, the only military unit in the area capable of carting the massive load, were at the Naval Support Activity "boat ramp" all night loading the massive tanks. Three of the tanks weighed just over 22-tons, the fourth tipped the scales at 47-tons. Navy Engineer Ensign Bernie Johnson, 25, from Gainsville, Florida was to ram-rod the convoy—a veteran of more than 25 convoys over Route ONE to Quang Ngai.

Following the Marine and Army sweep of Route ONE for land-mines that morning, the Seabee truck convoy moved out. The lead truck, carting the largest of the four tanks, the 47-
(Continued on Page 9)

They Did It, Again

CHU LAI, SOUTH VIETNAM—"It's all in knowing what formations to look for." Seabee driller EO3 Charley Bordner was talking about how to "put down" a well—and he should know, he and his crew are batting six for six. Charley, 24, from Dallas, Texas has worked on oil drilling rigs for over four years prior to entering the Seabee's DPPO program, and his experience is paying off, paying off for MCB 71's drill crew, and paying off for the thirsty servicemen of Chu Lai. Charley has brought in over six productive wells, three in areas where other drillers had failed to find water.

When asked what the secret is, Charley just shrugged and said, "I don't know. A spot just looks right, you go down 30, 40 or 50 feet, use the right slurry and pretty soon you've got water." Well, what ever Charley, Dick Stapleman and the team of UT's from Bravo Company are doing—they must be doing it right. They brought in another fresh water well this last week.

The Seabee convoy rolls south on Route ONE—passing under a coconut palm the four huge tanks lumbered along the dirt road to Quang Ngai.

Six work orders were received in the first week of August, any one of which could keep the Battalion hopping till the end of the deployment. But, the work orders all call for completion prior to November ONE—before the Southeast Asian monsoon season sets in. Battalion Officers and Chiefs are now determining how we can meet the fall deadline. Lieutenant (jg) Stephen Powers, Acting Assistant Operations Officer, expressed confidence in the Battalion's ability to complete the work on time, "providing," he said, "our equipment holds up." This work load will not only tax Alpha Company's operators, but her maintenance crews as well —70 per cent of the work involves massive earth moving operations. In addition the push will place a further burden on the builders, carpenters, plumbers, electricians and steel workers of "B", "C" and "D" Companies. A 24-hour work-day schedule is now being formulated for all companies, with the Fleet-bees—the office staff from Headquarters Company—taking over many of the non-construction Seabee duties, i.e., taxi and trash truck drivers, security and camp maintenance duties. An extensive "cross-rating" program will bolster the ranks of Alpha Company with additional equipment operators moved from other companies. A request for more heavy equipment and additional earth moving machines has already been placed with 30th NCR.

THE PROJECTS

The largest of the new projects will be adjacent to the South Heliport—to date MCB 71's only large project. Plans call for completion of "Phase ONE" of an "Ammo Supply Point" by November ONE. The project will include four observation towers, half-a-dozen 16 by 32 foot strong-backs, 20 underground munitions bunkers and two dozen covered ammo storage areas, all to house the arsenal of rockets, 500, 750 and 1,000 pound bombs and munitions used by the Marine Air Groups and Army helo squadrons in Chu Lai. When finished the Ammo Supply Point will be the largest single facility in the Chu Lai complex. Needless to say MCB 71 is tackling the largest undertaking of any of the Seabees in Chu Lai. Over 200,000 cubic yards of earth
(Continued on Back Page)

Front page of the August 1967 edition of *The Transit*.

By the time we finished it was afternoon, and the convoy started back on Highway One, heading home. By the time we entered the security gate at our camp, it was just past sunset. I was worn out—more from the stress of riding through unprotected territory than from the trip itself.

I spent the evening and a good part of the night in the air-conditioned darkroom processing, washing and drying my film, then making contact prints. The story filled a page in the August issue of *The Transit*.

Keeping the Marine A-4 Jets Flying

Just over the hill, a half-mile behind our camp, was a 1,200-meter-long SATS (Short Airfield Tactical Support) runway. MCB-10 laid down that strip in 1965 when they came ashore with the Marines to secure Chu Lai. This runway was still in operation and was now home to two Marine detachments of A-4 Skyhawk fighters. These wasp-looking jets screamed on takeoff, and as they cleared the hill that separated us from them, they were so loud you couldn't hear yourself talking.

I was sitting in Tuffy Lake's jeep next to the runway watching Chief Dick Wade and his crew from Charlie Company working to repair a section of damaged runway. A jettisoned bomb early that morning had blown a hole in the matting. "The strip will be shut down while the boys replace the matting," Tuffy explained. "Wade and his crew are out here every other day." The strip was not concrete, like the main Chu Lai runway, but was built with interlocking aluminum planks and steel mats, to create a smooth surface for landing and takeoff.

"In World War II, the Seabees used Marston perforated steel planking (PSP) on the coral islands of the Pacific," Tuffy went on. Marston planks are perforated steel planks 10 feet long by 15 inches wide. They each weigh about 66 pounds so could be carried

Steel workers from Charlie Company lay down smooth, interconnected steel plates to form a taxiway mat. The soft Chu Lai sand was replaced with gravel and laterite, providing a firmer base for the plates.

A dozer (out of frame) pulls out the "zipper plate" that connects two steel mats. The wheels of the grader hold down the mats. Oil lubricates the joints.

The zipper plate removed, a trio of heavy equipment drags a 30-ton section of runway mat out of the way. The damaged foundation will be repaired and the mats dragged back into place.

ashore easily and installed. The holes in the planks worked to reduce weight and provide drainage. We used Marston matting around our base as sidewalks, but not on runways. I asked Tuffy why, prodding him for a story.

"Chu Lai is all sand. Too soft. The thin Marston planks were okay on the hard coral islands of the Pacific in World War II, but here the sand is too soft to absorb the pounding of heavy aircraft landing at 140 mph." Seabees with heavy equipment were busy removing one of the zipper plates that held the steel mats together.

"We have to close down the strip while a crew is working," he added. "So the boys have to work fast. Chief Wade came up with this method of slipping out the zipper planks. See how the guys are pulling a plank out, with a dozer?" These aluminum alloy planks, I learned, are 12 feet long, two feet wide, and an inch and a half thick. They each weigh 144 pounds. The grooves along the edges are used to tie the larger steel mats together. The steel mats are made of individual planks, fitted together, into 150 feet long by 70 feet wide sections, each weighing tons. These formed the majority of the strip and refueling pads.

"When MCB-10 installed the runway, they leveled the sand with a grader and laid down the Marston planks, but that proved inadequate," Tuffy said. "The mats buckled and dented when a plane landed, due to the soft sand subsurface. So they removed much of the sand and laid down a sub-surface of crushed stone and laterite then installed the mats and planks."

"These runways are used all over Vietnam: Cam Ranh, Phan Rang, Khe Sanh, Dong Ha, Phu Bai, and here in Chu Lai—but they have their limitations. They need constant maintenance and repairs."

The Marine base at Chu Lai had grown in two years. The previous year, MCB-40 added a crosswind strip. "It's shorter than the main strip," Tuffy explained, "and it has arresting gear and a steam drive catapult system, same as used on aircraft carriers. This strip can be used as an emergency landing strip for carrier-based planes that couldn't make it back to their ship." Pilots landing on this SATS runway had to be carrier qualified. Trouble was, when these jet jockeys came in hot and short, the tailhook on their Phantoms could rip up the center line, which we would then have to replace.

Tuffy, the head engineer assistant with our outfit, had arrived with the advance party in March. He knew what was going on and had a hand in the plans for each of the unit's projects. This was but one of a dozen we were working on.

"Chief Steelworker Dick Wade and his crew from Charlie Company have been given the task of keeping these two strips operational," he said. "We make a weekly inspection, but Wade's crew is out here nearly every day, and many nights. They are on call 24 hours a day."

Tuffy and I climbed out of the jeep to talk with Chief Wade, an ingenious 39-year-old Seabee from Kalamazoo, Michigan. Tuffy explained as we walked over to meet Wade, "He's a father figure and boss to this eight-man team. He and his crew have managed to cut the repair time to less than half of the previous method."

The two men were engaged in a technical conversation that was beyond me, so I wandered around making photographs, watching a crew of steelworkers and equipment operators remove a zipper plate. They parked a road grader over the steel mats in the damaged area, with the tires straddling the zipper plate, then, with a dozer, a chain, and a liberal application of oil, they simply slid out the zipper plate. This allowed the crew to then tow the entire damaged blanket of matting out in one piece with a bulldozer, forklift, or any vehicle Chief Wade could get his hands on. Some of these mats could weigh over 30 tons. Once the mats were out of the way, crushed rock, one-inch-minus cement-grade aggregate and laterite were trucked in, dumped, bumped, smoothed and leveled. The mats were then pulled back into place and the zipper replaced, re-joining the mats.

Continuing his explanation, Tuffy said, "This runway takes a pounding. Landing heavy jet fighters every hour, at 140 mph, is bad enough. Occasionally a plane will lose a bomb on takeoff. The resulting explosion rips up a whole section of the strip. There's an occasional crash landing which tears up even more runway. Temperature expansion and contraction warps the metal mats, creating dimples in the subsoil. When the rain comes, there'll be erosion of the sub-grade at the edges of the runway. All this needs our attention."

The weekly rocket and mortar attacks that hit the strip couldn't help either, I thought. Good thing we were just a short hop over the hill.

Since World War II, Seabees have been inventing, improvising and improving on methods and equipment to get the job done—along with making life in the tropics a little nicer. During World War II the Seabees used empty 55-gallon fuel drums for everything from road culverts and bathtubs, to barbecues and chairs, to toilets and showers. Seabees still use old 55-gallon fuel drums filled with sand to create protective walls between the A4As. The West Indian steel band was invented when the natives on the island of Trinidad hammered the tops of 55-gallon fuel drums into the now world-famous musical instruments. Here in Vietnam the Seabees were again using their ingenuity to solve problems.

Charlie Company's clerk, Pete Peterson, told me this story. When the crew completed repairs on the SATS runway in the middle of the night, the Seabees and Marine airmen decided to have a little fun. The runway was a perfect drag strip. The men brought out their jeeps, trucks, and "the races were on!"

In the middle of one of these drag races, a security jeep pulled up. The MPs said the strip was shut down for drag racing. "There's a Major nearby. We can't have you guys making all this noise."

Out of one of the drag racers climbed a shirtless Marine. As he walked over to the MPs' jeep, he began pulling on his shirt. Once it was on, his collar lapels revealed two oak leaves. "Is there a problem here?" asked this Marine major.

"No sir!" announced the two MPs, climbing out of their jeep and saluting.

"Then carry on, Marines. The rest of us need to get back what we were doing."

Rebuilding the Main Runway

The year before we arrived, in 1966, the civilian contractor, RMK-BRJ, built a 10,000-foot-long concrete runway just south of the SATS strip. This two-mile-long runway provided taxiways and parking for Marine Aircraft Group 13 with three squadrons of F-4 Phantom fighter bombers. This was the strip onto which the C-141s delivered us in April.

Hot sun, monsoon rains, heavy use and frequent mortar and VC rocket attacks from the western hills had deteriorated the center seam of the runway. It was beaten up and needed to be replaced. Seventy-One got the job. As the runway would be closed to traffic, we were given only three weeks (22 days) to get it done. In the meantime, the A-4 Phantoms would have to take off and land using the nearby Marine SATS runway, putting even more strain on Chief Wade's crews. They'd now be working overtime and through most nights to keep the two SATS runways operational.

Thirty men from Charlie Company were given the

Seventy-One's Seabees used power saws with diamond blades to make four-inch-deep cuts on either side of the center seam of the concrete runway.

job to replace the center strip of the main runway. Using gasoline-powered rotary power saws with diamond blades, the crews made two four-inch deep cuts, seven inches apart, on either side of the center line where the two halves of the concrete runway met. As the two saws walked down the runway, right behind came the "breaker crews," which used pneumatic jackhammers to break up the old concrete, forming a four-inch-deep trench. Once the trench was cleaned, it was lined with a specially formulated epoxy. Before the epoxy had time to set up, a special mixture of concrete was poured in and leveled. The center seam expansion with the original lighting system was embedded and the job was completed in 18 days, four days ahead of schedule.

Seventy-One had delivered again.

Finding Water in a Desert

Repairing the runway: Pneumatic jackhammers broke up the damaged concrete before a special mixture of epoxy and concrete were added.

Fresh water in this sandy desert was hard to come by. Each encampment within the enclave needed its own water well. The job of finding water deep underground and drilling a well came to Seventy-One's water well drilling crew, attached to Bravo Company. The team had its own drilling rig and was under the command of Utility Chief Reimel. But the heart of the team was actually a Texas "wildcatter": Charlie Brodner, EO3, who the previous year had been drilling for oil in the Lone Star State. Brodner, a bespectacled Texan with a slight drawl, seemed to have a knack for finding water where no one else could. The team put down seven productive wells that summer.

The team of seven men from Bravo included Brodner and Ruddy Kanye, both equipment operators on loan from Alpha Company, along with George Hardwick, UT1; Rick Clayton, UT2; Denny Schlossar, UT3; Olie Oliver, UT3; and Norman Allair, UT3. They were busy all summer finding water.

When the Army's water well up at Task Force Oregon went dry in the latter part of June, Brodner and Chief Reimel were called in. Seventy-One was the only construction outfit in town with a drilling rig—so, who else you going to call? The team arrived on the site near the ice plant, and after walking around for twenty minutes, "taking in the lay of the land," Brodner chose a spot and the team set up the drill rig. In one day, they drilled a 32-foot hole in the ground. Nothing came up. It was a dry hole. They finished for the day and returned to camp.

When the team returned the next morning to move their rig to another location, they found the first well was overflowing. Brodner and the team had struck an underground stream that ran on top of the stratum of shale 32 feet down. The water was found to be safe and in sufficient quantity (at around 20,000 gallons per day) to satisfy the needs of the Army's ice plant, which supplied ice for the frontline troopers' beer coolers.

The team drilled six more wells in the Chu Lai Enclave that summer, every one of them productive. The team's grand total was 535 feet drilled, for seven productive wells, with 395 gallons of fresh water a minute. The wells averaged between 30 feet and 65 feet deep, with one well 260 feet deep.

Texas oil prospector Charlie Brodner, EO3, and Utility Chief Reimel with their team of drillers come in with another fresh water well. They drilled six more that summer.

Getting Wet with Our Underwater Team

Got a fighter jet that landed in the sea? A downed chopper in a river? A missing patrol? Do you have a leaking underwater pipeline that needs fixing? Did someone drive a jeep off the deck of an LSD? Seventy-One's Underwater Construction Team (UCT) was kept busy all summer with these kinds of tasks, and more. Our three-man team was called on for underwater operations by the Army, Marines, and Naval units not only in Chu Lai, but also up in Da Nang and over in Duc Pho.

The team's staple work was the constant visual inspection and maintenance of the Chu Lai POL tank farm's pipelines. These 8-inch and 12-inch ID, mile-long pipes ran from a floating platform anchored a mile offshore, out of range of VC rockets, underwater to the tank farm, located right next to our camp. The three divers connected, disconnected, replaced and repaired hundreds of feet of these pipes, often at depths of more than 60 feet.

"It is nice and cool at those depths," men of the team reported.

Chief Hayes, the senior diver, was assisted by Seaman Divers Bill Johnson and Craig Hutchinson. Chief Hayes, a Navy diver since 1959, reported to Seventy-One just before we left for Vietnam. He came to us from a much-publicized Navy diving operation off the coast of Spain—searching underwater for a lost atomic bomb.

LTJG Tony Smith, 24, had been the OIC for the Navy's swim school in Florida prior to his assignment to Seventy-One, and naturally wound up as our dive officer. Bill Johnson graduated from the Navy's second-class diver school and the new member of the team was newly arrived Craig Hutchinson.

Right: **Seaman Diver Bill Johnson rises to the surface amid a cloud of bubbles. He's using a double-hose, two-stage SCUBA regulator, ancient by today's standards.** *Bottom:* **The UCT divers worked in depths of up to 60 feet repairing underwater offshore pipelines. They were also known to retrieve downed and sunken aircraft.**

The chief and his team searched the Da Nang harbor bottom to recover equipment accidentally dropped over the sides of freighters, replaced propellers on the Navy Swiftboats, searched the sea bottom for a downed Marine jet fighter. They successfully raised a downed Army copter in 30 feet of water off Rosemary Point.

An Army Huey crew in Duc Pho was complaining about water seeping into their JP-5 fuel, so Chief Hayes and Diving Officer LTJG Tony Smith flew down for a look-see. They found that every one of the underwater hose connections were leaking. The following day our two-man team of divers, along with a Warping tug (more floating utility craft than a tug) from Da Nang, replaced over a mile of hose.

In August, the Army asked Seventy-One if our dive team could help search the bottom of the Tran Bong River for a missing patrol. This story is elsewhere in this book.

By mid-summer, our dive team had logged over 90 official dives and 65 hours of bottom time. That didn't count the "recreational dives" the team oversaw on the weekends. The UCT boys would take a few of us up to the coral reefs off Rosemary Point "to get wet" and swim around with the fishes in deep, cool water.

Playing with Our Tinker Toys

If you needed a road in the Central Highlands of Vietnam or a landing strip on top of the mountain, you had a problem. Getting our earth-moving equipment into such inaccessible locations had been giving construction engineers headaches for years. Until now.

The problem was somewhat solved when the military introduced a series of new "Tinkertoy" earth-moving equipment. Downsized dozers, graders, scrapers, trucks, front loaders, all reproduced at one-third size so to be airdropped or carried aboard small cargo aircraft capable of landing in hard-to-get-to places. All the of Seabee outfits in Vietnam received an allowance for these junior-size machines. Seventy-One had just made room for two each of the small dozers, scrapers, graders, trailer trucks and front-end loaders.

According to Alpha Company Commander LT Bob Sharp, some of our toy equipment was already in use. A Tinkertoy grader was in Duc Pho leveling building sites for 400 to 500 berthing huts for an Army Helicopter Attack Squadron and the 39th Marine Engineers. The body of the grader was flown down to the site on board an Army Chinook helicopter with the blade and turntable following aboard a second chopper.

LT Sharp also planned on using the smaller skip loader (front-end loader with backhoe attached) to assist in preparing the foundation work for the ARNV camp being carted down to Quang Ngai. One of the small dozers would be used at MAG-12 to complete the Ready Ammo Pad, as well as the ASP (Ammunition Supply Point). These massive, 12-foot-high berms were made of sand and topped with laterite. The smaller dozer was perfect for working atop the shifting piles of sand.

While Seventy-One was never assigned any major construction which would utilize the machines' airdrop capabilities, the addition of the smaller-sized equipment to the battalion stock allowed Seventy-One to be ready when a job came our way.

Chapter 10

Close Calls Come in Many Sizes

While this outfit was pretty safe inside the wire of the sprawling military enclave, occasionally the guys of Seventy-One experienced what the Marine and Army patrols were dealing with daily—getting shot at, dodging mortars, ducking a road mine or other explosive ordnance.

Stories Told in the Barber Shop

One of the places I could always find a story was in the barber shop. This was not a place to get a coiffure or close shave—everyone received the same buzz cut—but the shop was air-conditioned and always full of guys waiting for a haircut, or just there to cool off, but everyone there was swapping stories, some tall, others (mostly) true.

Once morning in late May, I was sitting in the barber chair reading *Stars and Stripes* when two Seabees from Alpha Company came in and sat down. The tall one asked, "Lyman. Want a story?"

"Sure. What have you got?" I replied, putting down the paper and taking out my notebook and pen.

There was no better place to catch up on world news and get a story for *The Transit* than at the air-conditioned barbershop.

"The Sand Ramp was hit last night."
"I heard."
"We were there," said the other Seabee.
"I'm all ears."
Here's their story basically as it appeared in *The Transit*.

It was a warm May night at the sand ramp five miles up the road from our base. Two of our Seabees were there loading their trucks for the trip back to camp.

Twenty-year-old Seabee Mickey Sarlo, from Reno, sat on the tailgate of his six-by, waiting for yard workers driving forklifts that were carting building materials from the cavernous hole of a nearby LST to his truck. The loading ramp was nothing more than a beach on the Bien Van River, by Rosemary Point, at the north end of the Chu Lai Enclave. Across the silent waters of the river was the dark island of Long Thanh Dong.

Unknown to Mickey, unknown to the 40,000 American servicemen stationed on the Sands of Chu Lai, Victor Charlie had put a handful of men ashore on that small island, men who had one purpose—destroy as much property and life as possible with the mortars they carried with them. Beside Mickey, who was smoking a cigarette, sat his buddy Dave Robinson, also 20, from Sparta, Tennessee. Dave was off duty but had tagged along to keep Mickey company during the all-night hauling operation, from the sand ramp to Seventy-One's camp and back again.

It was Saturday morning—the forklifts growled and smoked inside the huge LST as they carried pallets of cargo to Mickey's waiting truck. Mickey and Dave sat and waited.

WHOOMP! The first VC mortar round landed between the two outside LSTs—30 yards from the two startled Seabees. The explosion, muffled by the water, snapped them out of their early-morning reverie. The second and third rounds exploded closer to the outside one of the smaller LCUs—showering them with spray. The two Seabees were now on the run, heading for the yawning doors of the LST. They were joined by a few sailors and two Marines who were taking cover. Just as they got through the doors and into the huge cargo hole a fourth round exploded on the ship's superstructure, shaking the whole boat with a *BANG* that resounding throughout the cargo hold. That explosion fatally wounded a Filipino chief sleeping on the cargo deck above. A ship's officer ran into the cargo bay yelling for someone to call for medical aid and an ambulance.

With mortar rounds still showering down around the sand ramp, Mickey ran to the phone shack by the road and passed the word to the startled operator. "Get an ambulance down to the sand ramp—and damn quick," he yelled. "We're under mortar attack. We have wounded."

The VC were still pouring mortar rounds into the Naval facilities when Mickey pelted back to the cover of the LST. Explosions could be seen and heard as they landed at the nearby MCB-Eight camp, eventually killing one man. Mickey helped a Filipino sailor and two of the Marines to carry the wounded chief down the loading ramp and to a nearby pickup truck. The VC dropped over 30 rounds of 82mm mortars on the buildings and LSTs at the Naval Support Activity at Rosemary Point within just 20 minutes. Damage was reported as light. Destruction of materials and equipment was minimum. However, underreporting damage and causalities was SOP in Vietnam.

This was not a rare occurrence in Chu Lai. Chinese mortars and Russian rockets hit the runways, or some camp along the perimeter most every other night. Star flares continually floated down most nights, so the guys inside the wire could see movement in the fields and along the riverbank outside the perimeter.

Mickey and Dave stayed aboard the LST with their M16s to provide protection until the regular Marine security patrol released them a short time later. Both Seabees were short-timers, with only a week remaining before being shipped back to the States to rejoin their original outfit, MCB-Six.

Boom! Two Seabees Hit.

Wednesday, September 6, 1967—The Marine SATS runway was less than half a mile over the berm from our Camp. We heard the A4a Jet Fighters taking off all day long, providing cover for our Army and Marine grunts up in the hills.

Two of our guys, SW3 John Thierry, 19, from Detroit, Michigan, and CN Bill Miller, 19, from Dodgeville, Wisconsin, were standing by the guard shack at the top of the hill, waiting for a lift to Duc Pho. It was mid-morning, and hot.

Just as an A4a took off, its 500-pound bomb accidentally jettisoned and exploded at the end of the runway, spreading shrapnel as far away as our gate. Two men standing there in the open were hit by flying shrapnel, both receiving lacerations and one a broken arm. Both boys, from Delta company, were rushed to the First Marine Division Hospital up at Rosemary Point for treatment.

Bill Miller's injuries required additional surgical treatment, according to medical authorities. Proper medical attention by Navy doctors saved the arms and hands of both boys. According to reports, shrapnel wounds of the arm were the only injuries received.

Details Under Attack

Many of the small detachments from Seventy-One, those on projects far away from camp, occasionally came under attack and had to defend themselves. Our Seabee detail in Quang Ngai underwent mortar and small arms fire on August 30, then again on September 2, just prior to South Vietnam's general election.

A number of mortar rounds fell within 300 yards of the detail's tent camp site inside the MACV compound near the provincial capital. The compound itself received a heavy shelling as Viet Cong terrorists rushed into the city with satchel charges. They blasted open the doors to the jail and freed 1,200 VC prisoners.

LTJG Bernie Johnson (who had replaced LT Rüdiger as the detail's OIC) moved his crew deeper inside the MACV compound Friday and Saturday evening in anticipation of more attacks. The next night the Viet Cong again attacked, dropping 81mm mortar rounds inside the compound, nearly hitting the Seabees' abandoned tent camp. Casualties were light and no 'Bees from Seventy-One were injured. This wasn't the only time the Quang Ngai detachment was bothered by the VC.

The VC also attacked the ROK Camp at Bihn Son on the night of September 1. Seventy-One's detail there was building a hospital facility for the ROK Army and Marines. As with the incident in Quang Ngai, none of our Seabees were injured and we were back on the job the next morning.

This Is as Close as I Want to Get

It was a sunny morning in June, and already turning hot, as Stapleman and I drove through the gate on our base in Chu Lai. My EO buddy was driving a jeep, its ragtop off, the windshield down, to take advantage of the breeze. We were followed by EA3 Bob Wagnor's jeep and a survey team from Engineering. The two jeeps were off to the site of

Tower 7. We drove through the huge Chu Lai military enclave, exited the perimeter with a wave to the Marine guard and joined a line of traffic already filling dusty Highway One, heading south. Towers 6 and 7 were built and erected offsite, near our base. When the time came, these completed structures would be airlifted out to the work site and set in place (story in a previous chapter). We never did arrive to see it.

Trucks and civilian vehicles, heading in both directions, filled this narrow, lane-and-a-half dirt road. It was stop and go. A hot day. We were eating dust in the open jeep from the traffic ahead, so Stapleman hung back and we put up the windshield. We drove out of the flat, sandy landscape of Chu Lai area into the green countryside. Rice fields on either side of the road gave way to the occasional hamlets scattered along the way.

A few vehicles ahead, a Marine convoy with two six-by troop carriers full of Marines was shepherding a large 50,000-gallon JP5 tanker heading for a Marine Huey camp near Quang Ngai. We could just see the top of the tanker ahead.

Then it happened.

A tremendous explosion erupted up ahead. Stapleton slammed on the brakes and pulled the jeep off the road, nearly landing us in a rice paddy. Wagnor and his team behind us did the same. Dick grabbed his rifle and we both slid into four inches of mud amid small rice shoots in the paddy. A road mine had gone off up ahead. It had blown the dump body on the lead truck into the air. A mine explosion could be followed by an ambush—so the Marine instructors had taught us during combat training in Camp Lejeune.

"Get out of the vehicle, get off the road and take cover," the Marine sergeant had yelled at us in combat training school. "A road mine will stop traffic. A perfect time for the snipers to open up." Traffic stopped. The Marines jumped off the truck just ahead of us and ran past the tanker, searching the rice patties along the roadside for an ambush. I ran with them, my camera in one hand, my .45 automatic in the other.

The lead six-by in the convoy of three trucks had hit a road mine, blowing off the rear tires, throwing the dump body and its occupants through the air. Marines pulled the still unconscious driver and his passenger (aka his shotgun) out of the cab as the truck burned. The dump body had held four Marines and had not been sandbagged. Two Marines were found a hundred feet from the road in a rice paddy—dead. The other two, unconscious, were carried to the side of the road to be attended to by a Marine medic. I stood watching all this, beside the tanker as the driver and his shotgun climbed down. Both were shaking, their faces white under their tropical tans. The gas tank on the truck ahead let go, engulfing it in flames. During those few minutes we stood watching the Marines drag their buddies away from the flaming truck, time stood still.

All traffic on Highway One was stopped, in both directions. An hour later an Army EOD (Explosive Ordnance Disposal) team arrived to sweep the road for additional mines. People milled about. There was no ambush. As we waited, I chatted with the tanker crew, Lance CPL Burt Corbin, 20 years old, the tanker driver, and PFC Don Patterson, his shotgun. They were leaning on the front fender of their tanker, smoking nervously. Both were "short-timers" with less than two weeks left in 'Nam. These two young Marines were still in a state of shock from the explosion. They'd just witnessed the loss of two of their mates. Had their tanker, full of highly flammable JP-5 fuel used in military helicopters, gone up, the explosion and fire would have cleaned out the traffic for a mile on either side. I photographed the pair and took down their names and unit for a future story.

Lance Cpl. Burt Corbin, the tanker driver, and PFC Don Patterson, his shotgun, were short-timers—with less than two weeks left in-country.

An hour later, an Army EOD minesweeper with headphones approached, waving the disk on a stick back and forth over the road. He came right up to us, asked us to step aside, and swept the road under the truck, between the tires. He paused, swept the same spot again, took off his earphones and called over another EOD. They conferred, then told us they needed the tanker moved back around a hundred yards, along with the rest of the traffic. They'd found another mine under the front axle of the tanker. Corbin and Patterson were now visibly shaken. I noticed I too was shaking. I was standing within inches of a buried mine, next to a tank of flammable fuel.

It took an hour to move the traffic back up and down the road. By the time the tanker was safely out of the way, the EOD men had found a second unexploded mine further down the road. I photographed the EODs as they poked and prodded the roadbed with their K-bars (military issue knifes), outlining in the dust where the unexploded mines lay.

The VC had placed their mines just off the crown of the dirt road, where normal traffic would miss them. When two vehicles passed each other at that spot one would have to pass over the crown and detonate the device, catching two vehicles instead of just one. The EODs placed a block of composition C on top of each mine and told me to get the hell out of there. I walked off into a rice paddy on a raised footpath. After a few hundred feet I stopped, turned and waited to get a picture of what came next.

The Army EOD team cleared the area of personnel, placed wires from the explosives back to a detonator, and instead of digging up the mine, they blew both mines up in place. I made a photograph of the black mushroom cloud of dirt and dust, only to realize a few seconds later I had to crouch down and tuck the back of my helmet into the collar

Top: An Army EOD specialist found an undetonated VC mine with his sensing gear. With his K-bar, he would probe the mine under the road, outlining the mine's shape. He would then place a brick of Composition C and blow the mine in place from a safe distance. *Bottom:* Moments after the explosion on Highway One, a shower of debris, gravel and shrapnel rained down on the photographer crouching in a nearby rice paddy.

My story and photo in the June 19, 1967, edition of *Stars and Stripes*.

of my flak jacket, cradling my camera in my crotch, as shrapnel, gravel and stones showered down on me, splashing into the water in the rice paddy next to me.

After the dust settled, the highway was opened, but it took another hour for traffic to get moving. Dick and I turned our jeep around and headed back to base. It was midafternoon. We'd missed lunch, but we were alive.

On the way, we talked about what we'd seen and learned that morning. We realized we'd already learned most of those lessons during combat training in Lejeune. We also agreed, all of us—Army, Marines and Seabees—had been lulled into "complacency," as there had been no road mine incidents for the past four months. We now understood why our Gunny Sergeant Harrison insisted that all trucks heading off the base be sand-bagged, that flak jackets be worn, and zipped up, and to keep a safe "convoy" distance from the vehicle ahead.

The photograph of the explosion, along with my story on Corbin and Patterson, ran as a full-page story in *Stars and Stripes* in the June 19, 1967, issue.

We Are Under Fire!

"We have a squad of Marines missing in action."

An Army captain was talking to our Operations S-3, LCDR Martin. Not a pleasant situation nor a comforting term. "I've lost a squad—last seen returning from a patrol into VC country. They were floating down the Tra Bong River, on a Vietnamese sampan, just west of Tan Ky. We need divers to sweep the river bottom."

The Army needed our help. They wanted their men back, dead or alive, so they'd called Seventy-One. We were the only unit in Chu Lai that had a UCT (Underwater Construction Team). Chief Hayes and his two third class divers were all commercially certified. It was August when we got the request.

"Can you and your divers sweep the river bottom?" the Ops officer asked Chief Hayes.

"Sure can," said the chief, the dive team's leader. "We'll need protection and a dive platform," he added.

"I'll make the arrangements," chimed in LTJG Tony Smith, the OIC of HQ. Smith was only 24 but had served as OIC for the Navy's swim school in Florida prior to his assignment to Seventy-One. He wanted to go along as the officer, to get out of the office and get wet. This could be a good story, so I tagged along. Floating down the river would be better than staying in camp.

For two days, the team from Seventy-One drifted down the river on a Marine AmTrac (Amphibious Tractor, Personnel), LVTP-5A1. A second AmTrac shadowed us, drifting along the edge of the river, while we were out in the middle, sitting ducks.

These floating personnel boxcars were fitted with tank tracks so it could operate on land or maneuver in the water. The crew consisted of two Marines, a corporal driver, and his shotgun. An M60 machine gun was mounted on the turret next to the hatch on top, where the driver sat. These large, bulky, floating transport boxcars could hold a platoon within its body, but we were sitting topside, our feet dangling over the edge into the river. In addition to the Marines and our Navy team, the Army had provided a squad of grunts for each of the AmTracs for added protection.

Our Navy team, the lieutenant, the journalist, and our three divers pulled up to the river's edge with a truck full of tanks, flippers and masks, C-rations and water jugs. LTJG Smith met with the Marine and Army leaders and discussed the operation. One of the AmTracs would be our dive platform, anchored mid-stream. The divers would descend, make an ever-widening circular sweep of the bottom, then we'd move down river and repeat the procedure.

The Army grunts split up and boarded the AmTracs and we shoved off. The divers, the lieutenant and I moved our gear aboard and made our way into the middle of the waterway. The divers dropped an anchor, then geared up with air tanks, regulators and face masks. Down they went. From the anchor line, they began their search pattern. We sat atop the AmTrac, its decks hot enough to fry eggs—the men pouring helmets full of river water over themselves and the decks to cool off. We broke our C-rations, drank from our canteens and waited. The divers came up, we moved down river, reset the anchor, and began the process all over again.

The next day, we began the process anew. The divers went down, and the men on the AmTrac were enjoying dumping helmets full of water on each other. Zip ... zip ... zip ... we began taking fire from the shore. At first I didn't know what all the fuss was about. Then I saw, and heard, that bullets were making zipping noises in the water around the AmTracs. Then, a round ricocheted off the AmTrac's hull and

Half a dozen Army riflemen lounge on the hot deck of a Marine AmTrac. The driver of the floating tank, a Marine corporal (white tee-shirt), chats with LT Smith, MCB-71's diver officer, while two of our divers are below, exploring the river bottom.

went whining off into the distance. Zip, zip, zip, more rounds splashed into the water around us. In less than a second, the Marine corporal had armed his M60 and was hosing down the shoreline.

The Army guys opened up with M16s. The crew on the other AmTrac close to shore was fully engaged in returning fire. But no one really knew where the fire was coming from, just someplace over there in the trees.

Then silence, while everyone paused to reload.

By then, I'd managed to get my .45 Colt out of its holster and was struggling to get a round in the chamber. My piece was clean and oiled, but the ammo had sat in the magazine for months and was a bit dirty, I'll admit. While everyone was occupied reloading, I got a round chambered, and began firing in the general direction as had the others. The only sound now was the popping of my pistol ... then laughter. The men on my AmTrac busted a gut over the journalist and his totally unprofessional gunnery.

Top: A second AmTrac, loaded with more Army riflemen, floats along the river edge not too far away. *Bottom:* Diver Bill Johnson is helped aboard to change tanks, as the AmTrac moves to a new search position.

"Hey, Journalist!" one of them shouted, "shoot pictures. We'll do the real shooting!" and they opened up again. A few minutes later the three divers appeared alongside the AmTrac. They'd seen empty shell castings stream down from above and knew something was afoot.

Nothing more came from the sniper that day. The barrage we laid down had either killed him or scared the bejesus out of him and he was running for the hills. The men theorized that the shooter was either an old man, or had very poor eyesight, or both, as he was such a bad shot. No one was hit.

We continued for the rest of the day, sweeping the river bottom, but never did find the missing squad.

My story and photographs appeared in *The Transit*, and as a center spread in *Stars and Stripes* later that month.

My Medic Buddies Tell Me a Story

WHUMP! The explosion of a rocket hitting the Marine runway, just over the berm, interrupted my sleep. The base was under attack, the second time in a week. Fully awake now, I pulled on my boots, grabbed my gear and stumbled out of my office hooch in nothing but my skivvies. It was just four strides to the mortar pit beside my hut. I slid down the sloped banking of sandbags, into the soft sand at the bottom.

A minute later, the two medics from sickbay slid in beside me. No one appeared concerned about our lack of clothing; we were all clad in just our underwear.

"It's just the VC lobbing rockets on the airfield," one of the medics reported—as if he knew—to dispel the concern we all shared. This was the second time this week the three of us were sitting here in this pit talking about bowel movements and heatstroke. What else was I going to discuss with my medic buddies?

"What are the biggest medical problems you guys deal with in sickbay?" I asked, hoping these "experts" might shed some light on some base-wide issue I could write about.

"Besides hangovers and skin infections, it's VD and hemorrhoids," one said.

"There are fungal infections, and a few severe cases of heat rashes," said the other.

"Those are difficult to treat," said the first guy. "Some of the guys just need to learn how to clean themselves better."

"With all the heavy equipment these Seabees operate, it's a miracle there aren't more accidents," said his mate.

"Hangovers, I know about," I said. Many a morning I would stand in line with a dozen others at the sickbay hut to receive my APC, "All Purpose Capsule." "What's in those things?" I asked.

"APCs contain aspirin, phenecitin and caffeine. The phenecitin is to counteract the jitters from the caffeine which supposedly made the aspirin work better. Aspirin," said the first, "it's really just a good pain killer and the caffeine gives you a kick. We give out a lot of them."

"Well," I admitted, "they do work, to that I can attest."

THUD!

Another rocket hit the Marine strip. The guys from Charlie Company would be busy early tomorrow morning replacing the busted-up steel plates that made up the runway.

"If they get one of those Russkie rockets over the hill, they'll hit us."

"Yes, but if they hit the fuel depot next door, that would fry our collective asses for sure."

THUD!

"What's the next serious problem you guys deal with over there in that Quonset hut of yours?" I asked, still hunting for a story.

"VD, STD, you know the clap, the drip."

"That's a problem?" I asked. "We are a bunch of guys locked up here on this base. How are we supposed to have access to the ladies?" I ventured.

"You don't know. We do."

"Well, don't hold back. What's the story?"

"Nearly every Seabee returning from a week's R&R has a dose of the clap."

"R&R in Bangkok is the worst."

"But some of the guys are getting it from the girls off base, in the village."

"Trouble is," his buddy continued, "the strain of gonorrhea we are seeing here in Asia is not responding well to the penicillin."

"What are the signs?" I asked, having very little experience with the symptoms of VD. In fact, I had none.

"It takes a few weeks for the drip to start," he said, "followed by pain during urination." These guys were now into the medical lingo. "It can then take a month or more to get rid of the STD."

"The pills don't work, so it's a shot in the butt every few days."

THUD!

This VD story was interesting but not something I'd get past the CO, the XO, LTJG Smith or that colonel up in Da Nang. I kept prodding, wanting to get our collective minds off the idea of the fuel tanks next door going up in flames, ending in burning JP-5 jet fuel flooding into our camp.

"I hear it's the malaria pills that cause most of our problems," I said, for a personal reason, but also to change the topic.

Every Sunday, while standing in formation for inspection, our officers doled out malaria pills, Chloroquine. We were supposed to swallow these large brown pills, right there, on the spot. Many skipped the ritual, knowing of the side effects to come. These pills were supposed to prevent us from getting malaria, but the side effects could be pretty bad, which some thought worse than the disease itself: loss of appetite, mild dizziness, clumsiness, headache, nausea, stomach cramps. Worst was the diarrhea.

Within a few hours of downing the pills, there'd be a mad rush to the four-holers. Eight hundred men trying to get to the "shitter" would result in long lines. So we stood there trying to hold back the flood that was to come.

"When you gotta go, you gotta go." So the saying goes. "If you don't go when you gotta go, when you do go, you find it's gone."

This "anal retention" can result in a wave of medical problems, which, for many of us, remains with us to this day. The physical stress of holding back diarrhea, plus the mental and emotional stress of living and working in a combat zone puts a "strain" on those tender butt tissues, resulting in internal and external hemorrhoids, known as "piles." I'll not go into an anatomical description of this condition, other than to say it made life uncomfortable, and, for many, still does.

I learned more about hemorrhoids, first-hand, from my mortar pit mates.

"It's also the food they feed us," said Billy-O, one of the medics.

"It's also the booze we drink," the other added.

"The pills are really a form of Ex-Lax, in disguise," I offered. "I've visited sickbay three times so far. Last time, one of you told me: 'Put your ass in this basin of hot water. Just your butt, not your balls.' What's in this water?" I asked.

"Witch hazel. It'll soften up your hemmies."

"Then what?"

"The doctor will take a look at your ass and tell you what's next."

"What could that be?" I asked.

"He'll probably prescribe Preparation H. It's the usual medication. We go through cases of it. It has witch hazel in it. If your hemorrhoids are really bad, he'll lance them and remove the clot." I was not looking forward to this at all.

Sitting at my typewriter for long hours, sweat running down my spine to collect where I sit, only added to my discomfort. I'd sit on one cheek, then the other, dreading my daily bowel movements, which had become excruciating experiences.

"Do they award a purple heart for hemorrhoids?" I asked, rhetorically.

THUD!

Nothing had landed in our camp, except last winter, before we got here, a stray Russian rocket landed on the four-holer nearby. Splattered crap all over the place.

Flares floated down far out over the perimeter. The three of us sat in the bottom of the pit, talking. The flares finally petered out. It went quiet. The "All Clear" came, and we climbed out of the pit and plodded back into our respective hooches. But who could sleep after all that commotion? There was just too much adrenaline flowing to go back to sleep, so I lay on my office cot and imagined what it would like if we did get overrun.

I played these "what if" games in my mind weekly. What if a squad of VC came ashore from a fishing boat and made it through the beach perimeter? We had two M60 caliber machine guns set up at either end of the concertina wire barrier separating our base from the beach. There was a narrow maze that allowed us access to the beach, but the VC would have a hard time finding their way through, but if they did, what would happen?

I had nothing to do for the next few hours so I let the daydream unroll and fantasized about what it would be like to be in a real firefight. What would I do?

Sometimes, I was ripped out of a dream about skiing by the first bursts of machine gun fire from our security bunkers, followed by the return from the VC's AK-47s. I'd grab my stuff and dive headfirst into the mortar pit, roll over and settle against the sandbag wall, slip a clip into my M14, and chamber a round. Then, I'd buckle my helmet strap, snap closed the flak jacket, and poke my head over the top of the berm. By that time, others would have joined me in the pit. We'd discuss strategy, take up positions and wait for something to move "out there."

By now, flares would be floating down over us, bathing the camp in harsh orange daylight. I'd be fully aware, the adrenaline surging through my body. I'd be shaking, my mouth dry. "Wish I'd brought along my canteen," I'd say to myself. "It was sitting right there on my desk." Sporadic gunfire would be heard all over the base as our men began to engage the infiltrators, or they might just be shooting at shadows. My hands were sweaty, and I rubbed them on my skivvies, then returned them to my rifle lying atop the sandbags.

This daydream was an old friend. My imagination ran this dream weekly, like reruns of *M*A*S*H* or *Hogan's Heroes*. Sometimes the dream ended with me being shot, the medics in the pit working on me, the initial pain, then nothing as I drifted into a black hole and lost consciousness as the morphine reached my brain. In another dream, I was captured while taking photographs in a village, taken away and hidden. Then, blindfolded, I was marched up the Ho Chi Minh Trail to North Vietnam as a POW. There would be interrogations, torture, pain before I passed out. Would I break? In other dreams, I'd be charging out of the mortar pit, my rifle shooting at the VC running through the camp. Men would fall, return fire would miss me, and on I would run, chasing the VC out of the camp.

Seventy-One spent 210 days in Vietnam. I spent only 180 days in-country. That's seven months, four weeks a month, less the five days each month I was in Tokyo. That's 180 dreams. Sometime the dreams were conjured up, others came involuntarily during sleep, and I'd awake, sweating and shaking. These dreams were too real.

There was a level of fear I experienced the entire time I was in Vietnam, sometimes more intensely than others. This fear was not completely debilitating; it was like a dull toothache, reminding me that I was in a combat zone. It was fight-or-flight, but the only place to hide was in the mortar pit. We Seabees were not aggressors—like the Marine and Army guys—we were a defense unit. As in soccer, the strikers were down field trying to kick the ball into the enemy's net, while we, the defenders, sat back here, making sure the other team can't get their ball into our net.

Seems almost playful when you think of it that way.

Chapter 11

Outside the Wire

In Vietnam, fear was always present, a nagging feeling that something's not quite right. It was like being awakened at night by a noise, then waiting for the other shoe to drop. It was like a piece of undigested beef sitting in the pit of your stomach, a reminder of just where you were. That feeling was there throughout the day, but especially at night.

"Incoming!" the PA blurted. I'd already heard the thud of rockets hitting the Marine SATS airstrip just over the ridge, a half a mile away. Fear kicked in, the adrenaline began to surge, my hands began to sweat as I fished around in the dark for my helmet and flak vest. It's the feeling of fight or flight, but there's no real fighting in this situation for me and the only place to take flight is the mortar pit. So, that's where I ended up.

This fear stayed with me the entire seven months I was in 'Nam. The fear was there, but it did not stop me from doing what I was supposed to be doing and at times I was actually thrilled to be there—"thrill" defined as being just this side of "terror."

An Assignment in Da Nang

That fear level ratcheted up a notch as I boarded a Huey Slick for the 45-minute flight up to Da Nang. I was leaving the protection of the Chu Lai compound so I had on my flak vest, with my .45 Colt sidearm on my hip, and no helmet, just my Seabee green cap with my rate insignia. I was on my way to check in with the MACV Press Center in Da Nang—and while there do a story on our Cumshaw Boys, Seventy-One's Material Expediting Team. These three guys made sure our outfit got all the supplies we'd ordered, on time.

This would be an overnight assignment, so I stuffed my toothbrush and deodorant in my camera bag and boarded one of two choppers on the Army pad up by Rosemary Point—pads my outfit had built two months earlier. Each chopper was full of men going to Da Nang, some to fly home, others on TAD, to check into a hospital, or to be reassigned. Door gunners sat on either side of the Huey, pilot and co-pilot up front, and a row of seats against the aft bulkhead accommodated the passengers. There were no safety belts, no oxygen masks and the briefing was short, just: "Hold on. We'll be at Monkey Mountain in about 45 minutes."

The bird lifted off the pad, followed by the second Huey. Their blades slapped the hot air, making that familiar *whoop whoop* racket. The choppers spun around and headed north, out over the bay, climbing. I was seated on the port side, next to the open doorway,

The Army heliport we'd built earlier was where I could board a Huey Slick to hitch a ride up to Da Nang. The term "slick" came from the fact these choppers did not carry the firepower of the "gunships."

bent on photographing the trip along the way. We rose up to 1,000 feet. The temperature dropped 10 degrees—a welcome relief.

We flew along the beach on the South China Sea, passing over the village of Hoi An, its market crowded with Vietnamese in the morning light. We passed over the mouth of the Chu Bon River, its harbors packed with fishing sampans. We flew along the beach of white sand. This could have been Truro on Cape Cod. We flew past Marble Mountain, which is really four volcanic mounds that rise abruptly out of the flat, sandy landscape. Next was China Beach, with an expansive evacuation hospital complex, then we passed a military resort that MCB-Five and Eleven had built for sailors off their ships on R&R.

The two choppers turned to the northwest and the whole of Da Nang Bay came into view. It was a near perfect circle, a large and natural harbor, protected on all sides but to the northeast. It was crowded with freighters, tankers, LSDs, and naval combat ships at anchor.

To the east, the bay was protected by a peninsula on which sat Monkey Mountain, a 2,000-foot-high mound of volcanic rock that rose straight up out of the surrounding sand. A small, deep-water harbor lay below the steep mountain. Two cargo ships were tied to a long concrete pier some Seabee outfit had built. The Cau Do River emptied into the bay next to the ship terminal, then the city itself came into view, stretching along a gentle curving beach to the west and north, ending at the base of Hai Van, another hilly peninsula. From the air, the city appeared squished in between the river, the beach and the large military air base. Da Nang was busy—it was one of the few natural ports along the entire coastline of Vietnam.

As the chopper descended to land at the base by Monkey Mountain, we skimmed over Da Nang Harbor's fishing fleet.

From the open doorway of the Huey, I photographed the local fishing harbor, packed with small sampans and houseboats as we made our approach. Bamboo fish traps with netting were strung among the bank. The choppers descended sharply to land at an Army base at the foot of Monkey Mountain.

The Cumshaw Boys

The expediter team was there to meet me in their 1953 Dodge T-245 pickup. We drove to a Navy base close to Monkey Mountain, where the team was housed in a barracks with a spare bunk for me. The crew chief, EO1 "Goldy" Goldsworth, was a seasoned Seabee, savvy in the ways of the subculture of the military. He knew how to get the stuff LCDR Powers, our supply officer, had requested. Spare parts, fuel, motor oil, 600 feet of copper tubing, two loads of plywood, steel matting and corrugated roofing—oh, yes, and a pallet of San Miguel beer. Goldy and his crew of two, EO3 Lee Hoyt and BU3 Steve Lunt, were masters at the cumshaw racket. They knew the protocols for above, and below, official acquisitions.

We stood in line at the mess hall, and over dinner and a beer chatted about their job and what it was like to be working in Da Nang.

"The city itself is small and compact," they told me. "But the military infrastructure stretches the entire length of the beach, a few miles inland, toward the mountains and south past Marble Mountain." I learned there were two large military airfields here, the SAC base on the edge of the city, and a Marine base near Marble Mountain, the one we'd

Need anything from up in Da Nang? These are the men who will find it and get it down to Chu Lai: Chief EO1 "Goldy" Goldsworth, BU3 Steve Lunt (driving) and EO3 Lee Hoyt. These three men were Seventy-One's Expediting Team, better known as the Cumshaw Boys.

flown over. There were smaller heliports for various units of the Army Cavalry scattered around. It was the 95th Evacuation Hospital complex we'd flown over on China Beach. It looked like a city itself, neatly laid out on a grid, with Quonset huts, two-story wood barracks, metal buildings and a large helicopter landing area.

On top of Monkey Mountain was a radar and artillery installation, carved out by a Seabee battalion. Scattered all over the place were camps for Marine units, Army regiments and battalions. All this built by the Seabees and Army Engineers in just two years.

"HQ for Eye Corps is here—that's the designation for the five northern provinces just south of the DMZ," explained Goldy. "The ARVN forces are stationed here, out there on the other side of the airport. The Naval Support Activity HQ is over the river in the city. It's big cheese here, providing logistic support to all American forces in the Eye Corps. We are all under MACV, the Military Assistant Command Vietnam." For me, as an enlisted man, the chain of command went as high at our CO, but Goldy needed to know how the supply chain worked here, and it did not necessarily involve the official chain of command.

"I heard there were some fireworks up here last month. You guys involved?" I asked.

"We got to watch," said Lunt. "The attack happened on the night of July 15. Lasted most of the night and into the morning. The VC and NVA lobbed rockets into the airstrip over there."

"But the fireworks lasted well into the next morning," added Hoyt. "They hit the ordnance bunkers full of 500-pound bombs. We watched the explosions from here for most of the night. The ordnance kept cooking off until the morning." The Viet Cong hit the airstrip, the bunkers and barracks with a total of 83 NVA 122mm and 140mm rockets. The airmen at the base suffered eight killed and 175 wounded. Ten aircraft were destroyed and 49 were damaged. The rockets destroyed buildings, hangers, mess halls and barracks. All this I learned much later, when the actual numbers were released.

Da Nang is halfway between Chu Lai, 60 miles to the south, and Hue, 60 miles to the north. Hue, the ancient imperial city, once the capital of central Vietnam, was just 50 miles south of the DMZ. On the other side of the DMZ, I'd heard, were 40,000 soldiers of the North Vietnamese Army.

Da Nang, with its deep harbor, made an ideal port for MACV. I'd seen large ships at anchor and a steady stream of LCMs and LCUs were off-loading their cargo onto the beach landing area. Forklifts unloaded cargo, which was transferred to flatbeds to be moved to supply depots all around Da Nang. There were depots for lumber, refrigeration sheds for food, warehouses for clothing, bedding, weapons. There were bunkers for ammunition, bombs and anything that might explode.

Early that next morning, the four of us squeezed into the pickup and headed off on the team's morning rounds. First stop was an Army supply depot, across the bridge, out past the airfield. Goldy had made "friends" with the supply sergeant there. He got out of the truck and disappeared into the mammoth warehouse. I gathered that a few words were exchanged, and I don't know what else, but Goldy returned with a case of Scotch, Dewars I think.

Off we went in search of copper tubing—from one supply depot to another, the trio, with me in tow, began to assemble a load of materials, supplies, spare parts, food and tools for the boys back in Chu Lai. Last stop that morning was at the LCM loading ramp on the harbor edge. Goldy walked up the ramp to the empty cargo hold, a bottle in hand, then climbed up to the bridge for a chat with the captain. The vessel, we learned, was heading down to the Sand Ramp in Chu Lai later that day. Arrangements were made for space onboard for a large shipment of plywood, cases of steaks for the unit's party, copper tubing, crates of spare parts and beer. By the end of the morning's rounds, the case of Scotch was empty.

Nothing in the military gets moving without grease. Dewars, I gathered, was the preferred lubricant.

It was while driving around with the expediters that I began to realize the scope of this U.S. military operation in Vietnam. Case in point: we paid a visit to Beer Town to arrange for shipment of a few pallets of beer to our base. Beer Town was a two-acre parcel of land on the east side of the river, fenced in, where cases of beer were stacked on hundreds of pallets. We drove down San Miguel Avenue, turned right at Coors Street, then right on Budweiser. The pallets were stacked three high, forming city blocks of beer. It was all sitting outside in the sun, no roof.

"Doesn't make much difference," said Lunt. "The beer here will be gone tomorrow, replaced by more beer coming off the ships."

Before lunch, the Cumshaw Boys dropped me off at the MACV Press Center, and continued on their rounds of collecting stuff for the base in Chu Lai.

I Learn I'm Not a Real Journalist

The MACV Press Center was a walled-in villa on the west bank of the Song Ha River. The Cumshaw Boys dropped me off by the sandbagged entrance. I asked the Marine guard where the press liaison officer was. He pointed to what looked like the gardener's cottage, separate from the villa itself. "He's in there," he said.

I walked over, knocked and a voice inside told me to enter. A lone officer sat at an ancient wooden desk—a Marine major, in his fifties, I would guess. One of his jobs was to clear press releases, photographs and anything leaving the military units that was publishable. The military held its journalists on a tight leash. We were not real journalists. We were more like public relations flunkies, restricted to producing positive stories and photographs that showed the military in good light for the folks back home. It was our job to sell the war effort, show the American taxpayer the military was taking good care of their boys. Today, it's called—arguably—being "embedded."

The major must have liked me, for after my briefing on what I needed to do before sending out any of my unit's news, he invited me to join him for lunch in the officers' mess. We sat down at a linen-draped table and a steward took our orders. The restaurant was abuzz with military officers and what I gathered were civilian journalists also dressed in green fatigues, but with a lot less spit and polish, and no insignias. We sat overlooking the river and a fleet of fishing boats. The meal was the best I'd had since arriving in Vietnam.

The major, who I gathered was a university history professor doing his Reserve hitch, was eager to share his perspective of the Vietnamese and their history. He also wanted to instill in me why we, he and I, and the entire military force of the United States, were here in this backwater tropical rice paddy.

His lecture about Vietnam—a country I had never studied in school or was not even aware existed until shortly before I got here—occupied most of the lunch time. Here is his history lesson, or what I recall him saying, enhanced by research I've done since.

Vietnam itself is an ancient civilization. The Vietnamese as a people go back to before the time of Christ or the rise of Rome. From its earliest history the Vietnamese have been fighting—if not the Chinese, the Mongols, the French, or the Catholic Church, then each other. The Vietnamese people fought

Doug was one of the village elders in Hon Ba, the fishing hamlet on the beach at the mouth of the Song Tra Bong (River). His son was the village chief in the nearby village of Van An. Together they walked a narrow path between the foreign Americans who traipsed through their village by day, and the VC who came at night.

a thousand-year war to keep out the Chinese. This war ended in the tenth century. The Chinese returned, only to be beaten back, to be replaced by the Mongols in the twelfth century. The Mongols too, were pushed back, but the Chinese returned again in 1400, to be driven back after a 20-year war. The Chinese came back again but were driven out for the last time in the seventeenth century. Vietnam is rich in agricultural land, and with an industrious people, it's ripe for plundering.

Vietnam was then divided into three dynasties: Tonkin in the north, with its capital in Hanoi; Annam in the center, with its capital in Hue; and Cochinchina in the south, with its capital in Saigon. For generations, each of these provinces was ruled by a warlord family. At the end of the Sino-French War in 1885, France seized these three provinces and French Indochina came into being in 1887. The kingdoms of Cambodia and Laos were added after the Franco-Siamese War in 1893. France continued to rule Vietnam as a colony until the Japanese took over in 1942, at about the same time the Germans marched into Paris. The Japanese let Vichy France run things. But with the war over in 1945, the Japanese left and the Viet Minh, a communist organization led by General Hồ Chí Minh, declared Vietnamese independence. However, France didn't like that, so the French went to war and took back control of Indochina. An uneasy truce followed until 1954 when the Geneva Accords forced the French out of Indochina, and Vietnam was divided into two countries, North and South. Saigon was the capital in the south, Hanoi in the north.

The Vietnamese, I gathered, as a people, have always wanted to be a single nation, but personalities, egos, warlords and family infighting kept getting in the way. The communist North wanted to reunify all of Vietnam, and hostilities broke out in 1965, nine years after the French left. The Americans were invited in to help the South Vietnamese government fight off the Communists from the North and the local Viet Cong insurgents.

The difference between the North and the South was, as I understood it, economic philosophy. The North was a communist, one-party, totalitarian society; the South was free trade, capitalist and entrepreneurial, with all the corruption that goes with the free market.

The U.S. military took over Da Nang in 1965. We had to, the major explained. It was the only large seaport that could accommodate a large military buildup.

The city of Da Nang itself was settled in the seventeenth century and soon became an important trading center for European and Asian merchants. It was annexed by the French under Napoleon III in 1858, and was renamed Tourane. Da Nang had a lot going for it: a large, deep bay, a long beach protecting the harbor, lots of agricultural land nearby, rivers for transporting goods from the interior. Hue, the former imperial city on the Perfume River, is just 60 miles to the north. The French brought architecture, culture, the Catholic religion, their language and cuisine to this part of Asia. Saigon was the Paris of the Orient, Quang Ngai was the Riviera, Da Nang, with nearby China Beach, could have passed for the Biarritz.

End of the major's lecture.

A Fearful Walk Through Da Nang

Lunch over, I bid the major *au revoir*, and set off to walk through Da Nang to the airport to catch a flight back to Chu Lai. There were few scheduled flights in Vietnam, but choppers and fixed-wing cargo flights took off at all hours from the Da Nang Airport. The Cumshaw Boys told me I'd get a flight before dark, so I had a few hours to explore the city of Da Nang by myself. Within minutes of leaving the major's air-conditioned office I was drenched in sweat and beginning to think this walk through a Vietnamese city, by myself, might not have been such a great idea. As I walked down the avenue that ran parallel to the river, I noticed I was the only American, the only serviceman, dressed in green fatigues. I carried my Colt .45 in its leather holster on my right hip, spare magazines tucked into a pouch on my belt, my camera bag on my left shoulder. I tucked the holster's flap behind the pistol, for a faster draw—my hand on the pistol's handle made me feel better.

The city I entered was a compact and busy place, unlike any city or town I'd ever experienced. The avenue along the river was lined with walls, behind which I could glimpse expansive and expensive villas. It was evident the French had been here. They had left their architectural stamp on the villas, and on the government and commercial buildings that lined the riverbank.

I walked north, through what must have been a wealthy part of town. I had a visual map of Da Nang tucked into my brain, and knew if I kept going north, I'd run into the beach. If I turned left, and headed west, I'd run into the airfield. I couldn't get lost.

I turned west and entered the city proper. The streets were crowded, jammed with bicycles, mopeds, small cars and people. This was my first experience in a Third World city and I was as thrilled as I was scared. I was a woodsman, after all, not a city kid. I

A busy Da Nang street. Exhaust fumes were spewing from the tailpipes of ancient cars as well as modern mopeds, mixing with the smoke of charcoal and the scent of spices and body odors. This well-used and well-worn city is as much visual as it is sensual.

Top: Crowded open-air markets were the equivalent of supermarkets back home, as well as 7-11s and NAPA auto parts stores. *Bottom:* A foot-operated sewing machine was the center of the family business, a tailor shop tucked into a notch on a back street in Da Nang.

was out of my comfort zone. Da Nang was under U.S. control, but it was still a Vietnamese city and the VC were still able to infiltrate it, and occasionally a sniper would pick off a lone serviceman—like me.

The air smelled of exhaust from motorcycles and cars, burning trash, charcoal fires and pungent spices. It was a hot, dusty harbor city, at one time the gem of Indochina.

But it had seen better days. Parts of the city were in shambles, with abandoned and broken buildings, rubble on the sidewalks. But for the most part life went on. I walked past shops, many consisting of no more than a single room, their dark interiors a mystery. The signs above, written in a strange alphabet, were incomprehensible. In the deep shadows of one, I could see a woman at an ancient, foot-operated sewing machine, a mechanic working on an upturned motorbike. There was a barber shop, another tailor, a café with tables on the sidewalk, just like Paris. There were shops with piles of tin cookware spilling out onto the sidewalk, shops with colorful fabrics, a market with cages of ducks and chicken. As I walked through the crowds, I photographed a world I'd only seen in *National Geographic*. Now I was there. I was constantly dodging old cars, bicycles and kids. Even in the heat of the day, the place was abuzz with commercial activity. People still needed to eat, to buy and sell stuff. The markets (there were more than one) were noisy and busy places. Open stalls with ragged awnings above sold raw meat, fish, produce, and clothing. As I walked, the kids kept pestering me, asking for a handout, trying to sell me something. It was okay. With the kids around me I felt there was less chance a sniper would take a pot shot.

I walked on through the streets of Da Nang, I was sweating—as much from the nagging fear of being the only American serviceman among strange faces that only occasionally made eye contact—as from the heat and humidity.

Did Someone Just Step on My Grave?

As I plodded on through the streets of Da Nang, now away from the commercial activity and the kids, an internal conversation began to play itself.

"Has Death ever sat down next to you?" one side of my brain asked the other.

"I have no idea," came the reply.

"Yes, you do. Hiking up Mount Madison in New Hampshire, in a blizzard. The three of us. Your buddy, Allan, your brother and us. We came close to getting lost on that mountaintop and freezing to death that night."

"How about that winter we went on a SCUBA diving adventure on Cape Cod?"

"Which one? There were a few."

"Diving through the ice that winter off the beach in Falmouth."

"How many times have you been driving, half asleep?"

"Yah, that time I nearly had a head-on collision on the way back to the base in that Convair."

"We never did like that car anyway."

"I'm sure a bullet has passed nearby, without us being aware."

"Or we just missing stepping on a road mine a few weeks back."

"That was a lucky day."

Since that day walking through Da Nang, the only American serviceman in sight in a Vietnamese city, I've survived three hurricanes on my sailboat, been lost in a blizzard on a Wyoming mountain, sailed solo through fierce gales, and I'm still here to tell the tale. Why? Dumb luck? Could be, but the Irish call it "pluck," the luck you make by thinking through all possible dangers and preparing for them.

"What makes you think we'll get through this and get back to base alive—let alone get back to the States?"

"The Navy trained us to survive. The Marines gave us a mindset to protect ourselves when under attack."

Turns out I did learn a few things in the Navy.

Waiting at the Airport

I was getting light-headed and needed to drink something. I'd not brought my canteen, and we'd been told not to buy beverages in the markets, as they could be sabotaged with battery acid to kill Americans. Then I saw the chain-link fence topped with a string of razor wire; on the other side, the runway. I turned south and walked parallel to the fence until I came to the entrance to the airport. I showed my ID card and the two Marine guards waved me through. The Marine terminal, left over from the French occupation, was an open hanger, no air conditioning, no fans, lots of military around. Luckily, there was a canteen, or geedunk, nearby. I bought a cold Coke; two, in fact.

I checked in, added my name to a list on a clipboard for a flight to Chu Lai, sometime in the late afternoon. I had an hour or two to wait. I found a vacant bench in the shade and stretched out, my head on my camera bag as a pillow, just to make sure it wouldn't go missing should I fall asleep. I closed my eyes and regulated my breathing.

I acquired a valuable lesson in Vietnam: how to regulate my breathing and body temperature, manage the stress, and reduce the fear and frustration of being in the military and in the war zone. I learned how to meditate. I was never taught this, did not read about it, but need being the mother of invention, I discovered what others have known for thousands of years. The mind has some control over its own fears and the Ego.

As I began to regulate my breathing, behind my closed eyes I replaced the images of the Da Nang streets with the vision of a stream that runs along the edge of a meadow in Vermont. I visualized the sun filtering in through the green leaves overhead, leaving patterns on the deep green grass on which I lay. I could hear the gurgle of the stream as it tumbled over the rocks and roots of the trees that formed a canopy overhead.

Holding this vision in front of the internal eye was not easy. The noise and commotion around me, thoughts of what I needed to remember for the story I was to write, the danger I was in, kept trying to invade my thoughts. With concentration, I learned I could push those away and return to the stream. Within a few minutes, no more than three, I was gone. I could feel the stress, like molasses, begin to drain from my body, soaking into the wood bench on which I lay. I felt myself float out of my body, to hover a few feet above my physical self. I'd given up conscious thoughts of my physical body, yet part of me was still there, one foot remaining in reality. I was not asleep, I was meditating. There's a difference.

I've used this "guided visualization" meditation exercise almost daily since that time. I've found it one of the most valuable lessons I've discovered about life. The exercise takes no more than a few minutes to get into, and around eight to nine minutes to complete.

When the stress chemicals that have built up in my brain have drained away and some balance has returned to my mental state, I can feel my spiritual self return and enter my physical self. For years, I've set my watch aside as I lay down, and look at it when I come out of the meditation. Eight and a half minutes was the usual time I'd been away.

Away? Where? I don't know where. All I know is that I am renewed when I return, my energy has returned; that's why I still use this "nap" to this day. I may have to scoot over on my couch in my office right now for a short "nap."

Try it.

From deep in my daydream, I heard my name being called on the PA. I snapped awake, shouldered my camera bag, adjusted my utility belt and holster and followed a crew chief out to a Chinook, CH-47, a twin-engine, twin-bladed monster they call "The Hook," for its use in carrying heavy payloads on cables attached to the undercarriage. We used one to ferry concrete out to work sites where there were no roads. The interior can carry a couple of jeeps, a platoon of fully armed men, or a dozen pallets of beer. There were fold-down web seats along the sides for a few passengers, but the cargo this time were cases of artillery shells bound for the Army in Chu Lai. There were only five passengers, and the flight crew directed us where to sit.

As the Chinook wound up for takeoff, the whine of the two turbo engines and the flop-flop of the rotors was deafening. Most of my fellow passengers were stuffing plugs in their ears. It's the nosiest air ship in the world, and after half an hour riding in this flying warehouse I found I couldn't hear for two days.

Chapter 12

The Vietnamese People

There was a side of this war that people in the States seldom saw—the Vietnamese people. Even on the base we didn't get to see much of Vietnam or the Vietnamese. There were a few Vietnamese allowed in to clean the officers' quarters and run the gift shop. They smiled and bowed, but it was hard to engage them in conversation. A few of us got off the base and were able to see Vietnam while assigned to a detachment out in the boondocks, or riding shotgun on a convoy, or working on a Civic Action project in a village.

We had little insight into who these people were that we were supposed to be protecting. AFR and S&S didn't say much. We had no television on our base, so didn't even see what the folks at home were seeing. Combat reporters and photographers seldom, if at all, turned their attention to the lives of the Vietnamese, to the people in the towns,

A three-year-old Vietnamese kid salutes two ARVN soldiers on a moped as they avoid the kids and a pig in the middle of a busy Da Nang street.

Fishing nets on the beach. This is one of my favorite photographs from Vietnam. It was made with my Bronica square, medium-format camera. This camera was capable of recording greater detail and texture than my 35mm Nikons.

hamlets and the rural countryside. I got out of camp on weekly trips with our medical team to set up clinics in the villages. I covered stories of the Civic Action projects our outfit was working on out in the hamlets. I'd walked through Da Nang a number of times and visited Saigon a few times on my way back from Japan. But the Vietnamese were still a mystery. Hell, this whole experience was a mystery.

As a Navy journalist, I was expected to produce photographs to accompany my stories for publication. But photography, for me, has always been more than just journalism, it's been a way for me to see and experience the world, to produce a record, make Art … images I always hoped would enlighten, inspire, be provocative or touch the heart of the viewer.

The Vietnamese villagers around our base seemed to be an honest and hard-working lot. They led a simple life, far from the technology we Americans played with. I wished we could have left them alone. I took it as a personal mission to photograph these people, their villages, fields and families. Around the Chu Lai Military Complex were dozens of villages: Tung An, Dong Binh, Tri Bihn, Long Bin, An Tan, Sam Ha and the village of Chu Lai itself. I'd grown up summering on my uncle's farm in Vermont and found that these farming villagers dealt with many of the same issues as did my Vermont relatives. As a photographer, I'm always curious, and I found that the lives of the people interested me. I didn't understand their language, so it was hard to write their stories. My photographs of faces, body language, the way the people farmed, fished and conducted commerce in the markets—these would have to tell the story.

My Personal Assignment

"Come on, Scuzzy Skop, climb on board or we'll leave ya behind." It was Sunday afternoon, the outfit's only half-day off. A bunch of us were driving out into the boonies. I wanted to spend more time in the villages photographing the Vietnamese people, but since it was too dangerous to go by myself, I had to go with a squad. I'd signed out a

On Sundays we drove through nameless villages like this, exploring Vietnam and the way the Vietnamese lived. For me these expeditions were my own personal *National Geographic* assignment.

weapons carrier, and with Stapleman driving, six of us headed out of camp into the countryside. We'd armed ourselves to the teeth, piled on a case of beer and C-rations and off we went for an afternoon of adventure.

My small expeditionary force drove out of the Chu Lai compound, into un-secured territory, and down Highway One, that lane-and-a-half-wide dirt road that ran from Hue, through Da Nang and all the way south to Saigon. Every few miles, a village appeared out of the dust, some no more than a narrow place in the road where huts and open-air shops crowded in. The highway would open up for a few miles, rice paddies on either side, revealing farmers with oxen plowing fields. The occasional prosperous farm appeared hidden behind the hedgerows, its single-story villa set among gardens. Most of the houses we saw, though, were mere huts.

We saw no tractors or motorized farm equipment—the work was all done manually. Their irrigation system involved a bucket, with four lines attached. Two men, or two women, one on each side of the water-filled ditch, dipped the bucket into the stream, filled it, and then swung it up and dumped it into the paddy—over and over again.

A few miles south of the perimeter, we turned off Highway One onto an unmarked dirt path, heading east back toward the sea. We stopped at a small hamlet to buy bottles of Tiger Beer from a small shop. Whenever we stopped and got out of the jeep, kids

In this part of Vietnam life and agriculture went on much as it has for hundreds of years. I saw no tractors, no electric pumps, just Vietnamese working the land by hand. Irrigation was handled with buckets and two people moving water from a ditch or stream into the rice paddies.

Oxen were commonly used in place of tractors.

flocked around, climbing onboard and all over us jabbering in a mixture of Army English, French and Vietnamese.

"You want bang-bang my sister?"

"You number one Seabee. Souvenir me cigarette?"

The young girls stood back while the boys kept up a rapid-fire dialogue, their hands all over us, then a boy would scamper off with someone's wristwatch. "Hey! That little bugger! He took it right off my wrist! Hey you! Come back here you little thief! Chop-chop."

Giggles would spread throughout the entire herd of kids. Wherever we went the kids were trying to sell us their sisters, coconuts, palm frond woven bowls, Cokes. Yes, there was Coke wherever we went, even in the smallest hamlets.

As we drove through the countryside of Vietnam, the sweet scent of cow manure and the pungent smells of freshly turned earth made me think of my youth on that Vermont farm. The smell of men who work outdoors, no deodorant, just man's natural scent. It's a rare scent these days, everyone covered up by store-bought chemistry.

We drove through nameless hamlets, nothing more than groupings of families, past farmlands alongside the Tra Bong River, people bent over tending their rice paddies and livestock.

We arrived at Hon Ba, a small fishing village right out of Jack London's *The Cruise of the Snark*. Palm trees swayed, the waves splashed down on the hard sand beach lined with huts of bamboo poles, woven skirts of palm fronds, some with tin roofs, most with thatch. There was no poverty, as there was ample fish and rice at hand, but Vinh An and other nearby hamlets were primitive by American standards: no communications, one electricity line, no sanitation facilities, no doctor, and a population of a few hundred living close to the land and sea.

Wally Skop knew how to make friends—he brought pockets full of candy on our Sunday afternoon expeditions. The kids knew that.

A fishing fleet of wooden log boats lay at anchor, their sails wrapped around lateen booms. Boats made of woven reeds were pulled up on the beach and turned over as men painted the bottoms with tar. Fishing nets were spread out to dry on the beach. A photograph I made of those nets hangs on my wall today.

Fishermen with weathered faces, tending their nets, gave us shy waves. Kids ran around, old women hid in the shadows of the huts. It was rare to see a teenage girl, even a teenage boy. It seemed the Vietnamese were either pre-teen or over 50.

The Vietnamese are a thin people, at least the people I saw, for I never saw an overweight or plump Vietnamese. The girls, when we caught sight of one, were always pretty and shy. They dressed conservatively, in black slacks, a white flowing smock from neck to ankles, tied at the waist and slit on both sides for ease of walking. They wore wooden sandals or flip-flops and a reed-woven sunbonnet. Everyone did.

The freshwater wells in the hamlets were hand dug and lined with stone. There was no electricity, so no electric pump. Water was hauled up, often by the kids, in old metal buckets, and carted home, or to a building site where cement was being mixed for a foundation for a church or market.

There were no stores in this fishing village, commerce in the area was carried on at an open-air market over on the other side of the river in Tan Ky. There, fish, rice, chickens and the rare pig were exchanged for hard goods from Bin Son, Da Nang and Quang Ngai.

The villagers on the beach numbered no more than a couple of hundred—the larger town of Binh Thioi was upriver a few miles. The village of Tan Ky, where Seventy-One was helping build a new market, lay across the river. The main occupation in these villages

12. The Vietnamese People 165

The village of Hon Ba on the beach, where the Tra Bong River meets the South China Sea. Today, this village is an expansive community of well-built homes, paved streets, electricity, water and sewage. A large industrial center is across the river.

was fishing, which was done at night. The fleet of boats, with lamps hung over the bow, at night attracted schools of fish. These we saw from our base up the beach, their lantern lights reflected on the flat sea, blending with the stars overhead.

The fishermen were ashore during the day, and the nets were spread out on the sandy beach to dry, while older men sat in the shade of palm trees, mending nets by hand, their dark brown hands nimble and quick. They smiled at us Americans, but said little. I never knew what they thought of us. Were we invaders or liberators, or just a pain in the arse? Were their smiles just a way of tolerating our presence, as the Vietnamese have tolerated the French, the Mongols, and the Chinese throughout their 2,000-year history?

While I photographed the villages, the time-worn temples, and the kids, the adults tried to remain neutral while a full-scale war raged over, around and through their villages.

Kids were often tasked with drawing fresh water from the well.

At night the Viet Cong would creep into a village and harass the village elders, conscripting teenage boys for "the cause." During the day American, Korean and South Vietnamese soldiers and Marines would stomp along the streets and into their huts, looking for the VC.

Life went on in these hamlets and villages despite the screaming Marine Phantoms and A4s that passed overhead, and the chest thumping concussion from the blades of the Huey gunships that skimmed the treetops. At night, Army artillery pounded the hills only miles inland, allowing little sleep.

Between the VC and Americans, these fishermen, farmers, businessmen, traders and their families, along with the village chiefs and hamlet elders, were also trying to balance a conflict brought on by the government in Saigon. Most of these people were Buddhist, but Saigon was Catholic and the local representative of the Pope still held power here. The French had a hard time making converts of the Vietnamese, and the French had been occupiers for 100 years. The Vietnamese remained Vietnamese, they just dressed according to the current winds.

Despite the turmoil there was a seemingly abundant supply of kids. There was always plenty of laughter, much fooling around and always more games to play and things to do of an unproductive nature that there was time for. The kids were unafraid of the tall Americans, muscular and tan with belts full of toys and pockets stuffed with candy. We thought the kids were the greatest and vice versa.

The military tried, in a token way, to win the hearts and minds of the Vietnamese people whose lives, land and way of life we were stomping on, leaving behind bomb and mortar craters, burned-out hamlets, widows and fatherless children. Our unit was helping rebuild and construct new schools, orphanages, a church or a local market, but it all seemed hopeless. I felt we could do more for these people, or less—if we'd just give them the money the military was spending on this war effort and let the Vietnamese sort their differences themselves.

Tug was a successful fisherman from Hon Ba. He had two sampans, so the VC considered him a capitalist. Tug smiled and joked with the men mending nets, but said nothing to us. He could hear the war going on in the hills to the west, while overhead, the noise of slicks, gunships and phantom bombers was common.

CHAPTER 13

Civic Action Program

Of all the military units in Vietnam, the Seabees had the most connection with, and positive impact on, the local Vietnamese people. General Westmoreland, who was running things in Vietnam, had said: "The real war in Vietnam is winning the hearts and minds of the South Vietnamese people, to turn them against the encroaching communism from the North." To do this, all military units were encouraged to volunteer for Civic Action projects. These included rebuilding schools, orphanages, churches, markets, roads and entire villages destroyed by the war. The Seabees became the Navy's version of the Peace Corps. Why? The Seabees had construction equipment, savvy, manpower and

Polishing up the Seabee logo seemed a matter of life and death. The Seabees had a reputation among the locals as men who would help build schools and markets. Our vehicles, with the bumblebee logo, got thumbs up and shouts of "Seabee numba one" as we passed through the villages. The VC didn't seem to bother with us.

13. Civic Action Program

A dump truck from Seventy-One off-loads cumshawed lumber at the village of Ly Tra to help the residents rebuild their village, torn apart by the VC.

materials the people outside the wire needed to rebuild what this conflict was blowing up.

Chaplain LT Billy Dennis, a Methodist minister in real life, was our non-denominational clergyman. He was in charge of the socio-political relations with the local communities—the man the village chiefs looked to for help with a new road, a new school, a new well for drinking water. Chaplain Dennis negotiated up the "chain of command" to get materials, supplies and volunteers, then cajoled and encouraged the villagers to help themselves, alongside our volunteer Seabees who pitched in on their time off to help with the construction. This was Civic Action.

Help Is on the Way

It was now May, and we hadn't been in 'Nam more than a few weeks when our reputation had already spread to the Vietnamese villages outside the wire. Our chaplain, LT Bill Dennis, received a call from LT Henry Brown from a nearby Army unit.

"The village of Ly Tra was razed last night by the VC," LT Brown reported. "Can you help?"

Chaplain Dennis said he'd see what he could do.

The next day, a truck filled with scrap lumber and three of our Seabees drove the 45 minutes out to Ly Tra. The truck backed up to what was left of the village center, and began off-loading old packing crates, used pallets, empty wooden boxes, scraps of 2 by

4s and plywood. To the 'Bees, this truckload of scrap lumber seemed insignificant, but to these homeless Vietnamese this was the chance to begin rebuilding their burned-out homes.

The Doctor Is In

One mid-morning, Chaplain Dennis and his assistant, "Raunchy" Reedy, YN3, climbed into a jeep, which was followed by a "cracker box" (a military ambulance) with Dr. LT Jerry Hubbell, MD, and dentist LT Sam Whisper, DMD, and their staff on board. They were all headed north on Highway One to the village of Khuong Long.

Once the medical team arrived, the corpsmen and dental tech set up makeshift clinics in the middle of the village. The doctors begin treating a line of villagers for a myriad

"How do you say, 'Where does it hurt?'" Doctor Hubbell asked for translation help from PN3 Bruce Kohfield (back to camera). Kohfield was one of the few Seabees to have completed the Vietnamese language school back in Davisville. Kohfield joined the MEDCAP field trips each week to help the doctors and corpsmen communicate with the villagers.

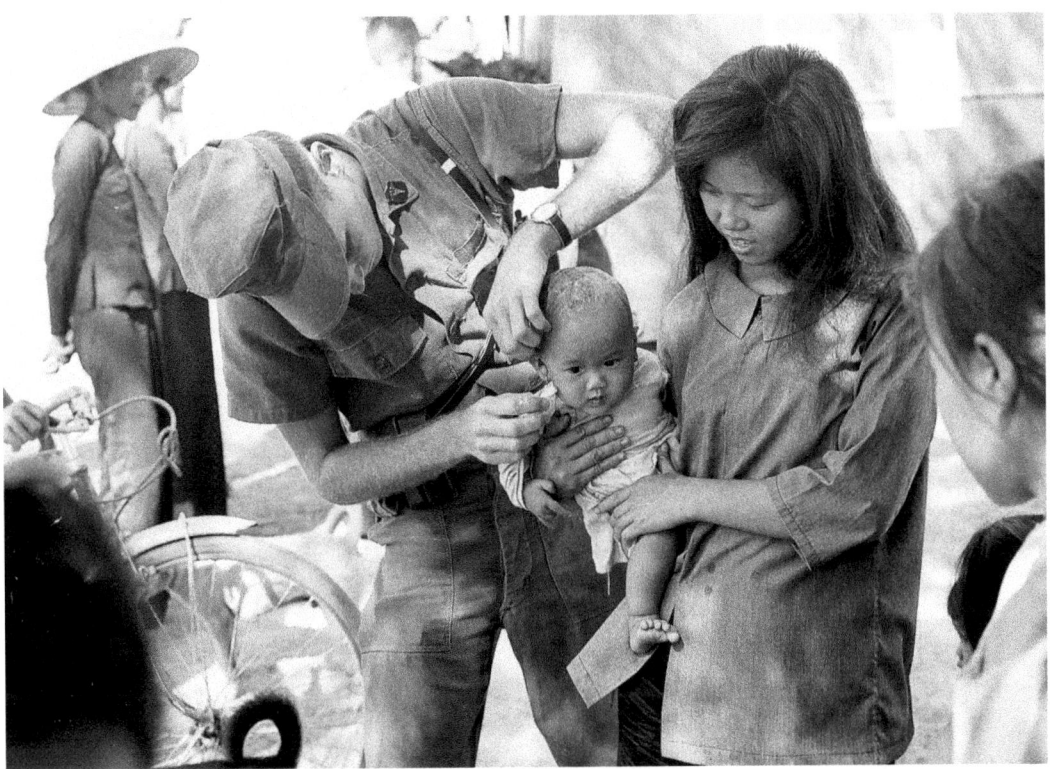

The gentle hands of Navy Corpsman Tim Findley, 22, from Fresno, California, clean the scalp infection of a 13-month-old baby. The young mother brought her child to Seventy-One's MED-CAP in the nearby village of Khuong Long each week.

of ills, sores, injuries, and complications common in these small underdeveloped villages. Most problems involved skin infections—inadequate sanitary conditions, heat and humidity complicate skin infections.

Corpsmen treated the kids for scrapes and passed out bars of soap, together with instructions—in broken Vietnamese and lots of hand-waving—on how to use the soap to prevent future infections. On the other side of the ambulance the dentist, LT Whisper, and his tech settled down to extracting teeth that were beyond repair.

"I'll make you a movie star!" joked the dentist—in a language his patients hardly understand. But his hands were skilled and reassuring as he went about his work. For many, this would be the first time they'd had relief from the constant pain in their jaw.

A Marketplace for Tan Ky

Tan Ky is a farming and fishing village along the bank of the Tra Bong River, 12 miles south of our base. The homes were mostly thatched huts, with a few constructed of cement block and stucco. The village was already a market center for trade between farmers, fishermen, and tradesmen who came down from Da Nang or up from Quang Ngai once a week with hardware and staples, cooking oil, canned goods and fabric. The village elders felt a new, more substantial marketplace would help the people in the surrounding hamlets. This market would stand as a symbol to the people themselves, but the Viet Cong weren't having it—they'd been stealing the villagers' building supplies, hindering progress, so the village chief asked the U.S. forces in nearby Chu Lai for help.

Enter John Murphy—a fifty-plus-year-old, former construction company owner back in the States. He'd re-enlisted in the Seabees as an IPO EO1, for only one purpose, to help the Vietnamese rebuild what the war was destroying. He got his wish. John lived in the villages where he worked, and I asked him to write about the experience.

John Murphy lived in Tan Ky at the construction site for a few weeks. He rarely returned to camp, so every few days a truck with building materials, supplies and food for Murphy arrived from our base. I would often join these trips to photograph the progress and talk Murphy into writing a story. His vivid reports, with my photographs, were in each month's newspaper.

A few of our 'Bees would volunteer to spend a Sunday at Tan Ky helping Murphy, but it was the Vietnamese villagers who were Murphy's regular crew. Old women shoveled sand, gravel, and cement into an ancient concrete mixer, then carted the wet

John Murphy, a first class EO, owned his own construction company back in the States, but signed up with the Seabees specifically to help the Vietnamese rebuild what the war was tearing down. He got his wish.

mix to the foundation in pails. The kids pitched in, carting water in pails from the well to the site. The market took weeks to complete, with a concrete floor, a thatched roof, and no walls.

As the project neared completion, Tuffy Lake, from Engineering, and I drove out to see Murphy at the market. As we approached, we saw Murphy jump up, grab his pump action shotgun and run toward the jeep. "Don't stop, just turn 'round, and get me the hell out of here!" he shouted. "The VC are gunning for me," he said as he dove into the back of the jeep. "Now get out of here, fast!" Murphy had worn out his welcome with the local VC commander.

I never did learn if the market was completed. Murphy moved on to another Civic Action project, closer to the base.

A Building Project in Chu Lai Village

Chaplain Dennis got Murphy involved in a Catholic church building project, in the village of Chu Lai, just outside the perimeter wire. It would mean building, from scratch, a Catholic church, a school and an orphanage. Chaplain Dennis was in charge of the project, but it was Murphy who did the work on site. My off-base correspondent wrote a short essay on this Civic Action project, from his personal perspective.

Dick Stapleman, EO3, struggles to shoulder two pails of water for the cement mixer.

Opposite: Murphy worked right alongside Tam Ky villagers preparing the forms for the concrete flooring for the new market.

Women are the constant workers on the market project—their men-folk are in the fields or aboard their fishing sampans. This "tamper" is common to all foundation construction, but this one was made, and is manned, by Vietnamese.

It took almost two months to prepare the market site for laying down the concrete foundation. Up to 25 volunteer villagers now work beside the "one American" to better their lives and those of the community. Is there a language barrier? "Who talks?" says Murphy, "we do a lot of laughing though."

CIVIC ACTION

One American Is A Beginning

PHOTOS and STORY by Dave Lyman

TAN HY, SOUTH VIETNAM—The villagers of Tan Hy and the surrounding hamlets had a problem on their hands. The Army unit that was supporting the construction of their small market had moved out.

The village chief and the Army Civic Action Officer from TASK FORCE OREGON turned up at a nearby Seabee camp looking for help. Chaplain Billy Dennis and his civic action coordinator, John Murphy, from MCB 71 were engaged in the completion of a school and orphanage in Chu Lai, but they'd give it a try.

In mid-July, Murphy began traveling the ten miles to Tan Hy, crossing the Song Tra Bong (river) by ferry, twice each day.

The market, planned by the villagers, would consist of a 5,000 square-foot concrete foundation with five or six small tin-roofed buildings, and most importantly, a concrete gate facing the road.

It took over five weeks to haul in the hand-crushed rock and hand-dug laterite for the foundation. American construction equipment was almost never seen. Murphy, and the few volunteer Seabees that accompanied him, worked with Vietnamese tools, using their materials and their methods. Murphy was a catalyst; his presence brought out the villagers and gave them confidence and support.

The project is not an important one to the Americans—to a newer and better Vietnam it is but a miniscule part. BUT it is important to the thousand fishermen, farmers, and small businessmen on the south side of the Song Tra Bong (river), AND it is important to one American, and one American is a beginning.

John Murphy, is a cantankerous old codger. If it wasn't for his lack of a New England twang, he'd pass for a full-blooded Yankee. But Murphy has a job to do, and as he sees it, there is but one way to do that job—his way.

And he should know. No other American in the area has won the respect, admiration, and trust of the Vietnamese people as has Murphy. He's not a legend—the Seabees in his own camp hardly know what he's doing in the nearby village within sound of daily small arms fire—but to his Vietnamese fellow workers he's "number ONE."

Murphy's just doing a job he feels needs being done AND he's getting it done despite the Viet Cong threats on his life.

"Ooops, not much water left." Murphy holds the water-barrel while one of his younger—and smaller—fellow workers gets down to "the last drop". Water for the concrete foundation is carried, shoulder-wise by elderly women, from a well half-a-mile away.

A couple of the boys from Tan Hy, pile scrap lumber, ready for foundation forms. None of the lumber, cement or other building materials have been missing from the site. The villagers value this project too much to make free with the materials.

Vietnamese construction methods are at first a bit strange to American Seabees. Mixing concrete, for instance, is done on the ground, at the spot where it will be used. Very little water is used—the mix takes 5-years to cure—but the results are surprisingly good.

Wearing a camouflage hat he bought from the villagers, John Murphy works side-by-side with the villagers. He's not a boss nor supervisor—just their friend. Murphy is a veteran of this type of people-to-people work; he served as a civilian advisor in under-developed nations in Central America.

The story of the Tam Ky market as it appeared in the September 1967 edition of *The Transit*.

Top: Compare Stapleman's struggle with these two kids, not yet 10 and a quarter the size of the Seabee, who cart water all day long. *Bottom:* Time for a rest. No sooner is EO1 Murphy seated than he's pestered by kids.

The Noise Understanding Makes
by John Murphy, EO1

A scolding female voice cuts through the noisy racket being made by the one-lunger concrete mixer. The Seabee operating machine knows instinctively what he did wrong. He spilled some of the precious water being carted in 10 gallon buckets by this tiny Vietnamese woman from the well to the construction site. The two are part of the team building an orphanage, Catholic church and a school in the village Chu Lai, just outside the perimeter of the military complex.

Part of a small group volunteers from Seventy-One, this lone Seabee is quick to understand the Vietnamese worker's good-natured impatience. Half an hour earlier, he was carrying water while the woman was shoveling sand into the mixer in 130° heat.

A sheepish, apologetic grin makes the bridge needed to keep the water coming. The mixer continues to clatter, while another "Georgia Buggy" (two-wheeled wheel-barrow) loads up with concrete and heads towards the concrete block school foundation, pulled by a Seabee and a young Vietnamese boy.

Understanding is a two-way street in a place like Chu Lai village, where the residents are surrounded by the sounds and sights of a big-time war. Round-the-clock, war planes roar in and out of the airstrip, the thump-thump of Huey blades swatting the hot tropical air overhead, the sound of heavy artillery hammering away at invisible targets in the mountains. Combat infantry patrols slog through the sandy village streets, through the schoolyard, searching for the latest VC terrorists reported to be in the area.

When the civic action functions properly, there's little that separates the Americans and the Vietnamese. The risks and burdens are shared, at first because the people involved are depending on one another. Acceptance of this condition quickly builds a desire to share viewpoints. The process of developing understanding and friendship has been launched, an effective pacification program moves forward.

When the project was completed, there was a ceremony and Murphy was presented with a gift from the village. Then, it was off to his next Civic Action project.

CHAPTER 14

Putting the Pieces Together

Standing in the shade of a pallet of plywood, I photographed two Seabee BUs (Builders) work without saying much. They were putting together a barracks. LCDR Powers and EA1 Tuffy Lake were nearby chatting with the chief running the job site. I was making the rounds of job sites photographing and gathering stories for the newspaper.

All summer, I'd been watching these builders and steel workers from Charlie and Delta companies create vertical projects—construction that went up. Teams from Alpha and Bravo companies worked with heavy equipment on horizontal projects: roads, runways, building foundations. As the men worked, they joked with and razzed each other.

"Hey! Spider Legs! Get that fat arse of yours over here. I need a hand with this siding," shouted one 'Bee to another.

"Keep your pecker in your pants, Fart Face," came the reply. Foul language is common in the Navy. I suppose it is in all the other services as well.

These jobs were routine to these men, something they could do in their sleep, while spinning yarns of conquests with high school cheerleaders, cars they'd rebuilt, bar fights, money made and lost. There was a lot of harmless name calling, as 2 by 4s, boards and sheets of plywood were cut, handed up and nailed into place. The Seabees got to put together things, real things, like metal Quonset huts and stick-built barracks. They laid down AM-2 aluminum slab matting to create runways, mixed and poured concrete for foundations, laid down asphalt roads. They sweated, grunted, and laughed all day long. They got their hands dirty. They did physical things. At the end of the day they'd be exhausted, but they had the satisfaction of having built something.

The fighting units out in the hills didn't get to share that same feeling of accomplishment—of completion. The Marines would secure a mountaintop or village and move on; the VC just crept back in when the coast was clear. This was not your traditional war (like World War II)—there was no real "front line" to advance.

I was envious of these construction workers and their camaraderie, their ability to do physical work as part of a team, to carry on a conversation about anything but the job itself.

As a kid I did get to put physical things together. I built a sailboat with my father and learned about "measure twice, cut once," how to hit a nail squarely with a hammer and not bend it over, how to toenail, drill, screw, plumb, and square a frame. I put together model airplanes, boats and ships, using strips of balsa wood, tissue paper, and model airplane dope—yes, dope. Small bottles of vibrantly colored liquid lacquer. A kid could get high painting his model. In my high school days, I put together HeathKit electronics kits that came in a box full of resistors, capacitors, diodes, vacuum tubes, sockets, terminal strips, transformers and bits of colored wire; oh yes, and a booklet of instructions on how to assemble the parts into a shortwave radio, FM radio, or 100-watt amplifier for record hops at the gym.

For me, putting stuff together was a solitary occupation, well suited for a loner like me. This new role in which I found myself, the unit's journalist, fit me perfectly. I was putting ideas and pictures together to build a story. Each month, I joined convoys, conducted interviews with officers, organized photo ops, and tagged along with the Operations and Engineering teams in the field to collect images and stories. My notes were turned into drafts, to be re-written perhaps half a dozen times before I'd show them to LTJG Smith, the PAO (Public Affairs Officer). He'd make corrections and suggestions, or tell me to run the story by the XO for final approval.

Each issue of *The Transit* had a photographic feature on the centerfold, while other pages carried photos and stories about individual projects, events on base, individual Seabees getting promoted, signing up for another hitch, an officer being advanced. The work our outfit was doing in the countryside with the local Vietnamese people got a page or two in every issue.

Putting things together. Construction men (CM) Dumphy and Baskin nail pieces of corrugated steel skin over a 2 by 4 frame on an ARVN barracks.

Fortunately, I didn't have to write or photograph everything that appeared in *The Transit*—the CO, XO and the chaplain each wrote a column for page 2. John Murphy, the EO1 who lived out in the villages, wrote a monthly article about what that was like. LTJG Tony Smith wrote the occasional piece, and Wally Skop, YO3, better known as Scuzzy Skop, wrote a monthly sports column. The two Navy photographers with whom I shared the darkroom contributed photos as well.

My role as editor also involved the paper's design and layout—how the publication "looked." I'd built a tilted layout table in my office onto which I pinned up layout sheets. On these, I sketched in where I might place photographs, headlines, text blocks, graphs, and cartoons to tell the battalion's story. As the graphic designer as well, I worked with column widths, type styles, point size, leading between the lines, justified or ragged right, boldface, italic or regular. Putting a page together on my layout table was as much fun as was any other part of my job. I also got to see, graphically, where there were holes in my coverage. A few stories needed to be shortened or lengthened, I needed to include a story on C Company, something about the detachments in Quang Ngai.

Once the texts had been reviewed and approved by the XO, it was off to the MACV Press Office in Da Nang to get the major there to approve what was to be published. Then up to Tokyo for a few days to work at *Stars and Stripes'* letterpress shop to get the paper set in hot lead and printed.

It took me a day or so to get to Tokyo, a few days to set type and get *The Transit* printed, then a day or so to get back, leaving only three weeks back in Vietnam to assemble enough interesting material for the next issue. *Stars and Stripes* printed six of our monthly newspapers, and our print schedule was set in stone. I had a deadline I could not miss. Talk about adding stress to living and working in the war zone!

Oh, well, that's the life I wanted. Be careful what you wish for.

I'm Off to Japan

"How long this time, Lyman?" LTJG Smith asked. As H Company's OIC, he was my boss. It was he who had to authorize my TAD (Temporary Additional Duty) orders to Tokyo.

"Six days, sir."

"Explain that to me again." Smith had been taking some flak from some of the officers for the fact I was the only man in the outfit to get out of Vietnam for a few days each month.

"It takes a day to get to Da Nang and get MACV to approve the pictures and text, sir. Then a walk to the airport and wait for the next plane headed to Japan, sir. By the time I reach Japan, it's been 24 to 36 hours."

"Yes?"

"It takes all day to get into Tokyo, check into quarters, and register with the Unit Publication office. It takes three days to set type and wait for press time to print. Then, a day or two to get back here, sir."

"That's six, or is it seven days, Lyman?" he exclaimed.

"You've always approved open-ended orders, sir. You know what it's like." LTJG Smith had joined me on my first trip to Tokyo—it took an officer to negotiate arrangements with *Stars and Stripes* for the printing of our monthly.

"All right ... open-ended then. Write 'em up."

"Right here, sir. Already made out. Ready for your signature." I handed over my orders, all filled in, with permission to wear civilian duds, once out of Vietnam. I'd learned how to "cut orders" while in the personnel office on the carrier I had served on just a year ago. I could have signed them myself.

My Black Market Trip

With photos, stories and a rough layout of the newspaper approved by the XO, civilian clothes packed, order signed, I was still anxious about getting it all together. A day or so before I was to depart, a few of the Seabees would come by my office with hundreds of dollars and a shopping list of items they wanted me to bring back. I could hardly refuse—I was leaving the war zone for a week; they weren't. It was the least I could do for my mates. They wanted cameras, tape recorders, radios, binoculars, watches, kimonos for their girlfriends, a Japanese hand-painted partition to be sent home to their moms. Officers came by with requests. I was running a black market, smuggling in equipment the guys could not get at the base PX, or even in Da Nang. Finally, cash and requests gathered, I was on my way. It was a grueling, 24-hour trip getting to Japan.

With a small suitcase of personal items and my briefcase full of photos and stories, I caught a jeep or personnel carrier up to the division HQ heliport, to await a Huey heading to Da Nang. It could take an hour, or half the day, sitting in the shade of the flight shack.

Once aboard, it was a 45-minute flight up to Da Nang. Flying up at 1,000 feet, the temperature dropped 10 degrees, a welcome relief. We flew along the beach, passing over villages, past China Beach, past Marble Mountain to land at a Marine base at Monkey Mountain, at the entrance to Da Nang Harbor. I'd hitchhike into Da Nang to be dropped off at the MACV Press Office, a former villa near the harbor. Here I waited to see the Marine major who would read over my stories, look at my images and stamp them "approved for publication." Occasionally something I'd written, or something visible in a photograph, would bring a scowl to the major's face. "This won't pass," he'd say, running his pen through the text. He was the military censor, pointing out that I could not show the dead, ours or theirs, or damaged equipment or facilities.

With my text and images approved, I left the MACV HQ for an hour's walk to the airport. Flying out of country, I could not carry my sidearm, so walking alone, unarmed, through this city gave me a feeling of vulnerability. I felt naked. But nothing ever happened, and I got to experience once again the Vietnam and the Vietnamese that we Americans were supposed to be fighting for.

As I've said, we servicemen knew little of why we were here, or what we were fighting for. It was enough, some of us believed, that our government had asked us, or, in the case of the draftees, ordered us, to go and kill the enemy. We didn't even need to know who they were, or why they were fighting us.

The Air Force terminal was an old, open hanger left over from the French colony days. There was a counter to register for a flight and check your luggage. Crude benches filled what I gathered was the waiting area. Dozens of military guys were lounging about, waiting for a flight to the States or to another base in-country. A Vietnamese family ran a makeshift canteen, a snack counter, just outside, where I could buy a Coke and a French baguette.

I registered for a flight to Japan, then camped out in the open-air waiting area to sit and read and wait. The wait could be a few hours or a full day. The adjacent men's room was a gallery of artful graffiti rendered in large Magic Markers on the walls, the doors to the stalls, on the windows, the mirror over the sink, the sink itself. These imaginative graphics, cartoons and limericks expressed what we all felt—trapped in this foreign land few of us cared for, fighting a war few of us believed in.

When my name was called I followed a crew chief out to his plane. It could be a C-130 Hercules prop, or a C-141 cargo jet or a commercial charter with real "stews," or female flight attendants. The flight up to Yokota Air Base in Japan took all night on the C-130, or just five hours on the C-141.

Flying in a military aircraft was not pleasant—it was noisy and cold and there were no creature comforts, no reading material, no inflight services, and just the bare minimum for "facilities." The seats were rudimentary web affairs that didn't recline and were nearly impossible to sleep on.

I was a wreck when I arrived in Japan.

How to Build a Newspaper

I arrived in Japan after an all-night flight, to face another experience altogether. Culture shock! The air base at Yokota was huge, a city by itself. But once through the gate and on the train into Tokyo, I was in another world. The countryside was flat, a mixture of small farms, some no larger than your backyard; hamlets, small commercial villages, residences, all small and all very neat and tidy. Japan was clean and orderly in contrast to Vietnam, and even to the States. The buildings began to grow in height as we neared and entered the outskirts of the city. Tokyo itself was huge, with skyscrapers, heavy traffic and people—lots of people.

The taxi from the train station dropped me at the military barracks in the Roppongi section of Tokyo. There, a three-story hotel for servicemen was adjacent to the *Stars and Stripes* building. I checked in, found my room, dumped my stuff and, groggy from an all-night flight, walked over to the *Stars and Stripes* building. This was a five-story building containing the editorial department, the make-up floor, engraving labs and the presses. On the top floor was a restaurant, bar and nightclub. I checked in with the Unit Publication Office on the third floor and found my assigned space. They were expecting me, as my unit's newspaper was scheduled for printing in just four days.

Stars and Stripes was a bit more formal than working at Misty's print shop in Somerville, where I learned typesetting and page mark-up. The "make-up" room was noisy and smelled of hot lead and oil. Military editors, some in uniform, others in civvies, like me, were working at the make-up tables. A dozen large typesetting Linotype machines clattered away, operated by non–English-speaking Japanese technicians. These people were turning out a large daily newspaper for the Pacific Command. The Unit Publication prep room, off to one side, was lined with make-up counters and tables. It was here the Army and Air Force editors worked on their respective publications. There could be four of us editors working at a time, each with a table on which we assembled our pages in lead type. This method of setting lines of type in molten lead had been around for 150 years.

This entire process took a few days. First, my typewritten pages of text, each marked with specifications as to type font, point size, and column width in picas was sent to the Japanese typesetters. These chaps set my prose in lead slugs on the Linotype—each slug, a line of text. I'd collect a pan or galley of a column of slugs, slide the slugs into a page frame on my work table. Here I would arrange the type into columns, text blocks, leaving a blank space for the pictures. Headlines had to written and marked up as to typeface and point size, to fit the text block. These headlines were set on a Ludlow machine from a hand assembled matrix. Photographs were sent to the process camera room, where my 8 × 10 photographs were reduced in size and turned into a screened negative. These would be added to the text page negatives in the Stripping Department. These composite negatives were then exposed to sensitized plates in a carbon-arc plate maker, then wrapped on the drums of the Goss Web Press to print the newspaper.

1943   U.S. NAVAL MOBILE CONSTRUCTION BATTALION 71   1966

Vol. I No. 2 — (Family Gram) THE TRANSIT June 1, 1967

Seventy-Oners
"CAN DO"—AND DID!

Wade, a Seabee heavy-equipment driver with MCB 71, revved up the huge scraper and slipped into low-low gear, pulling out of the project area and back on to the road. The engine screamed as the driver began going through the 12 gears, getting the mammoth piece of earth-moving equipment up to speed—heading back into the night. With no springs or shock absorbers the twenty foot high earth-mover lurched down the dirt road, dust and gravel streaming off the huge flotation tires.

The twenty year old driver with a combat helmet and flack-jacket on, with a service rifle on the seat beside him, sped into the night, the lights on his scraper stabbing through the dust of the scraper ahead.

Time was short, the earth movers had been shuttling back and forth for five days—24 hours a day. The giant thundered over the pot-hole filled road. The driver gripped the wheel as he lurched into the ditch to pass another scraper returning to the work site. He slipped into low range and the MRS scraper's diesel screamed as he lumbered out of the ditch and further up the road. Out through a hole in the barbwire perimeter, past the sentry on guard, out into open country. The driver opened up his rig—the engine whinning as he sped through the night. Over on the right three flares hung in the black sky, casting their red light over the hilly countryside. The earth-mover screamed along. A mile outside the protective perimeter, in enemy country, the driver slowed his rig and turned off the road into a laterite pit, past a heavily armed sentry who waved him by. The pit was a mass of organized activity. Dozers were (Continued on Page 4)

The Seabees of Seventy-One move in. The "71" shield, with crane and anchor, that came out of the Pacific with the original battalion is put in place by two of "C" Company's carpenters, Charles Liss and Clay Henderson. The battalion arrived aboard nine Air Force C-141's to replace fellow Seabee battalion, MCB 71, at Camp Shields on the beach of the South China Sea on April 10, 1967.
(Navy Photo by Phi Canupp)

A Marine A-4 soars skyward as Steel Workers from Charlie Company lay down steel matting at the Helo Pad site.

COMCBLANT Visits Chu Lai Seabees

Captain Greer A. Busbee, Jr., Commander of the Seabees of the Atlantic Fleet completed a tour of his battalions in Vietnam recently, and in doing so paid a visit to his Davisville based unit, MCB 71.

Following visits to Dong Ha, Phu Bai and Danang based battalions the Commodore boarded an Army "Huey" for the twenty minute hop, south, to Chu Lai and MCB Seventy-One, his newest "in-country" battalion. His prime reason for visiting the Chu Lai area was to check on the progress of his battalion, and if they were being amply supported in their work assignments. One other reason for his trip through Vietnam was a sentimental re-visit to the areas he controlled as Director of Construction in northern Vietnam—I Corps Area under OICC (Officer in Charge of Construction).

Many of the projects visited by the Commodore during his stay with MCB 71 were initiated under his administration this past year, before he was evacuated from Danang with a Purple-Heart following a Viet Cong mortar attack. The incident was followed by his re-assignment as Commander of the Atlantic Seabees homeported at Davisville, Rhode Island.

Captain Busbee also toured the project sites taken over by MCB 71 — these included the rock crushing facilities, the quarry, airstrip, Pascoe hangars and the tank farm, to mention a few.

He departed Chu Lai for Danang and the 30th NCB, and from there went on to Saigon where he attended the change of command ceremonies for Rear Admiral Vech, who re- (Continued on Page 6)

Navy Captain, Greer A. Busbee, COMCBLANT departs Army Huey at Chu Lai.

Seabee Sees VC Attack

CHU LAI—At the LST loading ramp in Chu Lai it was a warm still summer night.

A twenty-year-old Seabee, Hickey Sarlo from Reno, Nevada, sat on the tail-gate of his "six-by" waiting for yard workers to cart building materials from the cavernous hole of the LST to his truck. His eyes wandered across the silent water of the river—over to the dark island of Long Thanh Dong.

Unknown to them, unknown to the 60,000 American servicemen stationed on the sands of Chu Lai, Victor Charlie had put a handful of men ashore on that small island—men who had one purpose — destroy as much property and life as possible with the mortars they carried with them.

Beside Mickey, smoking a cigarette, sat his buddy, Dave Robinson, 20, from Sparta, Tenn., off duty now, but who had tagged along to keep Mickey company during his all night hauling between the sand-ramp and Mobile Construction Battalion 71's camp five miles south.

It was Saturday morning — the fork-lift trucks growled and snorted inside the huge LST's hole as they carried the cargo to Mickey's waiting truck. Mickey and Dave sat and waited.

The first Viet Cong mortar round landed between the two outside LSTs—30 yards from the two startled Seabees. The explosion, muffled by the water, snapped them out of their early morning daze. The second and third rounds exploded close to the outside LST — showering them with spray—the two Seabees were now on the run, heading for the yawning doors of the LST. They dove through the door huge cargo doors as the fourth round exploded on the ship's super-structure, shaking the hull and resounding throughout the cargo hole. That same explosion fatally wounded a Filipino Chief who was asleep on the cargo deck above. One of the ship's officers came running to the loading doors where the two Seabees, a few sailors and two Marines had taken cover, yelling for someone to call for medical aid and an ambulance. Mickey, with mortar rounds still showering down around the sand-ramp and over the nearby Seabee base of MCB 8, ran to the yard phone shack and passed the word to the startled operator, " . . . get an ambulance down to the sand-ramp—and damn quick."

The Viet Cong still were pouring mortar shells into the naval facility when Mickey pelted back to the cover of the LST. He found a Filipino sailor and two Marines carrying the wounded Chief down to the loading ramp. Still panting, Mickey helped the three carry the Chief to a nearby pick-up truck.

The VC had dropped over 30 rounds of 82mm mortars on the buildings and LSTs at the Naval Support Activity and MCB 8's camp on Rose Mary Point. The early morning attack ended 20 minutes after Mickey had witnessed the first round explode- (Continued on Page 6)

The front page of the June 1967 edition of *The Transit*.

I'd spend all morning and afternoon in the make-up room designing and assembling pages, fitting text blocks, and writing headlines and captions for the photographs. I'd get a page pretty much together and pull a wet proof. This involved inking the page of lead slugs then rolling a damp sheet of heavy paper onto the page. This would allow me to see what the layout looked like. I'd study the proof. What was missing? How could I create a better eye flow as readers scanned a page? I'd fine-tune the layouts, rewrite captions, re-set headlines and sub-heads, make adjustments, then pull another wet proof.

Adjacent to the make-up room was a small editor's room, with a long counter on which sat half a dozen typewriters. It was here editors wrote headlines, captions and additional stories.

With headlines, sub-heads and text in place, I'd pull another wet proof and pass it to the proofreaders—a team of U.S. servicemen's wives stationed in Tokyo—who would read and mark up my proof, correcting misspellings and typos. The proofs then went back out to the Japanese typesetters, and corrections were made, line by line, slug by slug. When I got the corrected slugs and the marked-up proof, I set about replacing each slug with the corrected one.

Being dyslexic, I found it quite easy to read the words on the lead slugs, which were upside down and backward. But having dyslexia had another effect. My typing was as bad or worse than my spelling. The ladies in proofreading called me in and lectured me about my sloppy work and typing errors. "You can't expect these Japanese typesetters to correct your typos. They set just what they see. You mistyped 'the' as 'teh' so they set 'teh.' We can't keep sending corrected proofs back due your sloppy work."

I saw their point, so the ladies and I came up with a plan. They would proofread my text *before* it went to typesetting. If need be, I'd re-type an entire page, this time being careful. That solved the problem, but I still had the Army officer in charge to deal with. Halfway through our deployment, the colonel called me in and dressed me down for sloppy, unprofessional and un-military-like work. He threatened: "This will be the last issue of *The Transit* we will print."

I had an ace in the hole. I handed the colonel a letter of commendation from the Department of Defense's Armed Forces Information School at Fort Meade, Maryland. *The Transit* had been awarded the "Best Small Unit Monthly Publication in the Service," citing design, use of photography and selection of stories and editorial content. I told him the ladies and I had come to an agreement on how to clean up my sloppy text. We got to print at the *S&S* for the rest of our deployment. *The Transit* was awarded the "Best in Service" for the two quarters we were in-country.

A Stars and Stripes *Correspondent*

On my first visit to *S&S*, I made a point to introduce myself to the editors of the daily newspaper—guys like me, petty officers and sergeants, located on the floor below typesetting. They were hungry for stories and photographs from Vietnam. After work, they would buy me beers in the bar on the top floor of the building, and drill me on what it was like in-country. On subsequent trips to Tokyo I would bring a stack of photographs and a story or two for them to consider. There was not a month that I didn't have a page or two in the daily newspaper.

The story about the Tra Bong River search, the one where I was told to "shoot pictures

Stars and Stripes carried a two-page spread with my photos and story of our drivers searching the Tra Bong River bottom.

and leave the real shooting to the pros," was a two-page spread. The road mine incident was nearly a full page, and there were others.

Having my work in S&S was a great ego boost. I got to meet and chat with the editors of other military publications as well as the boys downstairs in the editorial newsroom, who kept buying me beers.

After 3,000 copies of *The Transit* were printed, they were bundled, bound and packed on a pallet, then driven to the airport for a flight to Saigon, then up to Chu Lai.

Getting myself back to Chu Lai was often more difficult than getting the papers there. It was even more difficult than getting to Japan was.

Exploring Japanese Culture

By 3 o'clock in the afternoon, my mind was fried. I couldn't see straight from all the detailed work of making line corrections, spacing headlines, and moving chunks of lead around.

I'd knock off work, walk to the Roppongi subway station a block away, and take the train into downtown Tokyo to roam the Ginza—Tokyo's version of Times Square. Tokyo was bigger than Manhattan, cleaner, and a great deal more polite. When you hailed a taxi, the passenger door automatically opened for you, then closed as you sat down. Hostesses at the foot of the escalators in the department stores wiped down the moving handrails, bowed, avoided eye contact as they greeted you.

Spending a few hours in this brilliantly lit shopping district was enough to clear my mind. The Ginza is a visual extravaganza. Advertising signs flashing colored lights covered the entire sides of skyscrapers. The streets were full of taxies, mopeds and delivery trucks. The sidewalks were packed. It was easy to spot another American, even two blocks ahead—they stood head and shoulders above the sea of Japanese people. There were department stores, electronics and camera stores, bars, restaurants, nightclubs and showrooms for flashy cars, motorcycles and furniture. I'd window shop, visit my favorite camera store, stop in at the large Sapporo Beer Hall for a huge mug of beer.

At the bar, I might meet a Tokyo businessman or young executive. If they spoke any English at all, we'd strike up a conversation and I'd learn a bit more of life in Japan. The Japanese were eager to practice their English on us American servicemen.

"I notice that no one will cross the street unless the pedestrian light is green," I observed.

"Of course not. It is not done," the nicely dressed elderly businessman replied.

"But there is no traffic, in any direction," I noted.

"Yes, but it is still not permitted to cross." Japanese were certainly law-abiding.

"Most Americans would say, 'screw this,' and simply jaywalk."

"What is jaywalk?"

"It's a term that goes way back to the horse and buggy days, when wagon drivers went down the wrong side of the road. Now it refers to people who cross a street outside the designated crosswalks, or against the pedestrian light."

"So, people who jaywalk have no regard for the laws?"

"Well, true, but it's not a big law. I suppose you could get a ticket, if caught. But, if there is no traffic coming, almost everyone waiting will simply walk across the intersection, no matter what the light says."

"We would never do that. It would be too embarrassing." He should see Vietnamese pedestrians negotiate the traffic in Saigon, I mused. It was like taking your life in your hands, but everyone always made it across.

"Embarrassing? I don't think Americans think that way."

"To disobey the law would bring shame to our ancestors."

"Hell, we applaud anyone who is brave enough, takes a chance, even bending the rules a little."

"We have a saying in Japan, 'The tallest grass gets cut first.'"

"You mean, people in Japan do not want to stand out? Americans are eager to stand out. We go out of our way to stand out."

Conversations like this were enlightening, illustrating the difference between Asians and Americans. America is a place where you can be different, stand out, and people will help you succeed. Being creative, innovative, thinking outside of the box requires the ability to make mistakes, screw up, and stumble on your way to discovering something new. Americans are able to do this.

My beer finished and conversation ended, I'd wander the back alleys of Tokyo with my camera. There were erotic clubs with women who would give you a hand job at the bar, strip joints, seedy movie theaters, and pachinko parlors—noisy places where young Japanese men stood at vertical machines, a cross between pinball and a slot machine, for hours. I'd watch from outside on the street through the large windows. The point of the game, I gathered, was to maneuver small ball bearings as they fell

Narrow alleys in Tokyo could lead to more adventures and discoveries.

Young male executives in suits stand at vertical pinball machines in pachinko parlors. They would be entranced for hours, watching ball bearings bounce down the studded face of the machines.

down a nail-studded wall, bouncing around; if enough of them fell into a small hole, you won!

I'd look for a place to have dinner. Fortunately for me, the restaurants displayed waxed models of each dish they served—colorful and mouth-watering, in a window with labels that gave the name, price and a number. This made it easy for a *gaijin* like me to simply order by number. I got to sample a lot of Japanese food, which was far healthier than what I was getting from the military. I'd sit at one of the long tables—family style we'd call it—jammed in among the locals. I'd watch young Japanese men and women, many my age, using chopsticks, shoveling bowls of rice, fish, vegetables, tofu and chicken into their mouths. As they rose to leave, there would be a lot of bowing to each other, palms clasped before them. There was lots of smiling and politeness.

Tokyo had movie theaters as large as those at home. The marquee above the entrances were huge, advertising the latest films from the West. I got to watch James Bond in *You Only Live Twice*; Julie Andrews as *Thoroughly Modern Millie*; Raquel Welch in *Fathom* and Michelangelo Antonioni's film, *Blow Up*. The actor David Hemmings plays the part of a British fashion photographer who inadvertently photographs a murder in the park. The mystery was over-shadowed by one erotic sequence of Hemmings photographing two young female nude models romping around in his studio on rolls of backdrop paper. I saw the movie twice and was so inspired I went out and bought a Bronica, a Japanese knock-off of the Hassleblad Hemmings used in the film.

A movie theater in Tokyo, showing the 1967 James Bond film, *You Only Live Twice.*

My Japanese Guide

I was nursing a half-gallon of beer one afternoon in the Sapporo Beer Hall on the Ginza. Two young ladies walked in and looked around. One was a tall American blonde and the other a much shorter black-haired Japanese lass. They appeared to be looking for a place to sit. I was the only American there, so stood up and waved. They smiled and joined me. Martha, the American, was from California, in Tokyo to teach English at a local school. All she had to do, I learned, was to speak English (American English, to be precise) with her students. Takiko, her Japanese friend, worked for a Tokyo newspaper. We sat and talked about our lives. Takiko was the first Japanese person with whom I'd ever conversed. Her English was perfect, with just a trace of a Japanese accent. The girls seemed fascinated with my stories of living and working in Vietnam.

I shared dinner with the two women a few more times that trip, and felt I had made the first friend in a foreign country with whom I could communicate. When I returned the next month, I called Takiko. We met for breakfast one morning near the *Stars and Stripes* building. I was eager to see and learn about Japan and its culture. Being Japanese, Takiko was naturally eager to please. My first lesson came as I paid the bill. As we were about to leave the restaurant, suddenly, I stumbled, lost my balance and fell against Takiko. What was happening to me? I wasn't drunk, was I sick? Takiko helped me up and laughed. "That was just a small earthquake."

"What?"

"An earthquake. We get them all the time." In that moment, the floor under me, the entire world, seemed to change. I felt as if I was walking on a large bowl of Jello. The quake lasted less than a minute but left a lasting impression on me, just how fluid the earth's crust is. The quake stopped and I regained my balance, shaken but not stirred.

On the weekend, Takiko, her boyfriend and I visited temples, shrines, parks, the Asakusa district and the shopping district in Shinjuku. Her boyfriend was a reporter for the same daily newspaper as Takiko. The three of us visited their editorial offices one afternoon and I got to see the typewriters and typesetting machines they used. The Japanese, I learned, have three forms of written language—*Katakana* and *hiragana*, then the Chinese *Kanji* ideograms. The first two use simple brushstrokes to represent a phonetic alphabet; their spoken language. There are 46 characters in each alphabet. The other, *Kanji*, is made up of Chinese characters, more complex, multi-stroke ink-brush ideograms, which represent a thought or concept.

"To graduate high school, we have to know 1,200 ideograms," the reporter told me. The typewriters, lager than ours, had both sets of characters, on a cylinder. Since one language, my native English, was a struggle for me, I was impressed with the command of language my two friends possessed. They basically knew four languages, English included.

My new friends and I talked about many subjects, including religion. Takiko told me there are two religions in Japan, Shinto and Buddhism. "They are not religions as perhaps you know in the West," she explained. "They are ... more like traditions, the way we honor our ancestors, celebrate events in the lives of our families. You know, how we express our place in the natural world."

At the Benzaiten shrine, the stone basin is a "tsukubai," a public sink with natural running water, used for washing or purification, *misogi*, a common ritual before entering a shrine. This shrine is located in Tokyo's Inokashira Park and is devoted to everything that flows—including knowledge, water and music. This shrine was adapted from the Hindu goddess known as Saraswati and is recognized in both the Buddhist and Shinto traditions.

"Which one would you consider is your way?" I asked.

"My family, we honor both. We celebrate the more joyous events in Shinto traditions. Buddhism is the way for more profound events."

Seemed like a sensible approach to me. I was still trying to define what I believed in; it wasn't going to be any of the organized religions, or some free-form hippie spirituality. My grandfather was a Baptist minister, but I wasn't having any of that Bible-thumping rhetoric. I'd been on a perpetual search for something to believe in since I realized angels didn't reside in the clouds as I'd been told. I'd flown over the clouds and didn't see any. Someone had been lying to me.

I joined Takiko, her boyfriend and a few of their friends one evening for what we'd call a "pub crawl." While the Japanese outdid me with their mastery of language, theirs and mine, I could out-drink them.

On my last trip to Tokyo, Takiko invited me to her home in the suburbs for dinner one evening. There, I met her mother and father—neither of whom spoke English, so Takiko translated. Her father was a conservative businessman, her mother a homemaker. I stumbled through the customs, removing my shoes upon entering, bowing, sitting on the floor for dinner and it was there I learned one custom that continue this day—leaving a little on your dinner plate to show your host they gave you just enough to eat.

After dinner, I stood by the sliding doors to the patio, studying the family's traditional Japanese tea garden. There was a small pond amid the plantings, with a stone walkway that led to a small tea hut. The stone path wound from the porch, through the pond and to the tea house. But the stones were not evenly placed.

"The walkway, the steps through the pond appears to be unfinished," I observed.

"How do you mean?" Takiko asked.

"The stones ... they are set, well, haphazardly, and pretty far apart. It would be difficult to walk out to the tea house without falling into the pond."

"That is on purpose," she explained, with a chuckle at my ignorance. "The walk to the tea house is an intimate part of the tea ceremony. The pathway slows the observer, giving them time to contemplate the aesthetics of the whole garden. We call it *ocha* in Japanese."

"But what if you fell into the pond?" I chided, always looking for the humor in any situation. "You'd wind up at the tea house wet."

"That's the point," Takiko added. "It takes great care to walk the path of stone steps. You must concentrate, focus, pause, consider each step. And by doing that, you arrive at the tea house in a meditative state, ready to enter the tea ceremony." Dumb, ignorant and uncultured American that I was, I was learning what I wanted to learn—how other people lived and led their lives.

I was curious about Takiko's relationship with her boyfriend, so I asked her: "Do Japanese fall in love?"

"We, at least women, rarely *fall in love*. We do not experience romance as you Americans know it."

"Are you and your boyfriend in love?"

"I have read of your Western love. I do not know if we experience it here the same way you do, at least not the way I read in your books. It all seems too intense, too much trouble."

"Then what brings you together?"

"I would say it is respect."

"Is that a feeling?" I asked.

"I respect my parents. I respect my boyfriend, but in a different way. He would make a good husband."

"I suppose that's a better reason for getting married than that whirlwind love affair we Westerners experience. Too many of us fall in love too easily, and the relationship ends poorly."

Back to Work

As I wandered the streets of the Ginza alone, images of my newspaper pages would begin to run through my mind. By 9 p.m. I was ready to go back to work. I'd sneak up the back stairs to Typesetting and work for a few hours. But temptation resided one floor above. There was a nightclub up there, with a stage, bands, girls, dancing and booze. Tucked off in one corner was a separate bar with pinball machines. From there, one could hear the music from the larger nightclub, but to access this part of the bar there was no cover charge. Here, I could put away a few beers before last call.

The nightclub section was huge, crowded with enlisted men on R&R and Japanese call girls dressed in skimpy attire. When the lights came up to chase out the crowd after "last call," many of the ladies scampered away. I realized that a few, under all that make-up, must have been grandmothers.

My Black Market Shopping Trip

After three days in Typesetting, my newspaper was ready for press. But it had to wait for its turn on the press. Since my orders were open-ended, with no return date, I'd spend a day shopping. I took a train to the PX at the U.S. Naval base down in Yokohama to fulfill my black market shopping list.

The train ride took more than an hour and was a chance to see more of Japan, as we sped through the landscape, past the backyards of residents, through villages and neat farming plots. I was getting a sense for the orderliness of the Japanese people, their attention to detail, and how much they could produce in so little space. Living that close to one another on an island, I understood why people would have to be polite and well-behaved.

At the PX—less general store and more shopping mall, before there were such things—I filled requests with the money the men had entrusted to me. Presents for the folks at home were packed up by the Navy and mailed. I'd found a camera shop on the Ginza that was more than helpful. It was there I bought my cameras and lenses as well as gear for the crew back in Chu Lai. The store packed up my purchases for shipment, got the package through customs and had it delivered to the air base. I'd pick up the shipment at the airfield and check it onto the flight back to Vietnam.

A Night in Saigon

Getting back to Chu Lai could take a day or more.

Most of the time I'd be on the *Stars and Stripes* flight, with my pallet of *The Transit* newspapers piled in with a dozen pallets of the *S&S*. This was a whistle-stop flight on a prop-driven C-130, dropping off a pallet-loads of newspapers at military bases as we flew south: Okinawa, Taiwan, Clark Airfield in the Philippines, and finally into Tan Son Nhut Air Base outside Saigon. By the time I arrived in Saigon I was wiped out. The trip had taken 24 hours, with nothing to eat but crackers from vending machines at airports along the way. The plane was noisy and cold and the only place to sleep was on top of my pallet of newspapers strapped in among other cargo that filled the bay. Once in Saigon, I had to get myself back to my outfit in Chu Lai with all my stuff. An airman who ran cargo transfer service at the Tan Son Nhut Airfield took pity on me. Jake was the one who arranged for my pallet of newspapers and boxes of camera gear to head north to my base. He let me bunk in with him on those nights I was stuck, waiting for the next day's northbound flight.

Riding into the city on the back of Jake's Vespa, I got to see what was once the "Paris of the Orient," Saigon. We negotiated the busy streets of this once grand and beautiful city, passing countless refugees, cooking on fires on the curb as their families huddled in cardboard shacks against walls of former villas. The city stank. It was dusty and very hot that summer of 1967. The street traffic was a steady flow of mostly mopeds, street bikes, Vespas, pedicabs, a few old French cars and military trucks. The sidewalks were crowded with a sea of Vietnamese, walking in both directions, like shuffling a deck of cards. The crowds were tightly packed; you could smell the person in front of you.

There were few traffic lights, and those seemed to make little difference as the traffic never let up. I was surprised to see a city that was supposedly at war so busy.

A whiff of urine would come out of nowhere and I'd gag. In Paris, there are public urination stations on the sidewalks; men stand in these cubicles, looking out over the partitions, taking a pee, watching the world go by. No such cubicles in this former French city, not that I saw, but peeing on the side of a wall, in broad daylight, appeared de rigueur.

The entrance to the converted hotel in which Jake had a room was a maze of sandbags. "VC sappers on motorcycles have a habit of throwing a satchel charge into hotel lobbies," he said, as we climbed off and he locked up his moped. "The electricity goes out at odd hours, but the water in the shower is cool."

Rejuvenated from a shower, and in clean civvies, we went out for dinner at a family-run Vietnamese restaurant a few streets away. As we walked through the crowds of people, dodging the bikes, mopeds, cars and military trucks at the intersections, I felt naked again, still without my .45 on my hip. I understood now why our Western cowboys wore their six-shooters.

Tokyo streets were crowded, but not like here. The Japanese were orderly; they obeyed the traffic signs—here, no such luck. You took your life in your hands if you jaywalked. Those who braved the dash across the street among fast-moving traffic reminded me of the Japanese pachinko pinball game.

"For Chrissakes!" Jack yelled from the other side of a busy street, "don't stop in the middle of the street. They'll kill you. Just move. They'll steer around you." They did. I was amazed. As I jogged across the street, the traffic just flowed around me—like a fast-flowing stream flows around a boulder.

"See. It worked!" Jake congratulated me on my first near-death experience in Saigon. It would take me some time to learn how to negotiate Saigon traffic.

Jake had a restaurant in mind, down a narrow alley, all lit up on the outside with neon, while inside it was dark. We could have been in a Chinese restaurant in New York City or Boston—the decor was the same.

14. Putting the Pieces Together

The place was crowded, noisy, and smelled a lot better than the streets, with a mixture of spices, perfume and human perspiration. Jake found us a table and a very petite and sexy Vietnamese hostess seated us and chatted on in fairly good American. English, as in "from England," was not a language spoken here, but "American," with its slang, Western drawl, and curse words, was. The bar and the tables were crowded with a mixture of well-fed Vietnamese and American civilians.

"The better dressed Americans with no tan are CIA or from the Embassy," Jake pointed out. "The guys over there in rumpled duds are probably journalists. You can tell the few of us military guys, we have tans." Here, I saw my first fat Vietnamese. Up north, in Da Nang and in the countryside, everyone was thin, but not here.

The menu was in chicken scratching, the Vietnamese alphabet, so I let Jake do the ordering.

"This evening is my treat," I told my airman host—it was the least I could do for the night's lodging and his help in getting me and my "traveling PX" back to Chu Lai. "I have no idea what to order, but since this is my first time, and perhaps only time, here in Saigon, I'd like to taste some real Vietnamese food. You order."

I never did learn any Vietnamese, and spoke only a few words in the villages and at the snack stand by the Da Nang air terminal, but Jake had learned enough to get by. I guess you had to in this city. We started with fresh spring rolls, a collection of fresh vegetables rolled up in soft white rice paper. I was used to Chinese egg rolls, those crunchy crusted tubes filled with cooked veggies. These were the opposite. The inside was crunchy and the outside was soft. A dark brown peanut and garlic sauce came along for dipping. I could have eaten a dozen and called it a night, but Jake kept ordering.

Jake had a soup, called *pho*—pronounced, he said, "fuh"—with noodles, slivers of beef brisket and fresh veggies floating in a beef stock that I could smell from across the table. He let me sample and I could have eaten his entire bowl.

Next came a large platter with a sample of vegetables, slivers of chicken, beef and pork and small bowls of dipping sauce. And we hadn't even reached the main course.

The sampler tray was cleared away and a large bowl was placed before me, mounted high with colorful treats, along with two more beers.

"That's *bun nam-vang*," said Jake, "pronounced 'boon nam.' It's my usual dinner here. Got everything in it you could ask for that's Vietnamese." I found slices of pork, shrimp, carrots, cucumber, mint, and bean sprouts piled on top of soft white rice noodles—a whole lot

We had access to two Asian beers, as well as San Miguel from the Philippines. Tiger Beer, from Singapore, and "33" from Saigon, were drinkable, but inconsistent. Beer from the States took months to get here, and when it did it sat around in boiling heat for another month, so it was not much better. But what are you going to do? Go without?

better than spaghetti. I found this to be an awakening. Finally, I'd found something in Vietnam to really like.

These Saigon ventures each month were my only taste of Vietnamese food. Back at our base we ate what the Navy provided, from cans. We were warned against drinking the local beer or partaking of the local cuisine, as it could be poisoned. But here in this busy city, the restaurants were packed with civilian and military Americans dining alongside Vietnamese. The food was great. It was not Chinese or Japanese, it was Vietnamese.

"They use a lot of herbs here," Jake explained. "It's a more subtle way of cooking," he added. "There's nothing really hot, like Szechwan. I've sworn off on Chinese food," he concluded as we dug in.

After a few more Tiger beers to wash down our treats, I settled the bill and we walked off our large meal, wandering the streets of Saigon.

"This was once a beautiful city," Jake remarked. "The French left a mark here, but it's all becoming Americanized. The bars and clubs here are now for the American servicemen, not the Vietnamese." Three million people lived in Saigon in 1967; and half a million of those were refugees, whose homes and villages had been destroyed by the VC or the Americans. It must have been the most crowded city in the world.

"Is this city dangerous?" I asked. "Walking around here at night, just two Americans in civilian clothes?"

"No, not really," he replied. "Occasionally, something happens, a shooting, a satchel charge, but it's no more dangerous than Chicago or Detroit." We stopped at a bar-café, with tables on the sidewalk. We could have been in Paris. A few "tea girls" moved from prospect to prospect. We ordered another beer, but I was not comfortable there. Living on the base inside the Chu Lai Enclave had left me soft and not alert to danger.

Curfew time approached as we made it back through the maze of sandbags and into the hotel. The night was hot. I slept on a spare cot in nothing by my skivvies, air from an oscillating fan between the beds periodically sweeping over me to evaporate the sweat that collected, cooling me. At first I was a little nervous, wondering if Jake had invited me to share his room with a purpose other than hospitality. I was glad to figure out he hadn't.

In the morning, Saigon looked, smelled and sounded different. Maybe it was a good night's sleep after only napping on newspapers in the noisy cargo bay of a C-131. Jake took me to a French café near the hotel, where we ordered coffee and fresh and crusty baguettes. The coffee was strong and gave me a buzz that lasted until noon. The streets were busy at 7 a.m., as the sun was already above the rooftops. Traffic and people were on the move. As we sped out of town on Jake's Vespa back out to Tan Son Nhut Air Base, I saw commerce going on everywhere—stalls selling stuff, mostly black market or stolen American items, and there were car dealerships, appliance stores, and shoeshine boys bothering the men in the cafés. Yes, this was South Vietnam where commerce and free trade abounded. Entrepreneurs were everywhere.

Later that morning, I boarded another C-131 and resumed my place on my pallet of newspapers and PX boxes. We flew to Cam Ranh Air Base for a brief stop. What passengers there were deplaned while the crew unloaded and refueled. We took off, stopped twice more at bases whose names I never bothered to ask. All day, in and out of airfields, I worried about getting those large boxes of brand-new cameras and electronics all the way back to base. I was a nervous wreck by the time everything arrived. I never lost a thing in the six trips I made to Tokyo, but each time I arrived home, I promised myself that was the last time I'd do that. It wasn't. Of course.

Chapter 15

The End Is in Sight

The Monsoon Rains Arrive

In the last two months of our deployment, conditions were beginning to get really wet. By September, Seventy-One was getting a taste of what it would be like later that fall. Each day in the late afternoon and on most nights, the South China Sea came calling. Buckets of heavy rain would shower down on our camp for 15 to 30 minutes, then stop, only to shower down again. What does rain lead do?

Mud You Say…

A bunch of the guys were sitting on the porch of their hooch on a Sunday afternoon in early October. The rain was pelting down on the canvas awning they'd rigged for some protection. One of the guys spied an object in the middle of the muddy road that runs through camp from the guard station.

"Bill, what's that sittin' in the road?"

"Where?"

"Over there, in front of the EM Club."

"Looks like a turtle."

"A turtle? There ain't no turtles 'round here. None that I seen."

"You got a scope on that M14 of yours? Go ahead and take a bead on that thing then ya'll know what 'tis."

Bill gets up, reluctantly, disappears inside the hooch, to return with a his service rifle, outfitted at his own expense, with sniper scope. He kicks out the bi-pod on the front of the barrel and rests the legs on the porch railing. Crouching down, he jams his right eye to the scope's eye cup.

"Looks like a helmet," he reports to the gathered Seabees.

"What?

"A helmet, like the one you wear on your head."

"What's it doin' in the middle of the road?"

"Someone must have dropped it."

"Or it fell offen a truck."

"Been no trucks able to get down that road all week, what with all this mud."

"What you think?"

"Nothing. It's just a helmet sitting there. No, wait … it's moving."

"What do you mean, moving?

"It's creeping along. It's coming this way, right down the middle of the road." The four Seabees sit back in their Adirondack chairs and wait. The standard military issue helmet finally arrived in front of the men's hooch.

"Well, you going down and see what's under that helmet?"

"You go. You're the one so all fired up about what under it." Bill leans his rifle by the doorway and walks out into the rain. Reaching the road in front of the hooch, he gets down on all fours, lifts up the corner of the helmet, and says:

SPECIAL BIRTHDAY ISSUE

the TRANSIT

1943   U.S. NAVAL MOBILE CONSTRUCTION BATTALION 71   1967

Vol. 1 No. 6 (Family Gram)   CHU LAI, RVN   September 22, 1967

NEITHER SUN NOR RAIN

"Neither rain, nor snow, nor..." goes the old Postal saying. Vietnam Seabees are now saying... "Neither scorching sun, nor drenching rains will, etc...." Seabee Equipment Operators from Seventy-One find a large beach parasol just the thing for keeping cool AND dry as they work on MAG 12's Ready Ammo Pad.

THE PUSH IS ON

SEABEES RACE FALL MONSOONS

CHU LAI, SOUTH VIETNAM—A tense drama is being played on the sandy stretch of beach held by American Forces at Chu Lai, South Vietnam. Seabee construction crews are battling against time and the approaching monsoon rains to complete four top priority military projects. The contest has all the elements of a modern suspense story—at least for these time-pressed Seabees and their Navy Civil Engineer Corps officers.

The orders came down to MCB 71 in Chu Lai that three ammunition storage and supply areas will be built, along with a crash project to prepare Chu Lai's main service route before the eroding rains of the fall monsoons set in. One of the ammo storage areas to be built by MCB 71's Seabees will eventually be the largest single facility in the Chu Lai military complex. Covering more than 2.5 square miles, the Ammo Supply Point will house the vast arsenal of munitions used by Chu Lai based units.

Work on these four priority projects has been proceeding at full speed, but soaking afternoon rains have begun to make earth moving—the major portion of the projects—an increasingly difficult task. The pace is beginning to slow. According to Navy engineering officers, only good weather and ingenuity are needed to get the job done on time, but, with the weather getting wetter and wetter by the day, ingenuity will be playing an ever increasing role in the Seabee's race against the fall deadline.

Seabees are battling the afternoon tropical cloud-bursts while they install an adequate drainage system along the 5-mile-plus highway through the Chu Lai enclave. Rains are cutting into the soft roadside as Seabees install culverts, run-offs, drainage canals and put up retaining walls. The road, left unattended, would be washed into the South China Sea by approaching fall-winter monsoon rains.

TWO DETAILS UNDER ATTACK

QUANG NGAI, SOUTH VIETNAM — The Seabee detail from Seventy-One stationed in Quang Ngai underwent mortar and small arms fire Wednesday evening, August 30 and again on Saturday, September 2—just prior to the Vietnamese general elections.

A number of mortar rounds fell within 300-yards of the detail's tent quarters just inside the MACV compound in the provincial capital. The compound itself received heavy shelling as Viet Cong terrorists rushed the city jail with satchel charges, blasting open its doors and freeing 1200 communist prisoners.

Detail OIC, Lieutenant (jg) Bernie Johnson, moved his crew
(Continued on Page 3)

Admirals Visit Here

MCB 71 was visited September 2 by two Rear Admirals who were touring the areas of their command. Rear Admiral W. M. Enger, the Vice Commander of the Naval Facilities Engineering Command, and Rear Admiral James V. Bartlett, who only a few days before relieved Commodore A. R. Marschall as Commander of the Third Naval Construction Brigade, arrived at Camp Shields after viewing the project sites of Chu Lai and Binh Son by helicopter.

Upon arriving in Camp Shields, the Admirals and their party were briefed by MCB 71's Operations Department on "the progress of the battalion's projects. Following the briefing, they made a jeep tour of Camp Shields and the worksites in Chu Lai before proceeding to MCB 6 and from there back to DaNang.

The Admirals' party included Commodore Charles Turner, Commander of the 30th Naval Construction Regiment.

Seventy-One's "colors" fly for the first time, as the color guard troops them off the field ahead of the 400-odd men of the newly commissioned battalion.
(Photo taken at Davisville, Rhode Island on October 4, 1966)

A Year Ago

From Davisville to Binh Son, Quang Ngai, DaNang, Duc Pho, Vung Tau, to Camp Shields, Chu Lai, South Vietnam. MCB 71's Seabees have seen a lot of the world in the past year —there's still a lot to be seen and a lot to be done. This is Seventy-One's first birthday. Just one-year old on October 4, MCB 71 has come a long way from home and has come a long way toward completing her mission.

It was just about one year ago, on a brisk fall October day that just over 500 Seabees, fitted out in dress-blues, formed up. By that afternoon those men were officially members of the Navy's newest Construction Battalion, MCB 71. The work and training were just beginning.

The front page of the September 1967 edition of *The Transit*.

"Well, if it ain't Tut Tuttle, the Postman. Kind of muddy walkin' don't you think?"

"Walkin'?! Hell, I'm riding atop an AmTrac," comes the reply.

I couldn't resist retelling this traditional Yankee yarn, dressed up for the Seabees.

Building a New Drainage System

Luckily, our camp was built on the beach, so the rain soaked through the sand and we didn't have to deal with mud. Outside of camp it was a different story. A "gully washer" would pour down on the roads, runways, chopper pads—which were either concrete, asphalt or metal matting—then run off, eroding the banks, flooding the culverts, washing out roads and overpowering the drainage system that led back to the sea.

Tuffy and I were in his jeep one morning in September on our way to a job site. We were headed north on the MSR toward Rosemary Point, that high cliff at the north end of the enclave. One of our crews was working on replacing a culvert.

Short-timer Rick Hanratty, DK3, checks off another day on his "going home" calendar. We all had one of these.

"Back in August, LCDR Martin, the Ops Officer, asked LT Power and me if we could come up with plans for a better drainage system for the entire Enclave." Tuffy was giving me background on one of our current projects, as we drove up the MSR, the windshield of the jeep down for the breeze. "'Sure,' I told him," said Tuffy. 'First thing we need to do is get a series of elevations along the entire supply road. There was a bunch of 16-inch elliptical culverts along the road that needed to be rebuilt. When RMK [Raymond-Morrison-Knudson], the civilian construction company here before us, built this main supply road, they put in only half culverts. You see, when these culverts are shipped over from the States, they come in two halves, semi-circles. That way they can be nested together on the ship. The halves are supposed to be bolted together to form a full circle. Well, RMK didn't do that. They used just one half. Well, every time you double the size of a culvert, it will handle four times the amount of water. We need to replace these culverts with full-size pipes, or build concrete channel crossings under roads." That's what our men were doing.

During one of the afternoon Operations meetings, Tuffy told me, one of the officers expressed dissatisfaction with Tuffy's solution for base drainage. "He thought he, being an officer, had to know more about construction than an enlisted man. Well, LCDR Martin, the Ops Officer, turned to the junior officer and said: 'Tuffy Lake here has more construction experience than all 24 of us officers combined. We'd be smart to make use of that experience.' LCDR Martin then turned to me and said: 'Tuffy, you do it any way you want, just make sure it works.' 'Aye, Aye, sir!'"

By October we were getting some pretty serious rain. One night it rained 14 inches in four hours.

"Came down in buckets," Tuffy said. "Couldn't sleep for the racket on the tin roofs. I got up around 4 a.m., woke up the lieutenant and asked if he'd like to take a ride with me, see if the draining plan was working. He jumped into my jeep beside me and off we went in the rain. Every driveway we passed was intact, every culvert was doing its job. No washouts. Except one. At the far end of the enclave, the builders had torn off

Drainage improvements went on throughout our last two months. Culverts, bridges, and ditches were built to keep the monsoon rains from washing out the roads, the runways—heck, the entire enclave.

the forms from a concrete channel crossing, and left the lumber in the ditch, which created a blockage and dammed up the water, which then flowed over the road. But other than that, I was pretty proud of our work."

The Bob Hope Amphitheater

Bob Hope was coming!

To get ready for the 1967 Bob Hope Christmas Show, Seventy-One was given the job of building him an 8,000-seat outdoor amphitheater. The job was actually begun by MCB-40 before they left, then handed over to Seventy-One with roughly 5 percent of the project underway.

15. The End Is in Sight

The Bob Hope Amphitheater would seat 8,000 when we finished it just prior to leaving Chu Lai.

The theater sat in a natural bowl on the side of the hill atop Rosemary Point. The Seabees from Forty had made the initial excavations for the site, stripping the bowl of all vegetation, which proved disastrous. The September rains turned the bare soil into mud, which began sliding downhill into the South China Sea.

Seventy-One's Engineering Department with their "Can Do" spirit came up with a plan which included a series of interlocking concrete sidewalks to act as retaining gutters. These were arranged on the sloped seating area in a checkerboard pattern, to collect the rainwater and divert it into concrete spillways, away from the seating area down the hill and into the sea. Bob Wagoner, EA3, and Bob Timerson, EACN, from Seventy-One's Field Engineers, laid out the entire seating area for the carpenter and concrete crews.

At the bottom of the sloping seating area, in front of the stage, water was also collecting. LTJG Powers and Tuffy Lake came up with a design solution to deal with drainage here as well. Tuffy explained it to me: "We used 106 recoilless rifle shell casings, knocked off the ends, and welded them together to form long perforated pipes that lead out to sea." Those shell casings were already perforated, full of holes to release the blast gases when fired, reducing the recoil. The perforations allowed the rainwater to seep in and away.

"Worked like a charm," Tuffy told me.

Once the drainage problems were solved with crushed rock, concrete walkways and the "French drains," the installation of 8,000 seats began. Shell canisters were placed on end in concrete pedestal forms, onto which 3 × 12 planks were fastened, forming benches. The project was completed in time for Bob Hope and his 1967 USO Christmas Show, but by then, Seventy-One was already back in Davisville—all except for four of our Seabees from Engineering: Bob Timerson, Bob Wagoner, Charlie Brown and Rich Russ. Those four got to see the show, as they had transferred over to MCB-Six when Seventy-One left Chu Lai in November. This transfer allowed three of them, each on a two-year enlistment, to fulfill their remaining months in-country, thereby not having to return to Davisville and then back to Vietnam in the spring of '68. Bob Timerson, on a four-year enlistment, was transferred to the Department of Public Works at NAS Memphis in Tennessee. He would later return to 'Nam with MCB-74 and finish his enlistment with MCB-40 in-country.

We hoped the troops, and Bob Hope, appreciated their new outdoor theater built by Seventy-One. If you watch the Bob Hope television special, Bob comes out on stage wearing a Seabee-Six hard hat. It should have said Seventy-One! (The 1967 Bob Hope USO Christmas Show can be viewed at https://youtu.be/weFkkHuUb_c. The Chu Lai segment begins around 25 minutes into the hour-and-a-half TV special. An Army soldier filmed the show at Chu Lai and it is also available on YouTube: https://youtu.be/QrhvyBbbgTk.)

A Tropical Light Show

Wally Skop and I were sitting on the steps of my office hooch one night in late September. It was around 11 p.m. The EM Club had closed, but we were not ready to turn in. I had only a few more weeks in 'Nam, and was savoring (if I can use that word here) the last few moments we would have in this tropical hell-hole.

We sat and watched the light shows—two of them. One was off to our right, in the hills to the west of the base: orange flares floating down on small parachutes, the boom of outgoing 109s, the flashes of explosions; all could be seen on the hillside, followed a minute later by the distant rumble of shelling and the staccato chatter of a machine gun from some bunker on the perimeter. There was a war going on over there.

But there was another light show that held our attention—30 miles to the south, over the city of Quang Ngai. Cumulonimbus clouds had been building all day. The hot summer sun had sucked up warm ocean water out of the South China Sea, forming towering thunderheads, now drifting westward over land. As the clouds rose over the mountains, the fireworks began. Lightning flashed within and between the clouds. Some of those mountainous clouds rose to 50,000 feet, ten miles up. In the afternoon you'd see them billowing out over the ocean, changing shape before your eyes, growing. Now, at night, as the lightning flashed within the clouds, the flashes silhouetted the mountains and valleys within the clouds. The sky looked like the Swiss Alps.

"We call it heat lightning," Wally said. "We'd watch at night from our bedroom window next to the Hudson River."

"Yes, that's what we used to call them … heat lightning, but they are just ordinary lightning. The lightning flashes are just too far away for the sound of the thunder they create to reach us." I was remembering how my family and I would sit on the porch of our lodge, watching the summer lightning dance over the lake.

"Makes our little war seen so trivial," Wally added. "You could write about that," he observed.

"Yes, I suppose I could. Watching all that energy, it could be a poem." We'd both turned reflective.

15. The End Is in Sight

All afternoon, cumulonimbus clouds had been building over the South China Sea. As they moved inland and rose over the highlands, the lightning show began in early evening.

"What are you going to do when you get out?" Wally asked. It was a question all of us were asking each other, and ourselves. We had just two more months in-country. I'd then have three weeks after we got back before being released from active duty.

"I don't really know," I said. "I've been too busy since we got here to even think about it."

"Would you go back to college?"

"I don't think so," I said. "I know now what I wanted to know."

"Will you be writing?"

"Or photographing. I'd like to come back here as a civilian photographer for one of the wire services."

"You'd come back to this? You're nuts."

"Yes, I guess I would be nuts. But there is a lot more to learn and see about this war."

"You'd not catch me coming back here, not if I can help it."

"You've got another year in. What will you do when you get out?"

"Go to work for my father. Go to college. But I'm not coming back here."

My two-year hitch on active duty with the Reserves would be up right after we got back to Davisville. The officer in charge of re-enlistments tried his best to get me to sign up for an additional two years. He said I would make Second Class Journalist, with a pay increase, and could get most any ship or shore assignment I wanted. For a few days I thought about it. Where would I like to be, what would I like to see, to photograph, to write about? There was an opening for a Journalist on the Ice—the Seabees were part of the U.S. base on Antarctica. Now that would be a place to photograph and find stories! But the deployment was a full year and once on the Ice, there was no way to get you off until the following year—no leave.

I was now used to the Navy and the Seabees. I liked the fact that they fed me, gave me a bunk on which to sleep, and I didn't have to spend my pay on living expenses. The Navy even gave me my clothes, free laundry, and cheap beer. On the other hand I was eager to get out of uniform and get on with my civilian life and career as a journalist. Besides, I wanted go skiing come winter.

By early October, all of us were officially "short timers." We had less than a month left in Vietnam and would be returning to Davisville the first of November. My conversation with Skop a few weeks earlier had been weighing on my mind. Once back in the States, I'd have three weeks in which to lay out the cruise book before being discharged. What was I going to do as a civilian? I'd been waiting for this door to open for five years.

The MARS Phone Call

I knew now that I was a newspaper man, a reporter, photojournalist, a storyteller. The Navy and this hitch with the Seabees had shown me that. I was sure a newspaper would hire me, or give me a chance to prove myself.

"Hello, Mom? This is me … Frank, your son…. I'm in Vietnam. I'm talking to you on shortwave. Can you hear me? Over."

One evening, slightly bleary-eyed from the beer at the EM Club, I walked past the MARS shack, the shortwave ham radio connection we had with the States. I heard a man's conversation through the screens, talking to his folks back home.

"Hi Mom, it's me," the voice said. "Is Dad with you there? Over."

"Chuck! I don't believe it!" came a woman's voice back. "This you? Where are you?" Long pause.

"Mom, you have to say 'over' when you finish talking, then I can respond. I'm in Vietnam talking to you on the shortwave radio. Over."

"What? All I heard was shortwave radio."

"Mom, when I say 'over' then you can talk. When you finish say 'over,' then I know I can begin talking. Okay? Over."

I stopped to listen and wondered who the hell I might call. Mom and Dad? What would I say? "I'm fine. How are you all there?" Then I realized I could call Allan and Dick at Mount Snow. Why? Dick was the marketing VP at the resort I'd ski-bummed last winter. My buddy Allan was the staff photographer. They'd know if there was something I might do at the ski resort that winter when I got back. I went into the radio shack and signed up for a slot, then sat in line on the steps of the MARS shack to await my turn.

I gave the Seabee radio operator the phone number in Vermont, which he forwarded to the ham operator in California. There was some confusion on the other end, as I learned much later. Allan and Dick were running around the office trying to figure out what a collect phone charge would be for a call from halfway around the world.

"No, you only pay the collect charges from California," the operator told them.

Allan and Dick came on the line on a shared phone, and after, "How are you doing," we got down to the future.

"If you are up for it," Dick said, "I can offer you the position as director of communication here. You'd oversee the PR department, edit the *Mount Snow Valley News*. We want to make it a weekly. Oh, and you'd organize all of our special events."

That was it. I had the promise of a job when I got back and was released from active duty. I was thrilled. I would be doing what I know I could do, and skiing at the same time. I walked back to my office, floating on air, or was it that the beer had finally kicked in?

Your Seabee Is Coming Home

The last edition of *The Transit* was coming up. I wrote a warning to the folks at home about what to expect when their son, husband or boyfriend returned from Vietnam. Here it is.

Dear Folks Back in the States...

Your Seabee will be returning from Vietnam shortly, and he'll be a strange bird, indeed. And for those of you who will receive the front end of this particular individual's pent-up energy—a few words of warning are offered.

This tired, but "happy to be home" Seabee will need to be handled with much TLC—with the emphasis on the "L." For his actions will require, above all, a great deal of understanding. Be patient if he appears at the dinner table with his old hunting rifle and a strange assortment of stainless steel wear, that's his mess kit. Don't be alarmed if he squats on the floor to eat and prefers his fingers to a fork. His tastes may have become more Eastern during his stay in Southeast Asia: instead of your

We're on the way home. Seabees in their best greens wait on the Chu Lai runway to board a C-141 for the flight home.

steaks, hamburgers and a cold Bud he may prefer raw fish, sticky rice, a bottle of 33—a local beer over here. He will want to wash his own steel tray with the toilet brush in a garbage can after meals and he will drink strong iced tea and Kool-Aid by the gallon.

Your Seabee will have to watch *COMBAT* on television each week, just to stay in touch, and he'll regale you with a play-by-play of the "inside skinny" of what's going on. A loud noise or siren will bring stranger reactions: First, he'll sit bold upright and ask, "incoming or outgoing?" then fly out of the house to seek refuge in the rock garden.

Your Vietnam veteran will be speaking a different language when he returns. This new lingo is a combination of official military jargon, Vietnamese and French, for the French left a lot behind when they departed in the 50s. He'll be using a lot of Navy lingo as well. "The head" or "the shitter" is the toilet; his bed becomes a *rack*; his bedroom will be known as his *quarters*; going upstairs is to go *above*; to go downstairs is to go *below*; a doorway is a *hatch*; the floor is the *deck*. He'll shout into the telephone, using terms like: "Say again! Do you copy? Come back on that, over," and finish with "break it down. Over and Out."

You may find his lingo salted with foul language—he is a sailor after all. But while in Vietnam, he's picked another language, based on Vietnamese: "Di-di" means to get out pronto, like, "let's di-di out of here." "Numba Wan," means finest kind. "Numba ten" is given to any undesirable thing or person. "Chop-chop" is slang for food; "beaucoup" is more, much more, and "same same" means same as, or just like this. He may take to calling his mother *Mama-San*, and Dad as *PaPa-san*, or as *The Skipper*. *Dung Lai* means "Stop!" He may ask you to *Saddle up*, when he wants you to get in the car and drive him someplace. *Souvenir me* means please give me something. He may refer to dinner as *mess, chop chop* or as *C-Rats*. He'll begin using the phonetic alphabet, Alpha is "A," Bravo is "B" and Charlie is

"C"; Zulu for "Z." You'll have to ask him for the meaning for the military abbreviations and acronyms he'll be using, such as EOD (Explosive Ordnance Disposal); LZ, a helicopter landing zone; HQ is headquarters; EPDOLANT is Enlisted Personnel Distribution Office Atlantic Fleet; SNAFU, ROK, IPO, RTO, RPG—the list is endless. And when the shit hits the fan, he'll simply say … "hell, it ain't no big thing."

It'll all take some getting used to.

Your young boy, your son, husband or boyfriend, will return tan and wiry (we've all lost weight over here). The Navy, the Seabees, Vietnam, the war and its constant tension, the noise of jets taking off, the thump, thump, thump as a dozen gunships pass at treetop over the camp, their rotor blades beating the air. He's become wary of mortar rounds landing nearby, to the crack of rifle and machine gun fire. If you find him huddled in the basement, next to the furnace, it's because he's become used to the heat over here. All this has become part of his life. He may seem devoid of those good qualities you once saw in him, but with time and understanding he will shed some of these nasty traits and what will emerge may be a stronger, more worldly man—who has lived through a war, and seen a part of life that few have been forced to witness.

He's all yours now.

Chapter 16

The Last Month in 'Nam

The KIA Flight

October—my last month in Vietnam. Only two more months until I would be out of the Navy. One last edition of *The Transit* to do. The issue would contain a wrap-up of our deployment, pictures of Seventy-One's birthday party on the beach and a warning to the folks back home about what to expect when their sons, husbands and boyfriends returned from this war in Southeast Asia.

With my attaché case full of pictures and typewritten stories, I caught a Huey at the Army heliport up at Rosemary Point for the 45-minute flight north to Da Nang. After landing near Monkey Mountain, I caught a ride in a jeep to MACV HQ in the city to clear my text and images with the PAO major. Then, there was the walk through Da Nang to the airport—again without my sidearm, as I would be leaving for Japan. This time, I felt even more vulnerable … this being so close to leaving. All of us "short-timers" felt this way, as if we'd already used up our allotment of good luck staying alive this long.

I stood in line at the military counter waiting to check in. It was busy. A second counter nearby was for Vietnamese civilians who were flying out on what was left of their national airline, old tail-dragging prop DC-3s. I showed my orders and ID card, checked in my suitcase, but kept my camera bag and attaché case with me. Then I waited. Late afternoon, toward dusk, with thoughts of spending the night in the terminal, my name was called. I met the crew chief for a C-141 heading back to the States, with a refueling stop in Japan, where I could get off.

"I have to warn you," he said as we shook hands. "I'm required to tell you, this is a KIA flight. You okay with that?" What he said didn't really register. Any flight out of here was better than spending the night in the terminal, so I followed the airman out and across the apron to this mammoth silver bird, two engines drooping under each wing.

I followed the crew chief up the ladder and through the crew door. A single row of passenger seats, the web kind, was against the forward bulkhead. I dropped my gear in an adjoining seat, sat down and buckled in. As I looked up, toward the rear of the cargo bay, five feet away, I was faced by a wall of silver aluminum cases, stacked four across, four high, and they went all the way back.

Then the realization finally struck me. This was a KIA flight … Killed in Action. Those were coffins. Each contained the body of an American serviceman. This flight was taking my fellow Americans home. I tried to count. There must have been more than 100 of these KIA cases filling the cargo bay.

I sat looking at the wall. This was the first time in six months I'd fully realized: boys

16. The Last Month in 'Nam

A C-141 waits on the Da Nang runway. KIA flights took off twice a week, all year long. Each flight carried more than 100 "Killed in Action" to their families back home.

were getting killed over here. And that's what we were doing here in Vietnam—spending the lives of these guys, just as the Brass was spending millions of dollars on infrastructure, material and ordnance to fight this Old Man's War.

I tried not to think about who was inside that one case on the bottom row, third from the left. I could see a name, rank and serial number on a label in a holder. I did not want to know. Here I was, alive, flying up to Japan to work at *Stars and Stripes* then climb some mountains on R&R. My choice to sign up for the Naval Reserves five years before was the reason I was sitting here, and not in the Army, or in one of those cases. In a few months, all this would be behind me. I'd be out of Vietnam, out of the Navy—my whole life now ahead of me. These boys would not have that opportunity. They'd not be able to live out their lives, get laid, find a job, marry, start a family, raise a few kids, run for office, start a business, write a book.

Americans at home see little of—and think less about—death, or the dead, except at funerals. The process is all out of sight. Here in 'Nam, the locals saw death and the dead every week. They saw family and neighbors lying on the ground, blood beginning to pool under them. Kids saw this. It wasn't right.

So far, I'd not given death and dying much thought. Only one of our 'Bees died in-country and that was from a concussion during a basketball game. I started wondering why we were here anyway. To stop the spread of Communism? Why bother? When we were ordered to Vietnam most of us felt we were doing the patriotic thing—defending the American way of life. Some may still have felt that way, justifying what they were called on to do—kill other human beings.

Sitting there in that web seat on that C-141, I was changing my mind about this war, the waste, and the egos of politicians and the military generals. I began to realize what we were doing to my generation of boys, as well as what we were doing to this lush and rural landscape and its people. We were blowing the hell out of it.

Fortunately, just after take-off, the crew chief came down the ladder from the flight deck and spoke in my ear. "The skipper doesn't want you staring at these coffins for the next four hours. You can come up on the bridge with the crew." Relieved, I followed. Chatting with the crew chief in more favorable spaces, I learned that this flight took off twice a week, each time bringing the bodies of a hundred American service men home. (More than 11,000 Americans were killed in Vietnam in 1967, and that's not counting the South and North Vietnamese army and civilians we killed.)

Why Are We Here?

The flight to Yokota Air Base outside Tokyo took five hours. That was a long time to mull over what I'd just left in the cargo bay.

I'd come to this war in Vietnam willingly, to experience it and write about it. I wanted to write about heroism, experience firefights in the rice paddies, drag a wounded buddy out of the mud to a "dust-off" helicopter, or be dragged myself. When I left the States I had images in my mind of a black-and-white war, like the World War II I'd seen in newsreels and in the Sunday afternoon television series *Victory at Sea*. Here I was writing about building roads, fixing runways, constructing barracks for the guys who were doing the fighting. But every war needs guys like me, making sure there's food and ammunition on the way, that the paychecks keep coming, there's beer at the bar, and the mail and care packages from home get delivered—even if they do come late.

In my seven months in Vietnam, I never saw a dead Vietnamese, VC, ARVN, or civilian. I got shot at once, came near to getting blown up by a road mine, scared myself walking through Da Nang alone, more than once. I'd photographed the fishermen and villagers in unsecured territory. I'd sweated a lot and worked 60-hour weeks, like the rest of the guys in my outfit. I was doing my "service" to my country. Fate had handed me this deck of cards. As one of the chiefs on the carrier USS *Lake Champlain* (CV-39) told me, "Kid, you got two years in this man's Navy, so make the best of it." I was trying. Without me even asking, the Seabees gave me my graduate degree in journalism.

And here I was, reporting on the good work my unit and the Seabees were doing for the war effort, plus the Civic Action projects we were doing for the Vietnamese people—building orphanages, medical facilities, marketplaces, fixing roads. But now I was thinking: To what end?

The Last Edition

The C-141 touched down at Yokota Air Base, 28 miles outside Tokyo, sometime around midnight. I said my good-byes to the plane's crew and walked in the rain to the vacant terminal. A lone airman at the counter told me there was no way to get into Tokyo that night. I'd have to bunk in at the transit barracks and take a morning train.

The barracks were more like a hotel than the barracks I'd been used to in the Navy. After all, this was the Air Force, not the Marines, where you were expected to sleep in a foxhole. I checked in, found my private room—and it really *was* private, just one bed. I dumped my stuff and headed for the shower down the hall.

It was raining the next morning when I caught the base bus to the train station. The hour-long ride into Tokyo was through a damp landscape, with low clouds and the windows streaked with rain. The day mirrored my state of mind. I was still processing the flight up from Da Nang and the plane full of KIAs.

I went through the now familiar process of getting checked into the barracks and up to the *S&S* Small Unit Publication room. My heart was not really in it this time. I plodded through the work of assembling the blocks of lead slugs, photos and headlines into pages. My mind was on other things—my release from active service, a waiting job in Vermont—but what really bothered me was my altered state of mind about the war I'd come to experience.

Around me was a giant military machine, men in uniform, officers, and non-coms working at *S&S*. These guys had surrendered their lives to the service. Not that I objected, for the service is an honorable profession—it was the politicians and corporate CEOs I was angry with.

Outside, on the streets of Tokyo, Japanese civilians went about their business in a city that was newer and cleaner than any in the U.S. We'd destroyed parts of Japan just 22 years earlier, and here this nation of now peaceful people had not only overcome their defeat, they'd rebuilt, and I found them actually eager to meet and talk with an American—and we had been the ones who had defeated them. The Japanese had rebuilt their country, practically from scratch. No matter where I traveled in Japan, I saw little or no evidence of World War II. Could this ever happen in Vietnam, I wondered?

My Last Column in The Transit

Thankfully, I had written my last editorial before climbing onto that C-141 KIA flight, for the editorial I would have written after that experience would not have been so positive. My last column began:

> Are you going to miss Vietnam?
> After all the months we've spent in the hot, dusty, war-like place this may sound like a rhetorical question. Who would possibly miss this place?
> I for one, and one of many, will miss my days in Vietnam—if just a little.
> You Seabees returning to Davisville for training, schools, leave or just sitting around waiting to come back, you will miss Vietnam, like it or not. And why? We've been doing something important over here, supporting the troops in the field, putting our training and skills to use, and we're all learned a thing or two. Sometimes it's about construction, our trade, at other times it's about life in another country. Most importantly, we've learned what this war has been all about--and we've learned all this firsthand. Over here, we have all felt the work we've done has been valuable.
> Some of us will be transferred to other construction units, back to shore duty or back into the fleet, still others will be going back to civilian life, but all of us will remember our time as a Seabee with Seventy-One in Vietnam.
> True, we've had a hefty share of bad times—hot weather, hotter than any man is used to, the noise of the jets and constant racket of choppers overhead, and the tension, BUT there have been good times here too. One of the best of those times has been the camaraderie that has developed through our work. The Seabees have added their part to the war, to the struggle of the South Vietnamese people—if only in a small part. The fleet sailors have had an experience that will last a lifetime. The 'Bees are a singular experience!

VIETNAM—FINAL EDITION

1943 U.S. NAVAL MOBILE CONSTRUCTION BATTALION 71 1967

Vol. 1 No. 7 (Family Gram) CHU LAI, RVN October 21, 1967

MCB 71 IS GOING HOME

CHU LAI, SOUTH VIETNAM — Seabees, now on a rotational "two-trip" schedule to Vietnam are serving more time in-country than any other service. Battalions d e p l o y to Vietnam seven to eight-months at a whack, then return to their homeport for rest and retraining; each Seabee is required to make ONLY two of these trips, but this still places him in-country two to four months longer than Marine, Army or Air Force personnel. This month, SEVENTY-ONE finds itself on the short end of that rotation schedule AND is getting r e a d y to head home. The 800-man Battalion will board Air Force C-141's shortly for the 24-hour, 13,000 mile hop to Davisville, Rhode Island — and home.

The unit's men will be enrolled in formal Navy schools, undergo construction and military training, and as a unit, the entire Battalion will go through three-weeks of combat-in-fantry training with the U.S. Marines, before packing up and heading BACK to Vietnam this next spring.

WELCOME MCB 40

For photos and a hint of what's in store for MCB 71's relieving battalion, turn to page 5.

One of the world's "Most Beautiful" sights—an Air Force C-141, SEVENTY-ONE's Advance Party boarded this sleek cargo-troop carrier early this month for the 25-hour flight back to Davisville, Rhode Island to pave the way for the Main Body's arrival.

DEADLINE NEARS

CHU LAI, SOUTH VIETNAM—The Monsoons arrived a bit early this year. High winds, heavy surf and the seasonal rains swept into Chu Lai Tuesday morning, October 3. With the monsoons, plus that special date on the calendar nearing, SEVENTY-ONE's construction crews are rushing to complete the last of the Battalion's assigned projects.

The Pascoe buildings for MAG 12 and 13 are up with the subcontracting of wiring, plumbing and inside work well under way. The acre-and-half Ready Service Ammo Magazine for the two Marine Air Groups have been completed, with the a s p h a l t topping to the high berms being laid down just before the rains set in.

Work on the Main Service Route through the Chu Lai complex has been finished, with the extensive drainage system now being put to the wet test.

Phase ONE of the 6-acre Ammo Supply Point has been hampered, not only by the monsoon rains, but by the absence of SEVENTY-ONE's three huge EUCLID TS-24 earth movers. The three monsters have been de-lined due to a lack of hydraulic parts. O b t a i n i n g (Continued on Page 3)

XO Promoted

CAMP SHIELDS, RVN—Official word was received recently that Lieutenant-Commander George Brown, Seventy-One's Executive Officer, has been selected for promotion to the rank of full Commander in the Navy's Civil Engineer Corps. It is expected that he will receive the "paperwork" from Washington and don his new rank prior to return to Davisville.

Lieutenant C o m m a n d e r Brown joined the Battalion in September 1966 prior to the unit's recommissioning. He was promoted to his present rank in July 1964 while Head of the Management Department of the Caribbean Division, U.S. Naval Facilities Engineering Command, the position he held prior to joining the Seabees.

ADVANCE PARTY LEAVES

CHU LAI, SOUTH VIETNAM—A handful of men from Vietnam based MCB SEVENTY-ONE have departed the main body's camp in Chu Lai for the unit's homeport at Davisville, Rhode Island—home of the Atlantic Seabees. The group, MCB 71's Advance Party, boarded an Air Force C-141 early this month for the 13,000-mile hop home to pave the way for the 800-man Battalion's return to the States.

The Party, under Lieutenant (jg) Jim Dougherty, Seventy-One's Security and Training Officer, will arrange for barracks, administrative and storage space, and be charged with the organization and setup of the Battalion training schedule for the fall and winter months. A coordinator in each of the Seabee ratings has been assigned to the Party to help in planning training and school requirements. Training will encompass both f o r m a l and informal schools, the latter being the construction training handled by the 21st NCB. At present the Party is firming up quotas for formal Navy A, B, and C schools, plus other special schools for Seabees as well as the "Fleet" ratings.

Military training will not be scheduled until later in the homeport period, but will include a number of changes. The total military training period will be 6 weeks; three at Camp Fogerty (formerly Sun Valley) and three weeks at Camp Lejeune — although no dates have yet been set for the trip to the Marines' training facility in North Carolina.

TRANSIT Wins All Navy Award

CAMP SHIELDS, CHU LAI, RVN — MCB 71's monthly F a m i l y G r a m newspaper, the TRANSIT, was awarded one of twenty-four Merit Awards by the Navy's Chief of Information (CHINFO) it was announced in a recent issue of Navy TIMES. The awards were given in eight different categories for the April-June quarter of 1967. The TRANSIT and the other twenty-three newspapers and periodicals were chosen from among 500 different Sea Service publications.

Awards were for the "best" in each of eight fields, both Stateside and overseas. The TRANSIT shared its honors with the JACKSTAFF, a newspaper from the Naval Support Activity in Saigon, as the "Best Letterpress Overseas."

The TRANSIT, printed in Tokyo, Japan by PACIFIC STARS and STRIPES, is edited by Journalist Third Class Dave Lyman from Seventy-One's Public Affairs Office. This is the first award the Seabee newspaper has received.

The "Best Letter Press — Stateside" was awarded to fellow Seabee unit, MCB 7 in Davisville, Rhode Island.

Front page of the last edition of *The Transit*.

Each of us will have a story to tell about life in this Bee Hive. Vietnam has been an experience I would never have passed up.

David H. Lyman, Editor

The Return Stateside, or: What a Deer in Vermont Taught Me About the War in Vietnam

When I left the Seabees and got to Vermont that fall I felt I needed to get back into the New England woods. I needed to be alone among the trees, traipsing through the forest after the leaves had fallen, up hills and over streams. Being alone in the woods felt good. I'd grown up in woods like these, and was at home here.

Deer hunting was something I had done every fall since I was a teen. My dad was a hunter. He'd taught me stalking, how to read the forest floor for the sign of deer. I'd hunted with a rifle, a Winchester saddle carbine 32–40, but had moved to bow and arrow in more recent years—it was a bit more challenging. You have to get a helluva lot closer to the deer.

Hunting had always been a deeply soulful experience. Dad used to say, "It's not the kill, it's the hunt, the ability to put yourself into a position for the kill. That's the test of a real hunter."

I went in search of an abandoned apple orchard on the backside of Dover Hills, between Newfane and Goose City. I found what was left of a forgotten apple orchard, on an old farmstead abandoned sometime in the last century. The apple trees still bore small, worm-eaten apples in the fall. "That's where you'll find deer," Dad had told me when I was 15. I found a hemlock on the edge of the old orchard, one into which I could climb, partially hidden among the branches but with a view of the orchard. "Deer move in the morning and the late afternoon, just before dusk," he had coached me, the young hunter.

Three afternoons, toward the end of deer season, I found myself standing on a stout branch, hidden in the hemlock. Late each afternoon, four does cautiously, noiselessly, entered the orchard. They were delicate and very feminine. A few minutes later, the buck emerged from cover and followed the females to snack on the fallen apples. They moved on. I couldn't get a clear shot.

On the third evening, the same routine. The four-point buck followed the females, letting them test the safety of the orchard. He came within range.

I had an arrow nocked on the string, and slowly I raised the compound bow, straightened my left arm, pulling back the string with three fingers on my right hand, the string against my cheek, the index finger of my right hand tucked into the corner of my mouth. I sighted over the tip of the arrow, to a target just below the deer's shoulder. I held my breath. I was about to relax the fingers and let the arrow fly, when the young buck raised its head and looked in my direction. Had he seen movement in the tree? Dad told me a deer will be spooked if it sees a patch of light in the forest canopy change. Is this what alerted my deer? Had I made a noise?

I looked down the arrow over its broad-head tip with four sharp cutting blades, to see the deer looking back into the tree where I hid. An hour passed, or what seemed like an hour.

I released my left arm, my right hand still holding on to the arrow's nock. The deer moved on. I stood there in the tree, 15 feet above the ground, shaking. I'd come so close to killing that deer. And for what? I asked myself. For what? I didn't need the meat, much as I do like the taste of venison. I had not been looking forward to the mess of gutting the carcass, then carrying or dragging it to my Land Rover, parked two miles away. But there was something deeper that kept me from releasing the arrow.

Why was I in that tree, with a bow and four arrows, each tipped with a deadly killing tip? I had no reason to kill that deer. The thrill was in the hunt, not in the kill.

I removed the arrow, pulled the other three out of the branch above me, unstrung the bow, and wiggled down out of the tree. During the hike back to my car, through those New England woods, I talked with myself, much as I had done in Vietnam. I was still a hunter, but I'd overcome the need to prove it, to boast of the kill to the guys at Dunn's General Store, where I'd have to weigh and register the kill. The idea of killing repulsed me. I felt ashamed I'd even had the idea in the first place. Did I have a right to kill? Or was killing just my ego trying to prove I was superior to another living thing? We dehumanized the VC and the North Vietnamese soldiers back in 'Nam. We called them Gooks, Chinks, Slants, Dinks, Zipper-heads; anything to make killing them less humiliating, to fend off the guilt of killing another human. Killing these small, skinny Asians was no more a bother than swatting a mosquito.

I'd only been back from Vietnam for a few weeks, and while I'd never killed anyone there, not even seen anyone get killed, death was still very much a part of daily life in Southeast Asia.

I'd had enough of killing and of war. I sold the bow that winter, along with the arrows.

I still hunt, but now only with my cameras.

Appendices:
The End Is Never Really the End

This is the end of the story of my year as a Seabee. The story of MCB-71 and its men and officers continued, as has mine. The following bits and pieces are observations and thoughts, sources and histories, an attempt to share what I learned while in the Navy, serving with the Seabees and what I've learned since.

THE FACES OF VIETNAM'S FUTURE

That summer of 1967, I photographed these ten- and twelve-year-old kids in An Tan, the fishing village at the mouth of the Song Tra Bong (River). They would now be

in their 60s. Their small fishing village has been replaced by a sprawling, modern suburb. Across the river is an industrial park, with a ship-building facility. Chu Lai, 12 miles north, is now the Chu Lai Industrial Zone. The SATS runway is gone, but the concrete runway we fixed is now a commercial airport. Nearby is a KIA plant building cars and a factory building heavy equipment.

There is no trace of Camp Shields, yet just down the beach, not far away, is an upscale beach resort with a dozen cabanas and a free-form swimming pool. You can see it on Google Maps.

What Happened to MCB-71?

MCB-71 returned to Chu Lai in the spring of 1968 for one more deployment. This time they went to Camp Miller, the other Seabee camp on Rosemary Point—not as nice, I hear, as Camp Shields. The CO and XO returned, as did half the original Battalion, only to decommission Camp Miller later that summer at the end of the deployment. MCB-71 never returned to Vietnam, yet the war continued for another seven years.

The battalion completed projects on Antarctica in the summer of 1972 and 1973, including a base at the South Pole, and Camp Siple at (75°55'00"S 83°55'00"W), a four-man wintering-over research faculty. The battalion's last assignment was to demilitarize the NSA (Naval Air Station) on Bermuda in the spring of 1975. The unit was decommissioned in Gulfport, Mississippi, later that summer.

Lessons Learned

No experience is entirely complete until it has been thoroughly debriefed, and the lessons noted. The Navy instilled in me lessons that continue today. I still fold my towels (hem inside) and clothes the Navy way. The enterprises I established used the chain of command, and the schools I founded embraced a little of what I learned in boot camp and my experiences in Vietnam.

I learned to not call mistakes, "mistakes," but use another name that turns a mistake into a "learning experience." If you call a mistake a test, an exercise, an etude, an attempt to find a better solution, it ceases to be a mistake and becomes just a step in the process of growing wiser. The Navy and the Marines provided combat training to help us prepare for what might come. The time to acquire these learning lessons is during practice, while playing. Kids do it, young animals do it, and adults do it during sport and recreation. We learn lessons when it's safe to fail. I used that lesson in my lectures to students in my schools. "I give you permission to fail this week. In fact, if you don't, it means you were being too cautious, and are not learning all that a failure can teach. Besides, some failures, looked at from the other side, may be gifts of brilliance."

That Navy chief on the USS *Lake Champlain* showed me we are responsible for everything that happens to us. There's no blaming others, or shifting responsibility. I'd returned to the ship late from a weekend liberty pass skiing in Vermont and missed muster. I stood before the chief, my hat in my hand, while he read me the riot act. "You say you missed muster because you were stuck in a snowstorm? If you had even the slightest inkling there was goin' to be a snowstorm, and that you might get stuck, you shouldn't have left the ship. It is your duty to be here Monday morning for muster. No excuses. No passing the buck. It's your responsibility. No weekend passes for you, Seaman Lyman, for the next month."

I've passed many of the lessons I've learned on to my two children and to my students. I've sailed more than 50,000 miles through the Atlantic, most of that time solo. It is risky, but the Navy and my experience in Vietnam showed me how to assess risk, to balance the joy of success with the consequence of failure. "What doesn't kill you, you learn from."

OUR COMMANDING OFFICERS

While researching this book, I contacted the offspring of the CO and the XO to find out what happened to their fathers after the war. Cheryl Brown Cole, daughter of our XO, CDR George Brown, wrote a touching recollection of her father, who passed away in 1971 at the age of 43. I include an excerpt of her letter here, with her permission.

Mr. Lyman,
    I talked to both my mom and brother and while Dad did write and send us recordings, unfortunately, none of us have any of his letters or writings. Little did any of us know how precious those letters and tapes would become after he was diagnosed with Leukemia (AML) in Fall 1971.
    I'm a Civil Engineer, like my Dad, and not much of a writer. But I will attempt to share a few memories of when Dad was transferred to Davisville, Rhode Island from San Juan, Puerto Rico. I was 10 years old, and in fifth grade. My younger brother, Scott, was 4 years old. The first thing Dad did was get us set up in a little ranch house on Forest Park Drive in North Kingstown.
    When his battalion was preparing for deployment to Vietnam, I remember him packing his big footlocker with all of those green uniforms and his big black combat boots. For a young child it was a surreal time because I picked up on the fact that he was going to where a war was being fought but I had no real concept of how long he would be there or what our lives would be like.
    The day we put him on the plane, all I remember is a very big airplane with a long line of men in those green uniforms slowly walking up the steps and boarding. We watched through a glass window inside a terminal. It took forever for them to load and my Dad was one of the last men to board. My poor mother must have been just heartbroken and terrified. But Dad was strong and standing tall through the whole process.
    Dad wrote many letters and sent lots of recording while he was in Vietnam. I recall laying on the floor in our living room, listening to his voice on the audio tapes. He never let on that he was near the fighting or that a war was going around him. He always managed to sound so strong, confident, and in control.
    We learned how he worked with the young men in his battalion and did his best to help them with the personal issues and problems the deployment caused for their families back home. He was so obviously incredibly proud of all of those men. I have to admit, I was a little jealous because they had "my dad" and he was apparently close to adopting each and every one of them.
    We also learned that CDR Coughlin was the boss. Through my Dad's eyes and his stories we

learned Dad had an immense respect for this higher ranking officer as he told all kinds of impressive stories about the "Skipper." He existed as a kind of magic imaginary hero in my mind.

When Dad returned, I remember the joyous trip to pick him up at the base. It took forever for that plane to unload. I watched every man deplane, watching for him. I swear he was either the last or next to last man off of that plane. I just couldn't believe everyone else was hugging and laughing while we were still standing, waiting.

Mom had cooked a special dinner for Dad that night and I vividly remember the four of us sitting around that dinner table together for the first time. My brother dropped something heavy on the floor with a loud bang. Dad just about jumped out of his skin! Years later I came to understand what conditions his nerves must have been in, how exhausted he must have been, and the types of dangerous noises he was probably exposed to while in Vietnam.

Our lives continued pretty normally after two MCB 71 deployments, then Dad was transferred to DC to pursue an MBA at George Washington University and then ultimately to Little Creek Amphibious Base in Norfolk as the Public Works Officer. He was so proud of that base and his job.

It was during this time in Norfolk that dad was diagnosed with Leukemia. In typical Dad manner we moved off of the base and he bought our first house. He then proceeded to teach my mom how to exist when he was gone.

He fought a darn good battle until July of 1974 when he succumbed to his illness at only 43. He died on the 12th floor of Portsmouth Naval Hospital under the care of some wonderful Navy doctors. Scott was only 12, I was 18, and my poor mother was widowed at only 39. Mom made the decision to stay in the house they had purchased in Virginia Beach, and we continue to live in this area today.

Over the years I have watched the research on Agent Orange and often wonder if that's what caused his illness. The Navy has taken good care of my Mom but I have to admit that whenever I visit the Vietnam Memorial Wall in DC I feel some anger. His name isn't on that wall but I believe in my heart that he's gone because of the time he was in Vietnam.

Thank goodness I have these beautiful memories of all of those men he bragged about from his battalion. I know he must have done some good things while he was there with them. Ironically, I am now a civil engineer, as was he. I work in Public Works Operations in Virginia Beach, VA maintaining the community's infrastructure. My 190 employees often remind me of those Seabees, as my engineers design projects and my field crews operate all of that heavy equipment. Dad had a huge impact on who I am today although he's been gone for 44 years.

All my best,
Cheryl Brown Cole
ccole2@cox.net [email address included
at her request]

Commander Coughlin, the CO

In January 2012, Ted Coughlin, the CO's son, emailed me to say his father had passed away peacefully in San Diego, California, at the age of 81 following a 34-year battle with Parkinson's Disease. Much more recently I reached out to Ted, as I did the XO's daughter. Ted sent me a few pages of recollections of growing up in a Navy family with a Navy father. Later, we spoke on the phone about what his father did before, and after, his command of Seventy-One.

Mr. Lyman

Dad was called by his middle name, Dan.

He was very proud of the work the battalion accomplished in Vietnam. He had a scrap book with all articles and pictures that you took and published in "The Transit." When Dad showed us his book, he would tell us that his greatest accomplishment was being a CO of MCB71, and the thing that made him the proudest, was he did not lose a single man on his watch. Dad was a humble "old school" soul. I am very proud to be his son. I followed in his footsteps by becoming a Civil Engineer. Dad was very proud. Dad battled Parkinson's from 1978 to 2012 and for that he is my hero. What a fighter!

Dad was always very subtle, calm and collected when passing out life lessons and discipline to us kids. Dad also took his appearance very seriously and always presented himself in a neat and orderly manner. I guess the Navy teaches you that, starting with his NROTC training in college.

Unfortunately, being a Naval Officer, Dad was quite often absent. I struggled with that. I had no male role model. I was in awe of Dad when he was at home, but was always competing with the rest of the family and his friends for his attention. Being athletic, as he was, I never had the joy of having my Dad attend my athletic events.

Dad wrote many, many letters, but I wish he had written more to me. I have always wished that he had been there for me when I was bullied every day of the school year in 8th grade by a kid 4 inches shorter than me.

Dad was from a small town at the edge of the California desert, and it was to California he returned when he left the service. He retired out of the service in 1972, formed and ran a commercial building maintenance company until 1978, then worked for FEMA until 1988.

Ted Coughlin

What Are the "Boys" Doing Now?

Of the 800 men and officers that were aboard NMCB-71 in 1967, there are a few hundred of us still around. Many are still in touch with each other—thanks to Gerald "Jerry" Montecupo, EO2. Jerry has maintained a roster of the men in Seventy-One from 1966 through 1975, in part to help in organizing reunions.

I've been in touch with a few Seabees mentioned in this memoir, and they have shared many interesting stories of lives lived, careers had, families raised and retirement achieved. A few are presented here, to illustrate that there is life after Vietnam.

John Cliett, JO3, PAO 1967 & 68

John was a JOSN when he joined me in Chu Lai but wound up as a JO3 when I left. He became the editor of *The Transit* when the outfit returned to Vietnam in 1968. After his hitch with the Seabees, John was transferred to San Juan, Puerto Rico, where he served as an announcer on American Forces Radio until his discharge from the Navy. After service, John returned to college, graduating from Florida State University with a degree in anthropology. He later trained as an electroneurodiagnostic technologist and worked for the Department of Veterans Affairs before retiring.

Francis "Tuffy" Lake, EA1, Engineering

Tuffy got out of the Navy in June of 1968 and returned to Anchorage, Alaska, where he went back into construction and location surveys. A bunch of the boys from Seventy-One showed up: Bob Wagnor, Dick Stapleman and Broader, the Texas well driller. Tuffy organized the Alaska Seabee Reserve Unit, with 64 construction men. He did such a good job that the Navy offered him a job as a recruiter in Michigan for three years. He then returned to Anchorage to work on the pipeline, then back to Wyoming to become an oil prospector for a large survey company. Tuffy is retired now, living in Mountain View, Arkansas, and is still active in his late 80s.

Gerald "Jerry" Montecupo, EO2, Alpha Company

When Jerry got out of MCB-71, he had orders to CBU-201, the Antarctic support unit based in Davisville. He checked into 201 and as an EO2 was assigned to the MAA office but left service before deploying to the ice. He returned home, worked as a laborer in construction, moved up to an equipment operator in the United States Steelworkers union, then joined the Operating Engineers out of Pittsburgh. He was a volunteer fireman in Monroeville, Pennsylvania, his hometown. He worked as ambulance engineer/driver with the fire department. With another Seabee from Harrisburg, Jerry formed an "Island" in Pittsburgh for the Navy Seabee Veterans of America. After a few years he became a National Counselor and Trustee.

In 2001, Jerry received a call from John Allsworth, EO2, from Alpha Company asking for help in setting up a post for the WWII MCB-71 Seabees, so they could have a reunion. He and John have hosted reunions every other year since, nine so far.

Gerald "Pete" Peterson, BU2, Charlie Company Clerk

Pete was one those who returned to Chu Lai in April 1968 on 71's second deployment to Vietnam. The Battalion moved into Camp Miller at Rosemary Point, which he reports was not nearly as nice as Camp Shields. "It was also disappointing to see that many of the projects we'd built in '67 had been destroyed during the Tet Offensive in January." Pete, Chief Funk and Lt. Wells moved from Charlie Company to take over Operations. Seventy-One closed down Camp Miller in December 1968 and returned to Davisville. Following separation from the service, Pete worked for eight years as a draftsman, then returned to the family farm in North Dakota. He's been growing grain ever since; still is.

Barry Putt, SK2, Supply Department

After his tour in 'Nam in 1967, Barry went back home to Cheektowaga, New York, and married his fiancée. In March 1968, he returned to Chu Lai with MCB-71's Advance Party, to witness the damage done to the complex during Tet. He stayed until the end of his enlistment in August 1968. With an associate's degree in accounting Barry went to work for Litton Industries in Virginia for two years. He earned his bachelor's degree in accounting along with an MBA in finance. He and his wife have two children and over the years he worked for a series of corporations: Anaconda Copper & Brass; McGraw-Hill; followed by Engelhard Min & Chem.; then the Crane Company; Sea-Land, and finally Maersk Inc. Now retired, he lives at the Jersey Shore with his wife of 51 years.

Dennis Smith, HM, Corpsman, Medical Department

Dennis returned from Chu Lai, and despite being eligible for E-5 at the tender age of 21, he was not about to reenlist. He worked at several hospitals in Rhode Island, putting his medical training to good use. He got married six months later. He then joined MEDEX I, the first physician assistant program in New England, which sent 23 former medics and corpsmen out to work with New England physicians. Dennis went to Vermont and worked for his first physician for nine years. He retired in 2014 and is now snowboarding, sailing, SCUBA diving, and enjoying grandchildren.

Dick Stapleman, EO2, Alpha Company

Dick returned to Idaho and his family when he left the Seabees and went to work in construction for a few years. In the early 70s, Charley Boardner, the Texas well driller, called, saying he was going to Alaska to join Tuffy Lake in Anchorage. Dick bought a 1959 pickup and built a camper on the back, then drove the thing to Alaska with Charley. Dick went to work for Western Airlines as the liquor agent, and that got him interested in flying. He bought an old tail-dragger in Reno and flew it back to Alaska, with no pilot license, no radios or electronics—landing on the TransCanada Highway to fuel up at gas stations. As a bush pilot, Dick flew hunters into the outback, before returning to Idaho, where he bought another plane, and formed his own construction company putting in gas pipelines. Dick became an expert and inspector of gas and oil pipelines, still is. Retired? Not yet. He'll be inspecting and consulting this winter where it's warm. He lives part time in Washington State, when not on the road.

Robert "Bob" Timerson, EA3, Engineering

Bob was discharged from the Seabees in July 1969 on an early out program following his fourth shortened tour in Vietnam with MCB-40.

What he found on returning to San Francisco was no better than what he left in Vietnam. The citizens were revolting against all government authority over the Vietnam War. There were shootings, bombs going off, protesting by the thousands, of all age groups and races. The biggest protest was South Vietnam's President Thieu's visit. The police estimated 250,000 people were there.

Bob went home to New York, got to attend the Woodstock Festival with half a million other people from across the U.S.—who appeared opposed to the Vietnam War as well. He then drove across the U.S. to find out where the rest of America stood. Nowhere did he find support for the war.

Bob traveled through Canada and found little support there either. He worked for U.S. Steel in Vancouver, BC, Canada, under landed immigrant status. There he found many of the workers were U.S. draft dodgers. When they found our Bob was a 'Nam vet he became their mentor. He never chastised them because he went and they didn't. His understanding and advice made several dodgers return to the U.S. to face the music.

After several years of wandering around the U.S. and Canada, Bob returned to New York, got married, raised two children and had a long career in construction. Along the way he formed a CM Company, RWT Consulting, providing construction services for many clients. He retired in 2012 at age 65.

Bob Wagoner, EA3, Engineering

Bob transferred to MCB-Six instead of departing with us, then got out. He graduated from Arizona State University with a degree in civil engineering. He founded a civil engineering company, which he sold in 1991, becoming the vice president at Del Webb Corporation, a land development firm. Later he started his own land development company, then retired. He lives in Scottsdale, Arizona.

Tom Widmark, EO3, Photographer's Assistant

Tom was discharged in November of 1968 and upon his return to the States found work with an advertising photography studio. While he admits he loved the work, he decided to go to school for electronics in the mid-seventies and had a long career in a new profession. Tom and his wife Jane live in a suburb of Minneapolis, St. Paul.

THE ONE WHO DIDN'T RETURN

In Memory of Bill Sipple

Bill Sipple was from H Company. He died in his bunk, in June 1967. His death was the result of a subdural hematoma received while playing basketball. He went up for a layup and when he came down he fell on another player, then fell on the concrete court, striking his head. While he was still eager to play, the medics would not let him finish the game.

That night, when a mortar barrage awakened everyone at 0200, Bill didn't get up. Rodriguez, an EA and hut mate, tried to waken Bill, and when he was unsuccessful he ran next door to get one of the corpsmen. The corpsman, after checking for a pulse, ran to get Dr. Hubbel, who worked on Bill for some time, attempting to resuscitate him with CPR. Bill's hut mates carried him on a stretcher to sickbay.

Bob Timerson remembers: "We all just stood there silent, not knowing what to do. None of us slept the rest of the night. When the rest of us left camp that next morning for the field, one of the corpsmen was standing guard over Bill, lying in a vehicle outside the sickbay. I often think of his family and the girl he was to marry went he got back. We sent them a card and she sent a nice letter back."

"The Chaplain, Lt. Dennis, held a service for Bill the following Sunday. I was there," wrote Timerson, "but some of Bill's teammates were outside shooting baskets. Bill's name is on the Vietnam Vet's Wall, June 1967 panel."

THE HISTORY OF NMCB-71'S PACIFIC DEPLOYMENT IN WORLD WAR II

Included here is a short history of MCB-71's World War II deployment in the Pacific. This information is from the battalion's official report at the Naval History & Heritage Command. I have edited and shortened the text somewhat. You can read the original report at the links at the end. The Journalist who accompanied the battalion for those two years wrote a complete, and fun to read, history in the unit's cruise book, available online as a downloadable PDF at the same link.

Naval Mobile Construction Battalion 71 was activated at the U.S. Naval Construction

Training Center in Williamsburg, Virginia, on 28 April 1943. More than 150 Seabee battalions were formed during World War II, 39 special construction battalions, 164 construction battalion detachments, 136 construction battalion maintenance units, 5 pontoon assembly detachments, 54 regiments, 12 brigades, and under various designations, 5 naval construction forces. Of the thousands of Seabees, 80 percent of them were involved in the Pacific Theater for the last two years of the war.

After commissioning, MCB-71 continued its build up, and underwent combat and construction training, primarily at Davisville and Port Hueneme. The men trained in invasion and beach tactics, road, bridge and landing strip construction, wood and steel building techniques. The entire battalion boarded a troop transport in California on September 7, 1943, for the four-week sail to Kokombona Beach on the island of Guadalcanal, arriving on October 3. The battalion came ashore and immediately set up a staging area and campsite. The camp was only temporary, as a major invasion of Bougainville was in the works.

A month later, on November 1, 1943, a 14-man team of Seventy-One Seabees hit the beaches at Empress Augusta Bay on Bougainville with the first wave of Marines to establish dispersal areas and erect bench markers. The rest of Seventy-One came ashore two days later with detachments from the 25th, 53rd, and the 75th Seabee Battalions, under steady fire from the Japanese.

First order of business: support elements of the 3rd Marine Division. The battalions offloaded two transports, but due to shallow water, the LSTs were unable to reach the beach, so the Seabees erected portable ramps to offload the dozers and other heavy equipment to build roads, clear camp sites, and begin construction on an airfield—all under constant air attacks, mortars and small arms fire.

Construction began on two fighter strips, and a bomber field at one end of Bougainville. The Japanese still held two airfields at the other end of the island. More and more Seabees poured in. They set up a sawmill, erected Quonset huts, cleared staging areas. Within 22 days, Seventy-One had built a 40-foot wide taxiway. But, before the main runway was completed, the taxiway had to be used for emergency landings. By December 10, the entire airfield was operational, despite the fact that on several occasions battalion was pulled off the job to man defensive positions.

In late February 1944, intelligence warned of an impending Japanese attack on Bougainville. The Seabees were called to man the defense lines. The Japanese attacked on March 8, unsuccessfully. By the end of March 1944, the battalion had completed all its assigned projects and boarded a transport for their next deployment.

The transport, with Seventy-One aboard, stopped in the Russel Islands just long enough to pick up the 58th Construction Battalion. The two outfits spent an entire month on that ship, sailing back-and-forth picking up supplies, water and more Seabees—waiting for their next job. The ship arrived in the Admiralty Group in early April. The 58th Battalion landed on Los Negros Island, and on the 24th, Seventy-One landed on the beach on Pityilu Island, the smallest in the Admiralty Group.

On Pityilu, the Battalion built a permanent camp and on May 5, when the heavy equipment came ashore, the Seabees began clearing the site for the airfield. Given 35 days to complete the field, Seventy-One finished five days ahead of schedule, on June 10, 1944. The battalion was awarded a "well done" from ADM Spruance. Besides the airfield the battalion built auxiliary buildings for the brass and erected a telephone system linking all the other islands in the group.

On 26 June 1944 the battalion began work on a fleet recreation center, including basketball and hand-ball courts, a baseball diamond, bathing pavilion, lockers and showers, a boxing ring, along with a stage and outdoor theater for the Bob Hope USO Show. [Twenty-three years later, in 1967, Bob Hope would be performing on the stage we built in Chu Lai.] The Seabees built a large EM Club that could hold more than 200 sailors, Marines and Army soldiers.

During the spring and summer of 1944, detachments from the battalion were assigned miscellaneous jobs on neighboring islands, building mess halls, admin buildings, generators sheds, laundries, a dispensary, signal and air traffic control towers, tent villages, even retail stores. They built radar installations on mountaintops, carved roads out of the jungles, erected bridges over rivers, built a Seaplane Base and a prisoner of war camp.

The battalion worked in the Admiralty Islands for six months, until November 8, 1944, when the main body boarded the U.S. Coast Guard ship *Gen. Morton*, and sailed back on Guadalcanal, arriving on December 12, 1944. The entire battalion went ashore and took up residence in a camp adjacent to the First Marine Division. For the next two months, the battalion trained in rifle and machine gun combat, and learned how to build Bailey Bridges.

As the war moved closer to the Japanese home islands, the battalion headed off on its third major deployment, Okinawa.

In late February the first party from Seventy-One joined the Third Amphibious Corps aboard the USS *Dickman*, to be joined by the rest of the battalion over the coming weeks.

On April 1, 1945, Easter morning, landing barges headed for the beaches on Okinawa amid a curtain of smoke and the boom of heavy naval guns. Seventy-One had been aboard the *Dickman* for a month, waiting.

Detachments from MCB-71 went ashore with the assault troops, serving as combat engineers and to support the ground troops rebuilding and improving the native roads and bridges destroyed in the assault. They cleared away enemy mines, located, developed, and operated a water supply system for all units, cleared and repaired and extended abandoned enemy airfields. They installed communication facilities, provided engineering assistance for garrisoned troops. The 'Bees worked night and day in spite of Japanese sniper fire, artillery fire and air attacks.

By April 2, 1945, the remaining battalion came ashore, then hiked 5 miles, carrying all their equipment, to take over a former Japanese airfield, at Yantan. They bivouacked and on April 8, began grading Highway One—Okinawa's main road leading north. Seventy-One followed the Marines of the III Corps, rebuilding this narrow road to keep supply lines open to the advancing Marines. A spotter plane landing strip at Onna was begun on April 16, and within four days was ready for the first plane to land. On April 26, improvements began on Route 6, a road crossing the isthmus near the middle of the island at its narrowest point, a distance of 3 miles. The road was widened and new sections added to straighten the road to accommodate two-way traffic and larger trucks.

By April 29, the battalion had extended Highway One north to Nago, a distance of more than 20 miles. Japanese roads were narrow, suitable for their smaller trucks, requiring the battalion to widen all the roads for the larger U.S. vehicles.

On May 4, the main body of the battalion moved south with the III Amphibious Corps to establish Camp #2. By May 7, the battalion was working on widening Highway One to accommodate two-way traffic and repairing bridges. Heavy rains hampered construction, as the Seabees worked to keep the muddy road open for the flow of supplies to the front line. Toward the end of May, this roadwork went on 24 hours a day, often under sniper fire.

Early in June the battalion moved further north with the Marines, establishing Camp #3, which was subject to nightly barrages of small arms fire and sappers. Seventy-One continued to widen Highway One, repave wash outs, and bomb damage from Japanese planes.

[The fighting up to this point on Okinawa has been some of the fiercest of the Pacific Theater. The three-month battle, named Operation Iceberg, was the largest amphibious landing in the Pacific Theater of World War II. It also resulted in the largest loss in lives. Over 100,000 Japanese died, along with 50,000 men from the Allied forces.]

Toward the end of June 1945, all organized Japanese resistance on Okinawa came to a halt. The captured airfields on Okinawa now allowed U.S. land-based planes to strike Japanese forces in China and on the Korean Coast. Seventy-One continued to widen and improve Highway One, to straighten curves, and re-build narrow bridges. In July, Seventy-One went to work back at the Yontan airfield, lengthening and resurfacing the runway, adding cross overs, and warm-up aprons, all this while being hampered by heavy rains. Seventy-One also built a headquarters camp, with quarters for Generals MacArthur and Kinney. The project was completed on August 4. Ten days later, Japan announced acceptance of the Potsdam Proclamation, and the "cease fire" order took effect the next day.

A month later, on September 2, 1945, the formal surrender was signed aboard the battleship USS *Missouri* in Tokyo Bay.

A few days later, September 7, 1945, marked the second anniversary of Seventy-One's deployment to the Pacific. Work on Okinawa slowed down considerably with the end of the war and MCB-71 was inactivated in December 1945.

MCB-71 was on deployment throughout the Pacific Campaign, with no time off. For the majority of the two-year deployment, the battalion strength was over 1,000 men and up to thirty officers.

The Secretary of the Navy, in a citation signed March 8, 1946, awarded the Navy Commendation Ribbon to MCB-71. The citation read in part: "for exceptional meritorious service in support of the III Amphibious Corps, against enemy Japanese forces in the Ryukyu Islands from April 1 to June 27, 1945. Employed essentially on combat engineering missions throughout the Okinawa Campaign, Naval Construction Battalion 71 was responsible for improvement and maintenance of 38 miles of narrow, native roads vital to the uninterrupted movement into the forward area of combat supplies and divisions during a period of extremely heavy rainfall. Carrying out a large portion of this military engineering task the hours of darkness and during frequent lockouts imposed by enemy air attacks."

The men and officers of Seventy-One came home.

Author's Note: You can read the complete report of Seventy-One's 1944–45 Pacific deployment in official Navy documents, available as a PDF download from the Naval History & Heritage Command, at www.History.Navy.mil. There, you'll also find the official reports from Seventy-One's two Vietnam deployments, along with cruise books from Seventy-One's three deployments. Here is the direct link to the World War II report: https://www.history.navy.mil/content/dam/museums/Seabee/UnitListPages/NCB/071%20NCB.

pdf. In researching this book, I found a copy of that 1945 cruise book on the Navy History website. It can be downloaded as a PDF, available online at: https://www.history.navy.mil/content/history/museums/seabee/explore/wwii-cruisebooks/cruisebooks-ncb.html. MCB-71's cruise books (there are two of them, 1966–67, 1968) can also be found there.

The author on assignment in Scotland in 2017, 50 years after Vietnam (photograph by Renaissance Lyman).

Index

A-4 Skyhawk fighters 166, 124
The Acey-Ducey Club 66
AFR (Armed Forces Radio) 159
airport 2, 13, 150, 153–154
Albert, Norman 83
Allair, Norman, UT3 129
Allsworth, John EO2 218
Alpha Company 23, 24, 38–39, 74, 78, 90–91, 106–107, 113–115, 129, 177, 132–133, 218–219
AM-2 (aluminum slab matting) 177
AmTrac (amphibious tractor, personnel) 140
An Hoa Bay 59
An Tan 161, 213
Annam 153
APC (all purpose capsule) 143
Armed Forces Information School, Department of Defense 183
Armed Forces Radio (AFR) 71, 2178
Army Cavalry heliport 93, 104
Army Recon Unit 60
ARVN (The Army of the Republic of Vietnam) 95
Ashland, EO1 108
ASP (ammunition supply point) 132
Asphalt and Blood (Warren Bell) 3
asphalt plant 111; operations, Chu Lai 112

Bailie, G.W. "Bell" EO1 95, 102
barracks for the ARVN Regiment 195 -103
Bartko, Chet, CMA3 90
basketball 21, 49, 56, 62, 90–91, 207, 220, 222
Baskin, CM 178
Battle Cry (Leon Uris) 9
Benzaiten Shrine 189
Bien Van River 134
Binh Son 120–122, 161–164

Binh Thioi 164
Blow Up 187
The Bob Hope Amphitheater 199
Bones, T.W., Ensign 20, 78
BOQ (bachelor officers quarters) 19
The Boston Globe 12
Bougainville 221
Bowden, David, HM 80
Bravo Company 23–24, 77–78, 91, 129, 177
Brodner, Charlie, EO3 129
Bronica Camera 4, 160, 187
Brown, George, CDR (XO) 26, 73, 80, 85, 87–88, 119, 215
Buddhism 166, 189
bun nam-vang 193

C-130 Hercules prop 180
C-141 (Jet cargo) 46–48, 56, 128, 180, 206–209
C-rations 3, 31–32, 65, 100, 117, 120, 140–141, 162
USS *Caloosahatchee*, AO-98 13, 14
Cau Do River 148
chain of command 169
Charlic Company 106
China Beach 148–150, 180
Cam Ranh 126
Cam Ranh Bay 58, 126, 194
Cameron, LTJG 106
camp layout 51
Camp Lejeune, North Carolina 33
Camp Shields 49–72
Camper, Cleylon, Marine Gunny SGT 73
Cantonment 95
Carnahan, EO2 109
CAT scrapers (Earthmovers) 40, 104–106
Caterpillar D8 Dozer 24, 99–108, 125–127, 132, 221
Cau Do River 148
CBU-201 (The Antarctic Support Unit) 218

Cement mix plant operations 113
CH-3, Sikorsky helicopter (the Jolly Green Giant, or The Hook) 116, 119
CH-47, Chinook helicopter 132, 158
CH-54, Sikorsky Flying Crane, helicopter 116
Chain of Fools 71
Cherry Point, North Carolina 33
Chief Mitchell 95, 103
The Chiefs' Club 66
China Beach 91, 148–150, 153, 180
chloroquine 144
Chu Bon River 147
Chu Lai 1, 41, 48, 54–62, 71, 73, 78–79, 82, 88, 93, 95, 97, 101, 104, 106–107, 110, 115–116, 119–120, 124, 126, 130, 134–136, 140, 147, 151, 157–158, 161–162, 173, 175, 185, 191–194, 200, 214, 217–218, 222, 225; beach 68; concrete runway repairs 128–129; enclave 59, 104; industrial zone 214; military complex 53–59
Cinderella Liberty 103
Civil Rights Act of 1964 7–11
Clark, Earl, CM 77
claymore mines 108
Clayton, Rick, UT3 129
Cliett, John SNJO 5, 217
Cochinchina 153
Composition C-4 110
USS *Compton*, DD 705 10
COMRATS 19
concrete plant 111
Conroy, Jay, LTJG 106, 112
Corbin, Burt, Lance CPL 136
Curtis, Johnson, YO1, USN 11
Chu Bon River 148
Chu Bon River 147
crowded streets 154–155
The Cruise of the Snark (Jack London) 163
Cumshaw Boys 147

227

Index

Da Nang 2, 3, 12, 55–58, 70, 84, 93, 95, 104, 115, 116, 120, 122, 130, 132, 144, 147–151, 153–157, 159–164, 171, 179, 180, 193, 206, 206–209
Dancing in the Street 9
Davisville, RI 13, 18–26, 39, 41, 50–53, 58, 73, 99, 133, 179, 200–202, 209, 215, 218, 221
DC-3s 206
Delta Company 106
Dennis, Billy, LT, chaplain 169
DMZ (demilitarized zone) 3, 58, 99, 150–151
Dong Binh 161
Dong Ha 126
Dong Tam 93
Duc Pho 135
Dumphy, CM 178

editing and production 178, 181–185
The EM Club 67
Empress Augusta Bay 221
EOD (explosive ordnance disposal) 99, 120
EPDOLANT 15
Euclid trucks 108, 111

Fathom 187
Fielding, BU1 113
5th Marine Regiment 55
The Fighting Seabees 81
Findle, Tim, Navy corpsman 171
Findley, Tim, HM3 171
Fire Base Camron 1
1st Brigade, 101st Airborne Division 55
First Marine Division Hospital 135
fleet-bees 20
Franklin, Aretha 71
Franco-Siamese War in 1893 153
French Indochina 6, 152–155

Georgia Buggy 176
The Ginza 185
Goldsworth, "Goldy," EO1 149
gonorrhea 144
Gooks, Chinks, Slants, Dinks, Zipper-heads 212
Goss Web Press 181
Green, Green, Grass of Home (Claude "Curly" Putman, Jr.) 71
Guadalcanal 221
gunships, Huey 1, 2, 56, 148, 165, 205

Hai Van 148
Haley, R.J., EO3 103
Hanratty, Drick DK3 197

harbor 148
Hardwick, George, UT1 129
Harrison, Gene, Marine Gunny SGT 73
Hasselblad camera 187
heli landing pads 106
Hemmings, David 187
high stakes poker 72
Highway One 29, 58–60, 97–109, 120–124, 136–138, 162, 170, 222
Hồ Chí Minh, General 153
Ho Chi Minh sandals 2
Hồ Chí Minh Trail 56, 60, 145
Hoi An 147
Hon Ba 152, 165
Hotel Company 24, 30
Hoyt, Lee, EO3 149
Hubbell, Jerry, LT, doctor 170
Hue 3, 8, 93, 120, 151–153, 162, 166
Husak, Ted, CM 77

I Corps area (Eye Corps) 2, 56, 58, 59, 70, 93, 150
Indochina 153
Ingraham EO2 109
IPO (instant petty officer) 19, 25, 81, 94, 108, 172, 205
I've Got to Get Out of This Place 71

Jackson, Jimmy JOSN 53
Japan: earthquake 188; tea garden 190; traditions and culture 185–191
Johnson, Bernie, ensign 120–122, 135 F
Johnson, Bill 88
Johnson, Chris, YO1 11
Johnson, Lyndon, U.S. president 9, 71

Kennedy, John F., U.S. president 8
Khe Sanh 126
Khuong Long 170–171
KIA (killed in action) 206
Knight, C.B., BU1 95, 103
Knupp, PH1 115
Kohfield, Bruce, PN3 170
Kokombona Beach 221
Krulak, Victor "Brute," General 58

Lake, Francis (Tuffy), EA1 41, 80, 92–95, 114–115, 124, 126–127, 173, 177, 197–199, 217, 219
Lake Anthony, CMA 48
USS *Lake Champlain*, CV39 13, 18
Laterite Pit 57, 89, 104–107, 124–127, 132

Lawrence, Charlie, CMA 48
LCM (Landing Craft Mechanized) 151
LCUs (Landing Craft Utility) 134
Leaving on a Jet Plane by Peter, Paul and Mary 71
Life Magazine The photograph that changed my life 11
Linotype 42, 181
Little Creek Amphibious Base, 216
Long Bin 161
Long Thanh Dong Island 134
LSDs 22, 148
LST (landing Ship Transport) 56–57, 120, 134–135, 221
Ludlow machine 181
Lukanic, Terry, EO1 (EA2 with MCB-74, author) 3
Lunt, Steve, BU3 149
LVTP-5A1 140
Ly Tra 169
Lyman, David 14, 18, 53, 82, 103, 120, 133, 176, 211, 215, 225

M14 rifles 22, 30, 34–36, 73, 88, 145, 195
M16 rifles 22, 36, 135, 141
M1911 (.45 Colt Semi-automatic sidearm) 141, 147, 154, 188
MACV (military assistance command, Vietnam) 95; Press Center 147–152
MAG-12 132
MAG 13 (Marine Air Group) 56, 127
MAG 16 (Marine Aircraft Group) 116
Manencia, Mike, EO3 98
Marble Mountain 148–149, 180
Marine Phantoms 127–128, 166
MARS (military assistance radio station) 203
Martin, LCDR, S-3 140
MASH (mobile army surgical hospital) 2, 21
Material Expediting Team 147
MCB-3 86
MCB-5 148
MCB-6 56, 93, 135, 200
MCB-8 89, 104, 134
MCB-9 93
MCB-10 12, 22, 49, 67, 124–126
MCB-11 148
MCB-40 48–49, 55, 99, 198–200, 219
MCB-71 Organization 24
MCB-74 3, 93, 200
MEDCAP 170
Miller, Bill, CN 135
USS *Missouri* 223
Monetecupo, Jerry, EO2 89, 218

Index

Monkey Mountain 3, 147–150, 180, 206
The Mount Snow Valley News 43, 203
movie theaters 35, 50, 69, 186–188, 222
MSR (main supply road) 197
Murphy, John EO1 96–97, 100, 172–178

Naomi, Nick 83
Napier, Chief 13
Navy Commendation Ribbon 223
Navy Swift Boat 110
New Market in Tan Ky 164
Ngo Dinh Diem (President, South Vietnam) 8
Ngo Dinh Nhu (President Ngo Dinh Diem's brother) 8
Nikon cameras 4, 70, 160 225
95th Evacuation Hospital Complex 150
9th Marine Engineers 49
Noch Mon 122
Norman, EO1 108
NROTC (Naval Reserve Officers' Training Corps) 217

Officer in Charge (OIC) 20
The Officers' Club 66
Okinawa 222
Old Flintstone 107, 111–112
Oliver, Olie, UT3 129
105mm artillery 5, 88
196th Light Infantry Brigade 55
Operation Lawrence 55
Operation Moon Pie 36
Operation Starlite 12
Operation Union 56

pachinko parlors 187
Pacific Theater 221
PAO (Public Affairs Office) 52, 53, 178
Patterson LCDR (S4) 57
Patterson, Don, PFC 136
Perry, E.C., EO3 103
Peterson, Gerald "Pete," BU2 19, 78, 127, 218
Phan Rang 126
pho (Vietnamese soup) 193
Phu Bai 93, 126
Pityilu Island 221
POD (plan of the day) 20
POL (offshore pipeline) 130
Port Hueneme 78, 221
Potsdam Proclamation 223
Powers, Stephen, LTJG 92
Powers' (Observations) Towers 114–119
Preparation H 145

PSP planks 64, 124
The PX 70

QM Repair Facility 95
Quang Ngai Detachment 97
Quang Ngai Express (convoy) 120–122
Quang Tri 93
quarry operations 108
Quonset Point NSA 21, 113

rear echelon commandos 97
Reedy, Ron, YN3 19, 20, 25–26, 97, 170
Reimel, Utility Chief 129
Republic of Korea Marine Brigade 55
restaurant 187
RMK-BRJ (U.S. Contractor: Raymond-Morrison-Knudson) 113, 197
Robinson, Dave, EO3 134
Roche, John, EO1 97
rock quarry 109, 111, 112
ROK Camp at Bihn Son 135
ROK Marines 71
Roppongi 181, 185
Rosemary Point 56, 59, 6 8, 88, 90, 104–110, 114, 134, 147, 197, 199, 206, 218
Rüdiger, Edward, LTJG 95–96, 99, 101, 135
RVN (The Republic of Vietnam) 8, 58, 95, 100–101, 150, 159, 178, 208

SAC runway 111, 120
Sadler, EO1 109
Saigon 8, 12, 53–58, 70–71, 99, 153, 166, 186, 192–194
Sam Ha 161
San Miguel (beer) 193
sand ramp 56–57, 73, 120, 134, 151
Sapporo Beer Hall 188
Sarlo, Mickey, EO 134
Sarvie, Ed, HM 80
SATS (short airfield tactical support) 55, 58, 60, 79, 107, 108, 124, 127, 128, 135, 147, 214; runway 55, 58–60, 79, 107, 124, 126–128, 214
Schlossar, Denny, UT3 129
Schroeder, CM 90
SCUBA (self-contained underwater breathing apparatus) 130
Sea Knight helicopter (Marine) 101
Seabee detachments 56, 62, 71, 80, 125, 179, 221–222
Seabee inventiveness 127
Seabee Team 7101 96
2nd Squadron, 11th Armored Cavalry 55

Seeger, Peter 71
Sellers (storekeeper) 90
Sharp, Robert, LT OIC 107
Shinjuku 189
Shinto 18
shooting range 88
short-timer 135, 136, 137, 197, 202, 206
Shovels and C-Rations (Charles Thompson) 3
Sino-French War 153
Sipple, Bill 220
Skop, Wally (Scuzzy), YN 25–26, 35, 88, 89–91, 119, 161, 164, 178, 200–202
Slicks, Hueys 1, 104, 147–148 167
Smith, Dennis, HM 79
Smith, Tony, LT (S2) 85–86, 131–132, 140, 178
softball 88
Son Tihn 122
Song Ha River 152
Song Tra Bong 140–143, 171
SOP (standard operating procedure) 134
South China Sea 12, 49, 68, 148, 165, 195, 199–201
Stapleman, Dick, EO3 25–26, 29, 81–82, 103–104, 114, 135–136, 162, 173, 176, 217, 219
star flares 5, 31–39, 74, 104, 106, 134, 145, 200
stars & stripes (S&S) 2, 71, 133, 139, 140, 143, 179, 181–184
STDs (sexually transmitted diseases) 144
Stony Bay Camp (Camp Lejeune) 33
Sturges, Master Equipment Chief 107
Sun Valley (Mudville) 20, 30, 31

T-245 (Dodge pickup) 149
TAD (temporary additional duty) 147
Tales of the South Sea (James Michener) 79
Tan Ky 164, 171–172
Tan Son Nhut Air Base, Saigon 58, 192, 194
Task Force Oregon 56
Thierry, John, SW3 135
Third Amphibious Corps 222
3rd Brigade, 25th Infantry Division 55
32nd Naval Construction Regiment 56, 93
Thompson, A.J., BU2 101
Thoroughly Modern Millie 187
Tiger Beer 162, 193
Timerson, Bob EACN 199–200, 219–220

Tinkertoys 132
Tonkin 153
Tourane 153
The Transit 44, 118, 123, 174, 182, 210
Tri Bihn 161

underwater construction team (UCT) 130
underwater fuel line repair, Duc Pho 132
underwater pipe line repairs, Chu Lai 130–132
Underway Replenishment (UNREP) 14
Union 56
U.S. Army Special Forces 22
U.S. Naval Construction Training Center, Williamsburg, Virginia 220

US Navy Seabees—The Vietnam Years, 1967/68 3
USO Tours 74

venereal disease (VD) 144
Vichy France 153
Viet Cong Insurgents 8, 153
Viet Minh 22
village reconstruction in Ly Tra 169
Vinh An 163
Vung Tau 3, 120

Wade (UCT dive chief) 88
Wade, Dick, chief steelworker 79, 124–128
Wade, EO3 105
Wagnor, Bob, EA3 26, 35, 94, 135–136, 217
Walt, Amy, General 105–106

We Shall Overcome 71
well drilling 129–130
Westmoreland, William, General 168
Whisper, Sam, LT, DMD, dentist 80, 170–171
Widmark, Tom, EO3 115

YANK Magazine 96
Yokohama, Japan 191
Yokota Air Base 47, 181, 191, 208
You Only Live Twice 188
Young, Stephen B. 12

Zupon, EA (engineer assistant) 88

www.ingramcontent.com/pod-product-compliance
Ingram Content Group UK Ltd.
Pitfield, Milton Keynes, MK11 3LW, UK
UKHW050532150426
5217IPUK00026B/1900